Illuminate
Publishing

# OCR GCSE (9–1)
# DRAMA

ANNIE FOX

Published in 2019 by Illuminate Publishing Ltd,
PO Box 1160, Cheltenham, Gloucestershire GL50 9RW

Orders: Please visit www.illuminatepublishing.com
or email sales@illuminatepublishing.com

© Annie Fox 2019

The moral rights of the author have been asserted.

All rights reserved. No part of this book may be reprinted, reproduced, or utilised in any form or by any electronic, mechanical, or other means, now known or hereafter invented, including photocopying and recording, or in any information storage and retrieval system, without permission in writing from the publishers.

British Library Cataloguing-in-Publication Data
A catalogue record of this book is available from the British Library.

ISBN 978-1-911208-73-0

Printed by Cambrian Printers, Aberystwyth

07.19

The publisher's policy is to use papers that are natural, renewable and recyclable products made from wood grown in sustainable forests. The logging and manufacturing processes are expected to conform to the environmental regulations in the country of origin.

Every effort has been made to contact copyright holders of material reproduced in this book. Great care has been taken by the author and publisher to ensure that either formal permission has been granted for the use of copyright material reproduced, or that copyright material has been used under the provision of fairdealing guidelines in the UK – specifically that it has been used sparingly, solely for the purpose of criticism and review, and has been properly acknowledged. If notified, the publisher will be pleased to rectify any errors or omissions at the earliest opportunity.

Editor: Roanne Charles, abc Editorial
Design and layout: Kamae Design
Cover design: Kamae Design
Cover photograph: Chickenshed Theatre's 2016 production of *Kindertransport* by Diane Samuels, directed by Lou Stein. Copyright: Daniel Beacock.

**Text acknowledgements**
Extracts are taken from:
*Blood Brothers* by Willy Russell, Methuen Modern Classics edition published by Bloomsbury;
*Death of a Salesman* by Arthur Miller, Penguin Modern Classics;
*Find Me* by Olwen Wymark and *Gizmo* by Alan Ayckbourn published by Samuel French;
*Kindertransport* by Diane Samuels and *Misterman* by Enda Walsh published by Nick Hern Books;
*Missing Dan Nolan* by Mark Wheeller, published by dbda.

p94 'The Leader' from *Sky in the Pie* by Roger McGough © 1983, Kestrel – Penguin Books Ltd reprinted by permission of Peters Fraser & Dunlop (www.petersfraserdunlop.com) on behalf of Roger McGough.
p216 Extract from *Leave Taking* by Winsome Pinnock reproduced with the kind permission of Nick Hern Books.
p220 Extract from *Metamorphosis* by Steven Berkoff, copyright © Steven Berkoff 1981, first published by Amber Lane Press.

Extracts from the GCSE (9–1) Drama Specification reproduced by permission of OCR.

The teaching content of this resource is endorsed by OCR for use with specification GCSE (9–1) Drama (J316). In order to gain OCR endorsement, this resource has been reviewed against OCR's endorsement criteria.

This resource was designed using the most up to date information from the specification. Specifications are updated over time which means there may be contradictions between the resource and the specification, therefore please use the information on the latest specification and Sample Assessment Materials at all times when ensuring students are fully prepared for their assessments.

Any references to assessment and/or assessment preparation are the publisher's interpretation of the specification requirements and are not endorsed by OCR. OCR recommends that teachers consider using a range of teaching and learning resources in preparing learners for assessment, based on their own professional judgement for their students' needs. OCR has not paid for the production of this resource, nor does OCR receive any royalties from its sale. For more information about the endorsement process, please visit the OCR website, www.ocr.org.uk.

**The author would like to thank:**
Laura Ann Price and Christopher Fox for their contributions and support.

# CONTENTS

# INTRODUCTION TO OCR GCSE DRAMA

Welcome to OCR GCSE Drama.

This is an exciting course which will help you to develop many skills. One day, you might be creating an original piece of theatre; on another, sketching a costume design, or acting out a scene from a play.

You will have opportunities to explore, through acting or design, a set text and another performance text. You will also watch and evaluate a piece of live theatre.

You will learn how to organise your drama ideas in written form. You will also create your own, original devised performance, based on a selection of stimuli. Some parts of the course assess your written work, while other components assess your ability to contribute to a practical performance. Throughout the course, you will have the chance to reflect on your own work and that of others.

At the beginning of the course, like many people, you might not feel equally confident in all areas. Try to view this, however, as an opportunity to discover and develop new skills. No one expects you to be an all-round expert at the beginning of the course, but it is important to be open to learning a range of skills. During their studies, many students discover new talents that they didn't know they possessed.

## How you will be assessed

You will complete three components in the course.

| Assessment component | Assessment method | Marks available | Proportion of total GCSE | Content overview |
|---|---|---|---|---|
| Component 01/02: Devising drama | Non-exam assessment | 60 | 30 per cent | Learners will research and explore a stimulus, work collaboratively and create their own devised drama. |
| Component 03: Presenting and performing texts | Visiting examination | 60 | 30 per cent | Learners develop and apply theatrical skills in acting or design by presenting a showcase of two extracts from a performance text. |
| Component 04: Drama: Performance and response | Exam assessment: written paper (1 hour 30 minutes) | 80 | 40 per cent | Learners will explore practically a performance text to demonstrate their knowledge and understanding of drama. Learners will analyse and evaluate a live theatre performance. |

There is no set order in which the course will be taught, and you will find that skills learned in one component are likely to enrich your work in another component. For example, the technical vocabulary that you learn in order to evaluate a live performance is also useful when writing your devising log or discussing your set text. Similarly, you might be influenced by ideas or techniques from your set text or a live theatre performance when creating your devised piece. Keep building on your learning in order to advance your work throughout the course.

# How to use this book

This book is organised to support each of the assessed components of the course. They are covered in this order:

1 Component 04: Drama: Performance and response (written exam)

2 Component 01/02: Devising drama (non-exam assessment)

3 Component 03: Presenting and performing texts (visiting exam).

The guidance notes and tasks in Component 04 cover a wide range of skills, concepts and terminology that you can carry forward to the learning and activities in the following chapters.

In addition to specific guidance for the content of these components, there are brief introductory sections on theatre makers and performance and design in order to equip you with the necessary technical vocabulary and concept terms. At the end of the book is a glossary as a reference and to reinforce this learning.

It is not expected that you will read this book from cover-to-cover. Instead, you should work through the sections that are relevant to you in the order that best supports your progress through the course.

To help you get the most from the book, the following features are included:

**What the specification says**: This highlights what is in the specification about the unit and the skills you need to develop, as well as pinpointing the assessment objectives for each unit.

**Key terms**: Definitions of important vocabulary to help you understand how drama works and how to express your ideas accurately and fluently.

**Tasks**: Activities to develop your learning. These include group work and individual tasks and are both practical and written.

**Extension tasks**: Challenges and longer tasks, such as research, or more advanced activities to stretch and extend your drama skills.

**Practice questions**: Sample questions written in the style of those you will encounter in an exam so that you can practise writing answers and become familiar with different types of question.

**Sample responses**: Candidate-style answers from which you can learn possible approaches to exam questions. Some have annotation comments to show where the work has met assessment criteria or, instead, how it could be improved.

**Tips**: Advice on ways of approaching and improving your work and how to avoid common errors.

**Check your learning**: Checklists of the main learning points from the component to ensure that you have covered everything and can feel confident in your knowledge.

**Look here**: References to other sections of the book that provide further information and more details on a particular topic.

**TIP:**

You might be taught the course in a different order, but there are supporting ideas and vocabulary in each section which should be relevant to you. The 'Look Here' icons will help you to make these connections.

**WHAT THE SPECIFICATION SAYS...**

**KEY TERMS:**

TASK

**EXTENSION**

Practice question...

Sample response...

**TIP:**

**CHECK YOUR LEARNING**

 LOOK HERE

# 1 THE ROLES OF THEATRE MAKERS IN CONTEMPORARY PRACTICE

**WHAT THE SPECIFICATION SAYS...**

Learners should be able to:

- Evaluate the roles that theatre makers (from contemporary professional practice) have on developing, performing and responding to a performance text.

## Theatre makers

Theatre is a **collaborative** form. When you go to see a play, you might not immediately be aware of the many different people who contributed to the final production. Some, like the playwright, director and designers, were involved with creative decisions long before rehearsals began. Others appear onstage or work backstage. As an informed student of drama, you need to become aware of these different roles and the areas for which each is responsible.

### Actor

Plays a role on stage in a production. These performers may be the leading actor in the play or might have a small or **ensemble** role. Actors are cast in a role, learn lines and movements, rehearse and then perform before an audience.

### Costume designer

Responsible for designing and organising the costumes, make-up and masks worn by the actors for a performance. The costumes might be specially made for the production, or hired. The designer will ensure that costumes fit the actors and suit the production and its style.

### Lighting designer

Designs how lighting will be used in the performance, including any special effects. Understands the technical capabilities of the theatre and creates a lighting plot (plan).

### Playwright

Writes the script, including the **dialogue** and **stage directions**.

### Director

Responsible for the overall **artistic vision** or concept for a production. Works with actors and the creative team, including designers. Leads rehearsals, guiding the actors, giving notes to improve the work and agreeing the **blocking** (or moves) with the actors.

### Lyricist

In musicals, writes the words to the songs: the lyrics.

# Choreographer

Responsible for creating dances and movement sequences during the production. They will oversee the dance and movement rehearsals.

# Understudy

An actor who is ready, if needed, to take on a role usually played by someone else when there is a planned or unexpected absence. In preparation, they learn the lines and blocking for that role, but usually have a limited amount of rehearsal time.

# Sound designer

Designs the sound for the production. This could include sourcing sound effects, creating original sound effects and composing or sourcing music. Creates a sound plot and arranges appropriate **amplification** and projection of sound.

# Set designer

Creates the design for the play's set, which might include set dressings (additional objects on stage) and furnishings. Provides sketches and other design material, such as a **model box**, before overseeing the construction of the set.

# Stage manager

A member of the stage management crew. Stage managers are responsible for organising the backstage elements of the play, including the **props**. One stage manager is usually 'on the book', calling cues and being prepared to prompt actors if a line is forgotten.

## KEY TERMS:

**Collaborative:** Working with others; team work.

**Ensemble:** A group of actors. The term can be used for actors who form a chorus of a play or musical, or it might refer to a group of actors who all play equal roles, with no single actor being the lead or 'star'.

**Dialogue:** The words/lines spoken by the characters.

**Stage directions:** Instructions in the script indicating how the play might be performed or staged, including physical actions, location and sound and lighting effects.

**Artistic vision:** The choice of what is going to be emphasised in a production, for example where it is set or what themes will be stressed. These decisions influence the staging, performance style and design requirements. Also called 'artistic intention' or 'concept'.

**Blocking:** The actors' movements. These are usually set during rehearsals and noted by the stage management in the prompt book.

**Amplification:** How sound is increased, for example through speakers.

**Model box:** A box representing the walls of a theatre space into which a cardboard scale model of a set can be placed.

**Props:** Small items that actors can carry onstage, such as books, walking sticks or boxes.

## WHAT THE SPECIFICATION SAYS...

Learners should be able to:

- State advantages and disadvantages for the decisions made directing, acting and designing for performance
- Apply knowledge and understanding of the development of drama and performance to the studied performance text.

## TIP:

When thinking about staging, consider the relationship between actor and audience. How close are they? How well can they see each other? Does the experience differ depending on the viewer's position in the audience?

## KEY TERMS:

**Sightline:** The view of the stage from the audience.

**End on:** A configuration in which the whole audience directly faces the stage.

**Apron:** The area of the stage nearest the audience, which projects in front of the curtain.

**Fly space:** The area above the stage where scenery can be stored and lowered to the stage.

**Wings:** Spaces to the side of the stage, where actors can wait to enter unseen and where props and set pieces can be stored.

**Stage picture:** A still image created on stage. It might include the positioning of the actors in relation to each other and the set. It can also be called a *tableau*.

**Box set:** A set with three complete walls, often used in naturalistic designs to create a believable room.

**Fourth wall:** An imaginary wall between the audience and the stage. A performer might 'break' the wall and speak directly to, or otherwise interact with, the audience.

**Fly:** To raise or lower scenery, items or actors onto the stage from the fly space by a system of ropes and pulleys.

# Staging configurations

One of the early decisions made about a performance is in which space it will occur. The choices that the director, actors and designers would make when preparing a play for a large proscenium arch West End theatre, for example, would be very different from those for a show touring schools.

When blocking the play, the director needs to consider **sightlines** and how key scenes can be effective. They will decide where the best entrances and exits are and how close the performers will be to the audience. Designers will need to understand the technical aspects of the space.

**Proscenium arch**

The proscenium arch of the Royal Opera House, Covent Garden.

A type of **end on** staging in which there is a decorative frame around the stage. This is associated with older, larger theatres and opera houses. A heavy curtain usually hangs from the arch, which is raised when the play begins. The stage in front of the curtain is the **apron**. The area above the stage is the **fly space** and the areas to the sides are the **wings**.

## Advantages

- It is easy to accommodate large scenery and technical effects.
- **Stage pictures** can be effective, as most of the audience will look at the stage from roughly the same angle.
- Set changes can take place behind the closed curtain.
- Scenes can be played on the apron when the curtain is closed.
- **Box sets** can be used without obscuring sightlines.
- A 'fourth wall' is created between the audience and the stage space.
- There is room to store sets in the wings or to **fly** sets in from above.

## Disadvantages

- The sense of formality and distance does not suit all productions.
- It can seem old-fashioned and might distract from some set designs.
- Interaction with the audience can be difficult.
- Some sections of the audience might be far from the stage.
- Some blocking might seem unnatural, for example to ensure that everyone is visible in a scene set around a table.

# Amphitheatre

A large semi-circular stage with the audience seated in **tiers** around the front curve of the stage. It is associated with Ancient Greek theatres. More modern outdoor arenas include the Minack Theatre in Cornwall, and the Dalhalla, a former limestone quarry in Sweden. The design of some modern theatres, such as the Olivier Theatre at the National Theatre, is inspired by Greek amphitheatres, with its semi-circular stage and large fan-shaped **raked auditorium**.

The Odysseas Elytis Amphitheatre on the Greek island Ios.

## Advantages

- If outdoors, natural scenery can create a powerful backdrop.
- The size and appearance can create a sense of occasion.
- It is very effective for 'large' performances with big casts and spectacles.
- It can accommodate a large audience.
- There is space to use special effects such as pyrotechnics or light shows.

## Disadvantages

- It can be difficult to create intimacy or connection with the audience.
- Sound might be difficult to amplify and balance.
- If outdoors and uncovered, weather and environmental noises can cause problems and distractions.

> **KEY TERMS:**
>
> **Tiers:** Rows of seating arranged so that they slope upwards and the people behind can see over the heads of those in front.
>
> **Raked auditorium:** A sloped seating area, with its lowest part nearest the stage.

# In the round

The Young Vic Theatre in Waterloo.

> **TIP:**
>
> A theatre in the round is not necessarily circular. The stage might be a square or rectangle and the seating could be in four banks around the sides. If there is an audience on all sides of the stage, it is considered to be in the round.

Here, the audience is seated around all sides of the stage. There are some purpose-built in the round theatres, such as the Stephen Joseph in Scarborough and the Young Vic in London (although this is very occasionally configured to be end on), but more frequently it is a configuration that theatres adopt for certain productions.

## Advantages

- Creates intimacy with the audience.
- Actors usually enter and exit through the audience.
- The audience can see other audience members, giving a shared experience.
- Staging can be active and inventive so that all parts of the audience have interesting stage pictures.
- Acting can be subtle and naturalistic as the audience is so near.

## Disadvantages

- Set changes will usually be made in front of the audience.
- There are restrictions for designers, as backdrops, projections or high-backed furniture would limit sightlines.
- It is difficult to create stage pictures that work equally well for the whole audience at the same time.
- There can be technical challenges for lighting and sound.

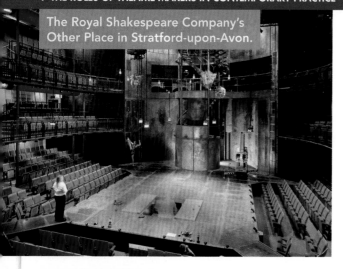

The Royal Shakespeare Company's Other Place in Stratford-upon-Avon.

## Thrust

A stage that protrudes into the auditorium with the audience on three sides. It was popular in Elizabethan times and regained popularity in the mid-20th century.

### Advantages

- It is dynamic, combining features of end on and in the round.
- The audience might feel closer to the performance as there are three first rows – one on each of the stage's three sides.
- Large pieces of scenery, backdrops and projections can be placed **upstage** without blocking sightlines.
- Interaction with the audience is easy.

### Disadvantages

- Sightlines might be blocked by large items placed **downstage**, and box sets cannot be used.
- Actors must be carefully blocked so that everyone can see them.
- Unified stage pictures are hard to create, as not all audience members see the action from the same angle.

---

**TIP:**

Most stages are flat, but some, including those replicating certain Elizabethan stages, are raked. A **raked stage** is typically highest upstage and slopes down towards the audience, leading to the terms 'upstage' and 'downstage'.

---

**KEY TERMS:**

**Upstage:** In a typical end on or thrust staging configuration, the area of the stage furthest away from the audience.

**Downstage:** In a typical end on or thrust configuration, the area of the stage closest to the audience.

**Raked stage:** A sloping stage.

**Audience interaction:** Involving the audience in the play, for example by giving them props, using direct address or bringing them on stage.

---

**EXTENSION**

Research thrust stages from Elizabethan or Jacobean times and the 20th and 21st centuries. From an audience's perspective, what are the advantages and disadvantages?

---

## Traverse

Aukland's Q Theatre's Rangatira stage set as a traverse.

A long, central stage, with an audience on both sides, facing each other. Often the extreme sides of the central area do not have an audience next to them, so these can provide more conventional acting areas. Traverse is rarely a theatre's permanent configuration.

### Advantages

- The audience might feel close to the action, as there are two long first rows.
- Audience members are facing each other so are aware of each other's reactions, providing a sense of shared experience.
- It suits certain play locations, such as a railway platform, conveyor belt or catwalk, or can help to depict a theme, such as a journey.
- It encourages dynamic, inventive blocking, and **audience interaction** is easy.

### Disadvantages

- Large scenery in a central section would block sightlines.
- It is difficult to create a stage picture that is the same for the full audience.
- The long, thin acting area can make some blocking challenging.
- Lighting needs to be carefully plotted and focused to avoid it spilling onto the audience.

# Black box

A simple room with black walls. Usually, there is no raised stage and the audience seating can be arranged flexibly. It is often associated with studio or chamber performances.

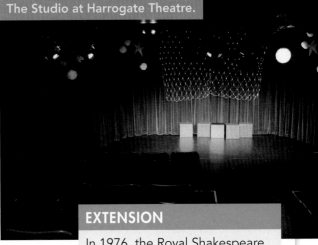

The Studio at Harrogate Theatre.

## Advantages

- It is a flexible space in which seating is arranged to suit the production.
- It is an intimate space with the audience close to the action.
- It can create an intense atmosphere.
- It is suitable for inexpensive or experimental work.
- Considered a 'blank canvas', it can allow a creative team to be imaginative and bold.

## Disadvantages

- The small space makes it challenging to create large, dramatic effects.
- Scenery needs to be carefully designed to fit the space and the configuration.
- It might seem plain or unexciting compared with other performance spaces.
- If the stage is on the studio floor, tiered seating might be needed.

### EXTENSION

In 1976, the Royal Shakespeare Company performed a 'black box' version of *Macbeth*, starring Ian McKellen and Judi Dench. Research the production and note benefits or disadvantages that you discover from reviews and production photographs.

# Promenade

French company Rara Woulib lead the audience around Greenwich in their production of *Deblozay*.

Here, the audience often stands and follows the actors through the performance. A promenade production might take place in a conventional theatre, or could be designed for a **site-specific** performance in an unusual location. Some promenade productions are **immersive**, where the audience participates, becoming part of the **narrative**.

## Advantages

- It is a very dynamic, active type of theatre, which involves the audience closely.
- It encourages an original type of storytelling, which suits certain plays.
- It creates a sense of occasion and event.

## Disadvantages

- The performers and stage crew must be skilled at focusing the audience's attention and ensuring that everyone can see and hear the action.
- Some audience members might find standing or moving around difficult.
- There can be health and safety risks.

### KEY TERMS:

**Site specific:** A performance in a location other than a theatre, such as a warehouse, office, museum or town square.

**Immersive:** A type of theatre that often includes roles for audience members, takes place in a specific, unique environment and has different narrative strands.

**Narrative:** A story and how it is told.

### EXTENSION

To learn more about promenade productions, research *The Passion*, staged over 72 hours in Port Talbot, or the work of Punchdrunk Theatre Company or dreamspeakthink.

## TASK 1.1

**A** Imagine you have been asked to create an original production of the fairy tale *Little Red Riding Hood*. Below are four goals for different productions of the play. For each bullet point, suggest a theatre configuration that might meet that goal well. Explain why your choice is suitable.

- Encourages audience interaction
- Scenery changes could be hidden
- The audience could follow the Wolf at one point
- Actors enter and exit through the audience.

**B** Using your chosen staging concept for *Little Red Riding Hood*, write a paragraph or draw a storyboard explaining how you would stage the first encounter between the Wolf and Little Red Riding Hood. Consider:

- What scenery would you have?
- Where would the items of set and the actors be positioned?
- How close would the audience be to the action?

## WHAT THE SPECIFICATION SAYS...

Learners should be able to:

- State advantages and disadvantages for the decisions made directing acting and designing for a performance.

Learners must know and understand:

- Acting skills, including:
  - Blocking
  - Characterisation
  - Improvisation.
- How meaning is communicated through:
  - The use of performance space and spatial relationships on stage.

## TASK 1.2

**A** Use stage directions to create a short scene from *Little Red Riding Hood* for an end on stage. Consider:

- Do your blocking choices help to make the story clear and interesting?
- How is the relationship between the characters revealed?

**B** Check that you have correctly noted the blocking, such as 'Wolf enters UR'.

## KEY TERMS:

**Cross:** Movement from one part of the stage to another.

**Counter-cross:** Movement in opposition to another character's cross: one going stage left when the other goes stage right, for example.

# Acting skills

## Blocking

Throughout the rehearsal process, the director and actors will decide on the moves the characters will make. This is the play's blocking and it influences how the audience understands the characters and the plot. For example, if a character turns and walks away from another character, this gives the audience clues to what that character is thinking and feeling.

Blocking is noted by referring to the different parts of the stage as shown in the diagram below.

When a character moves from one area of the stage to another it is called a **cross**. If an actor is moving from Upstage Right to Downstage Left, they might note in their script that they are crossing UR to DL. If a character is standing downstage of another character, they are closer to the audience. If they move behind another character, they are moving upstage of that actor. If one character crosses the stage while another crosses in the other direction, this is a **counter-cross**.

It is part of the actor's job to remember and repeat blocking in performance after performance.

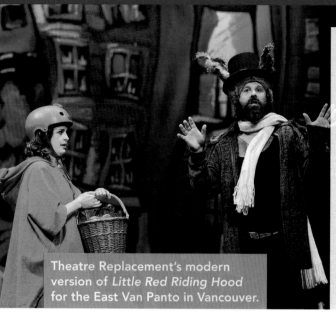

**Theatre Replacement's modern version of *Little Red Riding Hood* for the East Van Panto in Vancouver.**

# Characterisation

Throughout the course, you will be looking at how a sense of **character** can be created. The choices you make should have an impact on the audience. Think about the effects you are creating. Do you want the audience to:

- Like or sympathise with your character?
- Be amused or frightened by your character?
- Follow how your character develops?
- Understand what your character is thinking and feeling?
- Feel tense and involved with your character's situation?

To begin working on characterisation, you should think about your character's background, their **motivations** and their relationships to the other characters.

## TASK 1.3

**A** Working in a small group, discuss the characters in *Little Red Riding Hood*. In your version:

- What are the backgrounds of Little Red Riding Hood and the Wolf?
- What is their home life like?
- Why is this day different from usual?
- What does Little Red Riding Hood want?
- What does the Wolf want?

**B** Together, improvise or write a short scene in which an audience would see what each character wants when they meet in the woods and their individual ways of trying to get what they want.

**C** Then create three **still images** from this work, noting how the actors use their physical skills of facial expression, posture and gesture to show what they are thinking and feeling.

# Improvisation

Improvisation is acting without a script. It is a technique often used in rehearsals when developing a character, or when a script is being devised. During the creative process, it can aid understanding of a character and enrich the work. For example, in a rehearsal, you could **hot seat** the characters to discover more about them or have them improvise a scene that is not in the script, so that you understand what happened before the scripted scene.

**TIP:**

An improvised scene exploring what happened before a scripted scene is called a pre-scene.

## TASK 1.4

**A** In a group, take it in turns to hot seat both the Wolf and Little Red Riding Hood to find out more about them. You might ask Little Red Riding Hood why she has wandered from her path, for example, or ask the Wolf why he only hunts humans.

**B** Improvise a scene with the Wolf before he came across Little Red Riding Hood. Has he promised to get food for someone else, for example, or has he been teased for being a poor hunter?

**C** Now put together all the work you have done on this scene, including your blocking, characterisation and understanding based on your improvisations. How have you used the stage space and shown the relationship between the characters? Evaluate how successful your work was and suggest what you could do to improve it further.

**KEY TERMS:**

**Character:** A person or other being in a play, novel, film or other story.

**Motivation:** The feelings behind what a character wants or needs.

**Still image:** A frozen image showing the facial expressions and physical positions, including posture and gesture, of one or more characters.

**Hot seat:** A technique in which a performer sits in a chair (the 'hot seat') and answers questions in character.

**WHAT THE SPECIFICATION SAYS...**

Learners must know and understand:
- How meaning is communicated through:
  - The design of: set, props, costume, lighting and sound.

**KEY TERM:**

Colour palette: The range of colours used, for example earth tones, primary colours or pastels.

# Design

Throughout the course components, there are opportunities to explore design specialisms:

- Set and props
- Costume, including, as appropriate, hair, make-up and masks
- Lighting
- Sound.

## Collaboration

Typically, designers will work with the director to make sure that their designs support and advance the director's concept or artistic vision of the play. They might also collaborate with each other to make sure that their designs work well together. Set and costume designers, for example, will probably agree a time period and **colour palette** so that the set and costumes complement each other. Meanwhile, the lighting designer has to make sure that the lighting works in conjunction with the set and costumes, for example by using appropriate colour filters and ensuring that important areas are properly lit. In addition, the sound designer will ensure that the sound is suitable for the setting, for example by creating sound effects that reflect the correct period of time, mood or location.

Opulent costumes for a ballet version of *Little Red Riding Hood* in Beijing.

# Background research and design choices

In order to develop their designs, a designer might choose to research the period of time in which a play is set and recreate the furniture, fabric or music associated with that period. Many **naturalistic** productions do this in order to create a believable world that the characters inhabit. However, a director and designer might choose to create **abstract**, **stylised** or **minimalistic** designs. A design might be **symbolic**, emphasising a theme or idea from the play.

A set designer for a naturalistic *Little Red Riding Hood*, for example, might research the type of trees grown in the country where it is set and then recreate, as accurately as possible, a section of the woods appropriate for a specific season. By contrast, a symbolic set for the same play might emphasise danger, so, instead of recreating the woods, would have prominent 'Danger' and 'Turn Back' signs and flashing lights. A minimalistic set might consist of a simple **rostrum**, with a single artificial tree on it.

Another concept could be to update and relocate the setting, placing the action in a shopping centre or a nightclub. The designers would then need to decide how that would affect their choices of sound, lighting, costume and setting. The **semiotics** of these choices will convey particular information to the audience.

## KEY TERMS:

**Naturalistic:** Lifelike, realistic, believable.

**Abstract:** Not realistic or lifelike, but instead using colours, shapes, textures, sounds and other means to achieve a particular 'unnatural' effect.

**Stylised:** Not realistic; done in a particular manner that perhaps emphasises one element of the play or production.

**Minimalistic:** Simple, using few elements, stripped back.

**Symbolic/ism:** Using something to represent something else, such as a rose to symbolise love or an oversized map to symbolise property or a journey. Symbolic design might be dressing characters in white to suggest purity, or using the overly loud ticking of a clock to indicate the passing of time.

**Rostrum:** A portable platform upon which actors can perform. Some are constructed using modules, so that they can provide different levels.

**Semiotics:** How meaning is created and communicated through systems of signs and symbols. All the elements that make up a theatrical performance have meaning and an audience 'reads' or interprets them to understand the performance.

## TASK 1.5

**A** For a naturalistic production of *Little Red Riding Hood*, sketch a costume for Little Red Riding Hood and make a list of possible natural sound effects.

**B** For a stylised or abstract version, sketch a costume for the Wolf and make a list of abstract sound effects.

**C** Sketch two different sets for *Little Red Riding Hood*: one in the round and one for a promenade production.

**D** Imagine two different audiences – one made up of small children and one of adults – and make notes on how that might affect your ideas for the design of the play.

## CHECK YOUR LEARNING
### The roles of theatre makers in contemporary practice

**Can you...?**

✓ Explain what the three components for your Drama course are and what is involved in each.

✓ Give details of what the key theatre makers do.

✓ Describe all the different staging configurations.

✓ Provide at least two advantages and two disadvantages for each staging configuration.

✓ Explain how an actor can use stage space and physical skills.

✓ Define blocking, characterisation and improvisation.

✓ Explain the different design specialisms in theatre.

✓ Find definitions of key terms in this book.

# SECTION A
# SET TEXTS

## WHAT THE SPECIFICATION SAYS...

Learners will explore practically a performance text to demonstrate their knowledge and understanding of drama.

Through their practical study, learners need to know how characters and performances communicate ideas and meaning to an audience.

Learners are expected to:

• (AO3) Demonstrate knowledge and understanding of how drama and theatre is developed and performed.

## HOW YOU WILL BE ASSESSED

Component 4 is your written examination. It is worth 80 marks and 40 per cent of your final GCSE. Fifty of the marks are assessed in Section A, which consists of a series of questions testing your understanding of your chosen set text and how its meaning could be realised in a performance. For this, you need to demonstrate your insight into acting, design and directing choices, as well as the historical and/or social context of your chosen text.

No matter which set text you study, you will be expected to display certain skills and knowledge, such as how the stage space could be used effectively, how a character might be costumed or how the play (or a section of it) could be performed to achieve a particular effect. In your writing, you should use correct theatre terminology.

### KEY TERM:

**Genre:** A category or type of drama, such as comedy, tragedy or musical theatre, usually with its own conventions.

# How to read a play

For GCSE Drama, you are not reading your performance text simply as a piece of literature. Instead, you should think of it as a blueprint for a production. You must engage creatively with the text, imagining and practically exploring different choices that an actor, designer or director could make when staging a production of the play. These choices will have an impact on how the audience understands and is affected by the play.

The introductory pages here offer guidance and exercises to help you to discuss and write about any of the plays with confidence, while the following chapter provides specific study guides for each set text.

# Characteristics of drama

A play consists of dialogue and stage directions. The dialogue is spoken by the play's characters. Through dialogue and physical actions, the characters reveal their thoughts, feelings and motivations. Stage directions can help the reader, and ultimately the audience, to understand the world of the play, such as its period and location, as well as specifying any physical objects needed, such as furniture or props. Stage directions might indicate actors' tones of voice, use of props and movements, such as entrances, exits, fights, gestures and other actions necessary for the play. They could also indicate sound effects, lighting changes, costumes or music that could be used in the play.

What the playwright and director are trying to achieve might, in part, be determined by the **genre** of the play. There are many different genres represented by the set texts you might study:

*Blood Brothers* – musical theatre

*Death of a Salesman* – modern tragedy

*Find Me* – social drama

*Gizmo* – children's and young people's theatre

*Kindertransport* – historical drama

*Missing Dan Nolan* – verbatim theatre

*Misterman* – social drama/monologue.

# Requirements of individual plays

In addition to knowing the plot of your set play, you must be aware of the particular demands the piece makes on the actors, designers and director. A **verbatim play**, such as *Missing Dan Nolan*, gives voice to those who have suffered the loss of a loved one, a subject which, as an actor, director or designer, you must find a way of conveying sensitively.

Every play has a **context**, including when it is set and when it was written. If a play is rooted in a particular historical context, such as *Kindertransport*, which moves between two distinct and different time periods, you must consider the choices to be made in order to clarify these shifting time periods for your audience. You might also need to consider the social context of the play, such as attitudes towards mental health, as seen in *Find Me*, or the effects of unemployment as portrayed in *Blood Brothers*.

You should also consider the **performance style** of the play. *Death of a Salesman* is usually performed in a naturalistic style, whereas *Gizmo*, with its demanding physicality, is more stylised. Some plays combine styles. *Kindertransport*, for example, is largely naturalistic, but has stylised sequences involving the Ratcatcher.

As you work on the play, be aware of whether you would be creating a piece of drama that is realistic and lifelike or if the play requires a heightened, theatrical effect. Given the style of the play, you may use certain **performance conventions**, such as **mime**, **narration** or audience interaction. Ideally, the acting, design and direction will all work towards a unified performance style.

## TASK 2.1

**A** With a partner, discuss the style of the play you are studying and decide whether it is naturalistic, stylised (or 'non-naturalistic') or a combination of the two. Describe at least three moments from the play to support your point of view. (These moments might include dialogue and/or stage directions.)

**B** Describe how you think those three moments should be performed, directed or designed. Justify your choices through brief explanation of your artistic ideas and reference to the meanings, themes, form and/or style of the text.

# Performing a text

## Acting choices: physical skills

From the moment an actor walks on stage, the audience begins interpreting their character. The audience will note their physical characteristics such as their build and age, and form assumptions about the character. In order to develop their characterisation, an actor will use their physical and vocal skills to add to these initial impressions. Their choices should help the audience to understand and engage with the character's role within the play. Typical physical skills an actor uses when interpreting a character include:

**Ways of moving** / **Gestures** / **Facial expressions** / **Posture**

**KEY TERMS:**

**Verbatim play/theatre:** A type of documentary theatre that uses the words of real people.

**Context:** The circumstances of the setting of a play, such as the location, period of time or conventions.

**Performance style:** The way in which something is performed, such as naturalistically or stylised.

**Performance conventions:** Theatrical techniques used in particular types of performance, such as speaking directly to the audience (direct address) or miming the use of props rather than having them on stage.

**Mime:** To act without words. This might involve using gestures or movements to express emotions or creating a scene to suggest the presence of props or other physical items when none are present, such as 'pretending' to open a door.

**Narration:** A commentary or background to a play or other story.

**WHAT THE SPECIFICATION SAYS...**

Learners must know and understand:

In relation to their performance text:

• How meaning is communicated through:
  • The use of performance space and spatial relationships on stage
  • The relationship between performers and audience
  • The design of: set, props, costume, lighting and sound
  • An actor's vocal and physical interpretation of character
  • The use of performance conventions.

John Malkovich and Dustin Hoffman in *Death of a Salesman*.

## TASK 2.2

A Work with a partner to choose a section from the play you are studying in which a character enters a space (this might be a room or simply an area of the stage). Take turns to experiment with how the character enters by trying different uses of:

- **Movement**, for example quick or slow; graceful or awkward
- **Gestures**, such as arms at sides or waving or pointing
- **Facial expressions**, perhaps smiling or anxious
- **Posture**, for example upright or hunched over.

B Discuss with your partner your impressions of each entrance. What did you learn about the character? How was this conveyed?

C Now talk about where the character has been before they entered the space and why they have now entered. Consider:

- Are they looking for someone?
- Are they escaping from somewhere or someone?
- Do they want to be there?
- Are they familiar with the space?
- What are they hoping will happen?
- Are they in a hurry, or do they have all the time in the world?
- Are they alone, or are they with someone?
- What other factors influence how they enter?

Once you have agreed the character's motivations, experiment again with the entrance, making sure your posture, movements, gestures and expressions reflect your character's motivations.

D Make notes of the physical choices you have decided on for that entrance in the play. Write three sentences or so, explaining why you made those choices.

E Next, locate a moment in the play that you believe to be the play's **climax**, when the action is at its most tense. Create a still image with your partner that shows one of the character's physical reactions to this important moment. What emotion is your character feeling and how can this be shown through expression, physical position and posture?

F Sketch the position you have chosen for your character and write a few sentences explaining how this use of physical skills is helpful to the audience at the climax of the play.

### KEY TERM:

**Climax:** The most intense moment in the play, often shortly before the resolution.

## Acting choices: vocal skills

An actor's voice is one of their most essential tools. With their voice, an actor can suggest a character's background, emotional state and intentions. Examples of vocal skills include:

- **Volume:** How loudly or softly a line is said
- **Pitch:** How high or low the vocal register is or if it suddenly changes
- **Timing/Pace:** How quickly or slowly a line is said or if there are particular pauses or changes in rhythm or tempo
- **Intonation:** The tone of voice, such as tender or harsh, or the emphasis or colouring of certain words

- **Phrasing:** How lines are shaped, such as emphasising the poetry of a line or speaking informally or haltingly.
- **Accent/Dialect:** Pronouncing words in a way that is associated with certain geographical regions or social groups
- **Emotional range:** Showing the character's feelings, for example by laughing, crying, sighing, shouting, or vocally trembling or choking while trying to control an emotion (such as attempting to hide sorrow or fear).

## TASK 2.3

**A** Working with a partner, choose a small section of dialogue from the play you are studying. (In the case of *Misterman*, you may choose a section of the monologue and alternate saying the lines.) A section of about ten lines would be ideal. Stand back to back and say the lines to each other, listening carefully to how your partner delivers their line before you say yours. What do you notice about your partner's volume, pitch, pace and intonation?

- Are they speaking quickly and quietly?
- Do they speak slowly and harshly?
- Does the pitch of their voice vary (perhaps getting higher or lower at the end of sentences)?

**B** Now facing each other, experiment with the same lines, but by imagining the following situations:

- You are both very frightened and afraid of being overheard.
- One of you is very angry, while the other is trying to calm you down.
- You both need to finish this conversation as quickly as possible.
- You are from different parts of the country or world and find it difficult to understand each other.

Discuss how these different situations affected your vocal choices.

**C** Focus on what you know about the character or characters who are speaking in this scene. Make notes on:

- Their background (including where they are from)
- Their emotional state
- What they want in this scene.

**D** Now read the scene again, using your understanding of the character's background, feelings and intentions to influence how they use their voice.

**E** Complete these sentences:

This character, _____ [name] uses the vocal skills _____ to show _____. From this, the audience will understand or feel _____.

**F** Lastly, choose three moments from the play when you think one of the characters requires specific vocal skills and explain what you learn about the character from their use of their voice. For example:

Mr Bishop is a Yorkshire farmer, so speaks in a dialect of that region. He uses a stern intonation when he is angry at his son for not helping with the work on the farm. He uses pauses and shows his emotional range in his final speech, when he begins to express his feelings on the line 'Go if you...', but is choked up and can't continue. This will suggest to the audience that, despite his gruff exterior, he has tender feelings.

Cillian Murphy in the original production of *Misterman*.

**TIP:**

The sample candidate-style responses in this chapter are based on an imaginary play. When reading them, however, note how the ideas are organised, the type of terminology used and how ideas are justified. These skills can be applied to any of the set texts.

## KEY TERMS:

**Concept:** A unifying idea about a production, such as when it is set or how it will be interpreted and performed.

**Proxemics:** How spatial relationships between one performer and other performers and between performers and their stage environment work and create meaning.

# Directorial choices

The director is responsible for the overall **concept** or artistic vision of the play. They might decide to concentrate on a particular theme or set it in a specific location or time period. The director might consider the playwright's intention, for example a certain message about injustice, and how they hope the audience will react to their play. The director will guide the actors' performances, including how they use the stage space and interact with each other and the audience. The director might also choose the staging configuration and work with the designers on how the space is used.

## Staging

In the round/minimalistic (*Equus* set design by Kerry Bradley).

Thrust/naturalistic (*The Odd Couple* set design by Timothy Mackabee).

Traverse/period (*55 Days* set design by Ashley Martin-Davis).

Proscenium arch with a combined naturalistic and stylised backdrop (*The Hotel Cerise* set design by Ellen Cairns).

---

## TASK 2.4

**A** In a small group, study the four stage configurations above and decide which would best suit the play you have studied, and why.

**B** Try to recreate the staging configuration in the room you are working. If you have chosen theatre in the round, for example, mark out a circular area, so you know where the audience is and where entrances and exits are.

**C** Now choose a scene from the play to act. One member of your group will act as director and will block the scene, indicating when and where the actors need to move. The director should consider **proxemics**, including between the actors and the audience, and how this affects the audience's understanding and sense of involvement.

**D** Discuss if there were any moments that might have been unclear or ineffective for the audience.

**E** Stage the same scene again, but this time using a different staging configuration.

**F** After discussion, write down two advantages and two disadvantages of each of the staging configurations you tried. You might consider:

- Was it easy for the audience to see what was happening, including facial expressions and relationships between characters?
- Did the proxemics of the characters, to each other and to the audience, suit the performance and help to convey the action and characterisation?

- How could a set design or set furnishings suggested by the script be used in the staging configuration or be altered to suit it?
- Are the actors' entrances, exits and positioning on stage effective?
- Is it necessary that all of the audience sees the production from the same angle so that specific stage pictures are created?
- Would moments of audience interaction be improved by a certain stage configuration?

## Themes

**TASK 2.5**

When arriving at an artistic vision for a play, a director might consider the play's themes.

Below is the beginning of a 'theme' mind map for a play. Using this example, draw a mind map with a theme from your set play. Depending on the play, you might choose, for example: family, love, violence, community, mental health, money, social class, modern technology, memory, truth or fate.

Dialogue · Symbolism · Staging

Message · **Theme: Family** · Effects on the audience

Design · Performance style

# Design choices

Designers contribute to a performance in many areas, including:

**Costume** / **Set** / **Props** / **Lighting** / **Sound**

As you study your set text, make notes of opportunities for creative choices in each of these areas.

## Costumes

When designing a costume, you might consider:

- The style of the production (Is it realistic/naturalistic or stylised/non-naturalistic?)
- The period and location of the play
- The personality and occupation of the character
- Fit and silhouette
- Colours and fabrics
- The condition of the costume (Is it clean and new or dirty and well worn?)
- The effect of the costume on the audience's perception of the character.

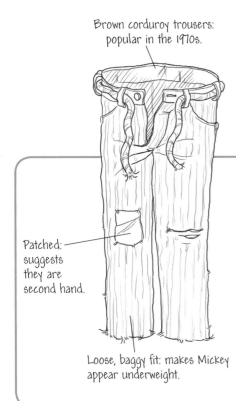

Brown corduroy trousers: popular in the 1970s.

Patched: suggests they are second hand.

Loose, baggy fit: makes Mickey appear underweight.

## TASK 2.6

**A** Research potential costume choices for a character in the play you are studying. Depending on the demands of the play, you could do this by:

- Looking at photographs from the period (for example, 1960s–70s for *Blood Brothers* or the Second World War for *Kindertransport*)
- Observing real-life characters who resemble those in the play
- Noting suitable clothing you come across in films, newspapers and magazines and on television and websites
- Examining paintings or photographs for ideas
- Exploring websites of costume designers for inspiration.

**B** Based on your research, draw some costume sketches for your chosen character and annotate them to explain your choices, as in the example on the left from *Blood Brothers*.

### EXTENSION

Some designers create mood or inspiration boards to collect their ideas for a design. These might include fabric samples, photographs, sketches, colour swatches and any other images that they find aids their creative process. Try creating your own inspiration board for a costume or set of the play you are studying.

A costume research board by designer Laura Ann Price is provided here as an example.

GRAHAM
A CHIP IN THE SUGAR

### KEY TERM:

**Theatrical metaphor:** Comparing something in the play to something else in order to make a point. For example, to indicate conflict, you could use the theatrical metaphor of placing the action in a boxing ring or at a football match.

## Set and props

When designing a set, consider the requirements of the play, including:

- The period and location of the world of the play
- Any location changes and ways of showing these.
- The colours, textures and materials used in your set
- The exits and entrances and, if needed, the levels, of your set
- If there is a theme to reinforce with your set through symbolism or **theatrical metaphor**.

## TASK 2.7

**A** With a partner, make a list of any props mentioned in the play.

**B** Choose one and either draw a sketch or write three sentences describing how it will look and be used in the play. Explain why it is important in the context of the drama.

**TIP:**

Remember to consider the impact that your design choices will have on the audience and how your designs will help to tell the story of the play.

## TASK 2.8

**A** Using one of the staging configurations shown on pages 8–11, draw a set design for the opening of the play you are studying.

**B** Complete the following sentences:
- The set I have designed is appropriate for this play because…
- For this set design, the audience will (learn/think/wonder/feel)…

# Sound and lighting

Both sound and lighting add immeasurably to the impact of a production. When designing for either of these, consider:

- How does it contribute to the period or setting of the play?
- How does it help to establish the mood or atmosphere of the play?
- Will it help with transitions, perhaps showing passages of time or changes in location or mental states?
- What equipment will be needed to produce the design?
- How will it help to tell the story of the play?
- What effect will it have on the audience?

**LOOK HERE**

For more information about how lighting and sound effects can be created, see pages 224–229.

## TASK 2.9

**A** Below is a short excerpt from a candidate's writing about sound and lighting. List all the technical terminology used.

In the beginning of the play, there will be a blackout **[1]** and the audience will hear a recording of the beeping sound of a hospital monitor. **[2]** The lights will fade up **[3]** to reveal a hospital room with a group of people gathered around a bed. The lights will have a green filter, **[4]** which will emphasise the green hospital gowns the doctors are wearing and also make the actors' complexions look green and eerie. **[5]** Off stage, an actor using a microphone **[6]** will say the first line.

**B** Choose a section from the play you are studying (between one or two pages) and note opportunities for sound or lighting design. Aim to include technical vocabulary, as in the example above.

**[1]** Identifies the opening lighting state.

**[2]** Suggests a recorded sound effect.

**[3]** Identifies how a lighting transition will occur.

**[4]** States a choice of colour filter.

**[5]** Justifies choice and explains effect.

**[6]** Suggests a form of amplification.

**TIP:**

Remember to use correct theatrical terminology when writing about your performance and production ideas. Revise the key terms defined in this chapter so that you can use them with confidence.

## BLOOD BROTHERS
### by Willy Russell

The OCR specification identifies editions of the texts that are used to set questions in the 'Drama: Performance and response' (Component 04) examination paper. It is not required that centres use these editions for teaching this component.

Here, page numbers refer to the Methuen Modern Classics edition of *Blood Brothers*, ISBN-13: 978-0-4137-6770-7, one of the editions used by OCR for question setting.

# Plot synopsis

## Act One

The play opens with the Narrator's 'story of the Johnstone Twins'. The Narrator invites the audience to 'judge' Mrs Johnstone, the working-class mother of the twins.

Mrs Johnstone sings about her past and how, by the time she was 25, her husband had abandoned her, leaving her with seven children and pregnant again.

Mrs Johnstone works as a cleaner for the Lyons, a middle-class couple who have been unable to have children. When Mrs Lyons learns that Mrs Johnstone is expecting twins, she asks for one. Mrs Johnstone reluctantly agrees when she sees the advantages that a child raised by the Lyons would have. Mrs Lyons makes Mrs Johnstone swear on the Bible to make it a 'binding agreement'.

When the twins are born, Mrs Lyons takes Edward, while Mrs Johnstone keeps Mickey. Mrs Lyons fires Mrs Johnstone from her cleaning job. Mrs Johnstone tries to take Edward back, but Mrs Lyons plays on Mrs Johnstone's superstitions and tells her that the boys will 'immediately die' if they ever learn that they are related.

Seven years later, Mickey meets Edward. The boys strike up an immediate friendship, becoming 'blood brothers'. When Mickey appears at the Lyons house, Mrs Lyons tells Edward he should never go 'where boys like that live'. Edward swears at Mrs Lyons, who hits him, which she immediately regrets.

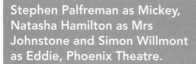

Stephen Palfreman as Mickey, Natasha Hamilton as Mrs Johnstone and Simon Willmont as Eddie, Phoenix Theatre.

On the street, Sammy (Mickey's brother) and other children tease Mickey, but school friend Linda is protective of him. Mickey introduces Edward to Linda and the three get into mischief, eventually being apprehended by a Policeman.

The Policeman visits both the Lyons and Johnstone homes. He threatens Mrs Johnstone with 'the courts', whereas he tells the Lyons that the children's misdemeanour was 'more of a prank'. Mr Lyons, concerned by his wife's worries, agrees that they should move away. Edward arrives at the Johnstone house to say goodbye and Mrs Johnstone gives him a locket with a photograph of Mickey in it.

The first act ends with the Johnstones discovering that they are being moved to a new area, with Mrs Johnstone declaring it a 'bright new day'.

## Act Two

Seven years have passed. Mickey and Edward are now 14 and experiencing adolescent worries and insecurities. Linda openly declares her love for Mickey, but a self-conscious Mickey can't express his feelings.

Both Mickey and Edward get in trouble at their schools: Edward for refusing to hand over the locket to a teacher, and Mickey for misbehaving in class. When Edward returns home, Mrs Lyons is upset to discover that Mrs Johnstone gave Edward the locket.

Linda and Mickey take a walk in a field, but Linda storms off when Mickey doesn't respond to her flirting. Edward and Mickey see each other from a distance and each wishes he was like the other boy. When they speak, they realise that they were childhood friends and resume their friendship.

Mrs Lyons goes to Mrs Johnstone's home and accuses her of following the Lyons and spoiling her relationship with Edward. She attacks Mrs Johnstone with a knife, but is fought off.

A deeper friendship between Linda, Mickey and Edward develops. This happy period ends when Edward departs for university and Mickey gets a job in a box factory. Although both boys love Linda, neither has declared his feelings. Edward encourages Mickey to let Linda know how he feels. Linda and Mickey finally kiss.

Linda becomes pregnant and marries Mickey. Mickey is made redundant. When Edward returns, Mickey and he argue. Sammy offers Mickey money to help with a robbery. The robbery goes wrong and Mickey goes to prison.

Some years later, Mickey emerges from prison, depressed and addicted to pills. Edward is now a city councillor. Mrs Lyons sees Edward and Linda together and tells Mickey. Mickey bursts into a council meeting and threatens Edward. Mrs Johnstone tells him not to hurt Edward as they are brothers. Mickey is outraged to learn that he could have been like Edward. He waves his hand and his gun 'explodes', killing Edward. The police shoot Mickey.

While Mrs Johnstone mourns the deaths of her sons, the Narrator asks what lessons can be learned from this tale: 'Could it be what we, the English, have come to know as class?'

**TIP:**

You might want to consider the playwright's intentions in writing the play. For example, what might Willy Russell be saying about class, social injustice and family relationships?

## TASK 3.1

**A** Working in a small group, create a two-minute version of the play, making sure that you cover what you all agree are the most significant events in the plot.

**B** Given your understanding of the play's plot, answer the following questions:

**1** What is the effect of the 'binding agreement' with Mrs Lyons on Mrs Johnstone's actions in the play?

**2** What is Mrs Lyons' reaction to seeing the locket Mrs Johnstone has given to Edward?

**3** When Mickey loses his job, how is his life changed?

**4** What is Mickey's reaction to discovering Edward and he are twins?

## KEY TERMS:

**Foreboding:** A feeling that something bad will happen. Associated with **foreshadowing:** a warning or hint of something that is going to happen.

**Protagonist:** The main character of a narrative.

**Direct address:** Speaking directly to the audience.

# Genre

*Blood Brothers* has elements of several different genres. As it features songs and music, it is an example of musical theatre, but it also contains many comic elements (misunderstandings, funny dialogue, exaggerated characters) and tragic aspects (a sense of **foreboding**, violence, the death of **protagonists**). Additionally, it has some features associated with political drama, including a social message (the unequal treatment of different social classes) and use of **direct address** to the audience by the Narrator to emphasise this message.

## TASK 3.2

**A** Read the first meeting between Edward and Mickey (pages 27–30). With a partner, experiment with how this could be performed to emphasise the comedy of the scene. Consider:

- The differences between the boys, including their costumes
- How they might interact with each other
- How they might use gestures and movement
- How they might use vocal skills such as accent, volume, diction and pace.

**B** Look closely at the argument between the older Edward and Mickey (pages 90–93). Explore how this could be performed to emphasise the conflict between the characters. Consider:

- What has happened to Edward and Mickey before this scene
- How costumes can highlight the differences between them
- How they might interact with each other
- How they might use vocal skills, such as accent, volume, diction and pace.

**C** Choose one of these two scenes and write a paragraph, or create a series of images for a storyboard, to explain how it could be performed and staged. Look especially to highlight the importance of these features in establishing the relationship between the characters and the mood of the scene.

Jordan Phelps, as the Narrator, surveys the ominous scene of the street outside Mrs Johnstone's house, Theo Ubique Cabaret Theatre, Chicago.

# Structure

*Blood Brothers* is divided into two acts. The first covers roughly seven years (from Mrs Johnstone's pregnancy to the boys at the age of seven), and the second act spans approximately ten years (from the boys at 14 to their deaths in their 20s). The structure of the play can be described as book-ended because the Narrator and Mrs Johnstone start and end the play. The Narrator's speech of rhyming lines spoken at the play's opening is completed in the play's final moments.

# Style

Due to the use of narration, verse, songs and multi-rolling (such as the same actor playing the Milkman and the Gynaecologist), the style of the play is sometimes considered non-naturalistic. However, other scenes, such as those between Mrs Lyons and Mrs Johnstone, Linda and Mickey or Mickey and Edward are usually performed naturalistically.

**A** From your knowledge and understanding of *Blood Brothers*, identify examples of the following structural or stylistic features:

- Narration
- Climax
- Conflict
- Foreshadowing
- A passage of a large amount of time.

**B** Read the statements below about the play. Then work with a partner to put them in order, with the one you agree with most as 1, and the one you agree with least as 5.

☐ The play is about social class and the injustices associated with it.

☐ The play is a modern fairy tale or myth.

☐ It is a love story.

☐ It is a modern tragedy exploring the difficulties of the working class.

☐ The play shows the effects of one bad decision.

# Context

In 1981, Willy Russell first wrote *Blood Brothers* as a youth play. He then developed it into a musical that was first performed in 1983. It enjoyed great success, including winning the Olivier Award for Best New Musical.

## Historical context

*Blood Brothers* is set in Liverpool. Although Russell does not mention particular years in his play, the action is thought to span the late 1950s or early 1960s to the early 1980s.

In the 19th century, Liverpool was a thriving city, with its port attracting industries and workers. During the 20th century, however, Liverpool's economic fortunes began to fail as major employers, such as the docks and manufacturers, experienced difficulties. This was particularly severe in the 1970s and early 1980s, when many people lost their jobs.

Russell depicts this when Mr Lyons sings 'Take a Letter, Miss Jones' while firing employees, including Mickey. The anxiety and desperation of those out of work is shown when Mickey explains what job-hunting is like: 'But, but after three months of nothin', the same answer everywhere, nothin', nothin', down for y', I'd crawl back to that job for half the pay and double the hours.' (page 92). In 1983, a Liverpool MP spoke in parliament about the effects of unemployment in Liverpool, where one in five people were '**on the dole**' and, in some districts, half the inhabitants were unemployed.

Unemployed workers wait outside the Ministry of Labour office in Liverpool, 1962.

Teenagers kill time with an abandoned car in 1970s Liverpool.

**KEY TERM:**

**On the dole:** Being out of work and receiving unemployment benefit from the government (from 'doling' or handing out of money).

27

A bronze statue of the Beatles in front of the Port of Liverpool Building.

## Cultural context

Mrs Johnstone is compared to Marilyn Monroe, a beautiful Hollywood star who would have been popular when Mrs Johnstone first met her husband. Music, such as that of the Beatles, was very important in the 1960s and Willy Russell was a semi-professional singer, making the use of contemporary pop music particularly appropriate for the play. In the 1960s and 1970s, Liverpool was at the forefront of youth culture, including fashions, such as mini-skirts and long hair. Clothing was often brightly coloured or patterned and items such as waistcoats or leather jackets were popular for men. The architecture of Liverpool at the time ranged from grand civic buildings to poor tenements. Some areas were still severely affected by the heavy bombings that Liverpool suffered during the Second World War.

## Social context

Middle-class people, like the Lyons, generally experienced fewer ill effects caused by the 1970s economic **recession** and had more opportunities for education and employment. Mickey and Linda, like Willy Russell himself, attend a non-selective secondary modern school. Edward goes to a private boarding school, spending term times at school and returning home for the holidays. Both are depicted as being flawed, but Edward's school has higher aspirations for him ('Talk of Oxbridge', page 63), while Mickey's teacher wonders if Mickey will ever be employed: 'Just how the hell do you hope to get a job when you never listen to anythin'' (page 67).

Although there had been some improvement for women's rights with the passing of the 1975 Sex Discrimination Act, a woman's role of wife and mother was still considered by many to be their most important. In *Blood Brothers*, none of the lead female characters is shown as having a powerful job outside the home, suggesting the importance of their domestic roles.

A middle-class 1970s couple window shopping.

### KEY TERM:

**Recession:** A period of economic unproductivity or decline, which is often associated with high unemployment and rising prices.

The 'quiet room' of a boys' boarding school, 1966.

Workers at the Liverpool Tate and Lyle factory, 1961. They would often pack sugar from 6am to 2pm before doing the family wash in the corporation laundry.

## TASK 3.4

Look at the list of key moments from the play below and write one or two sentences about each to explain what it tells you about the social or historical context of the play. (The first one has been completed for you.)

**1** Mrs Johnstone is afraid the social services will take away her children.

*This shows how working-class single mothers were judged by others and often struggled to make ends meet.*

**2** The Policeman treats the Lyons and Mrs Johnstone very differently.

**3** Mickey and Edward go to different schools.

**4** Mickey is unemployed and turns to crime.

When depicting the context of the play, there are a number of factors to consider, such as:

- How much money a character might have
- Fashions of the 1960s to 1980s
- The influence of youth culture and celebrities – such as rock musicians, movie stars or football players – on fashions
- The occupation of the characters
- The ages of the characters
- Props characters might use, such as toys or books from the period
- Types of houses and furnishings available for working-class and middle-class families.

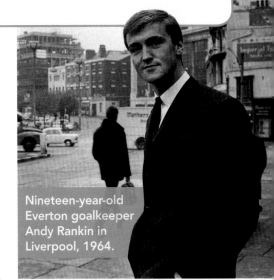

Nineteen-year-old Everton goalkeeper Andy Rankin in Liverpool, 1964.

## TASK 3.5

**A** Look at the list of costume items and props below and sort them into whether they would be more appropriate for Mrs Johnstone or Mrs Lyons:

> Light-blue cashmere jumper and cardigan (twin set)
>
> Flowered apron    String of pearls    Feather duster
>
> Casual, knee-length polyester skirt    Leather clutch bag
>
> Low-heeled, well-worn shoes    Baggy orange cardigan
>
> New leather shoes with heels    Tweed skirt

**B** Then draw a sketch showing how you believe the characters should be costumed in the scene in which they first appear together. What are the most noticeable differences?

**C** Annotate your sketches to explain what the costumes indicate about the characters and their contexts.

**TIP:**

In your exam questions, alternative wording might be used instead of 'context', such as 'reflect the time in which the play was written' or 'show when and where the play is set'.

One of the **Raywarp** ways with nylon

DRIP-DRY PETAL-SOFT

*Brushed Nylon*

Wash, drip-dry and wear again all on the same day – for Raywarp's quietly distinguished lines cannot sag – the pure brushed nylon tricot never loses its petal-soft luxury.

**Raywarp**

A magazine advertisement for a twin set and jacket. Mrs Lyons' would more likely have been cashmere than brushed nylon, but the style and colours could be similar.

A Liverpool housewife cleaning her front door, 1964.

## TASK 3.6

**A** At the opening of some productions of *Blood Brothers*, the exteriors of the Lyons and Johnstone homes are shown, highlighting their differences. Draw a sketch to show how you would depict the two homes. Consider:

- The materials from which the homes would be made (brick, wood, concrete and so on)
- The style and colours of the homes (Victorian, 20th century; large, small; types of windows and doors)
- What is outside the home (garden, street-lamp, bin, toys, pathway…).

**B** Write two paragraphs in response to the following question: 'Describe how you could show the social or historical context of the play by your design choices for the costumes and sets for Mrs Lyons and Mrs Johnstone.'

Semi-detached houses in a 'middle-class' suburb of Liverpool.

A backstreet in a working-class neighbourhood.

## EXTENSION

Research Liverpool from the 1960s to 1980s to gain a better understanding of the context. Some possible topics include:

- Social context: families, schools, housing, roles of women, unemployment
- Cultural context: fashion, music, architecture
- Historical context: economics, news and political events.

Make a note of anything that helps your understanding of the play and how it could be staged or designed.

## WHAT THE SPECIFICATION SAYS...

Learners must know and understand:

- How meaning is communicated through:
  - An actor's vocal and physical interpretation of character.

# Interpretations of key characters

You must demonstrate that you understand the main characters in the play, including different ways in which they could be interpreted. Brief descriptions of the main figures in *Blood Brothers* are given on the following page.

## Mrs Johnstone

A working-class single mother. At the beginning of the play, she has seven children and is a cleaner for Mrs Lyons. When she finds out she is expecting twins, she is afraid she won't manage and social services will take her children. She agrees to give up one of her twins, but quickly regrets this. Although the Narrator describes her as 'so cruel', she is shown to be warm and affectionate.

## Sammy

Mickey's wild, older brother, the leader of their childhood gang. Sammy's misbehaviour grows into crimes by the time he is 16, including stealing from a bus conductor. A few years later, he involves Mickey in a robbery, during which a man is shot.

## Mickey

Mickey is the twin that Mrs Johnstone keeps. At seven, he is a lively, friendly boy who is sometimes teased and bullied, particularly by Sammy. At 14, he is an awkward teenager, uninterested in school. He is attracted to Linda, but is unable to express his feelings. His friendship with Edward is important and Edward encourages him to let Linda know how he feels. He marries Linda, but loses his job and commits a crime. After leaving prison, he is almost unrecognisable due to depression and addiction.

## Linda

At seven, Linda is a confident girl, and protective of Mickey. She isn't afraid to confront Sammy or to shoot an airgun with the boys. At 14, she declares her love for Mickey, but he doesn't respond. When Mickey eventually asks her out, their relationship moves quickly. She becomes pregnant and they marry. When Mickey returns from prison, Edward helps them to get a house and a job for Mickey. She begins secretly seeing Edward.

## Mrs Lyons

Mrs Johnstone's employer. Initially, they have a pleasant relationship. Mrs Lyons convinces Mrs Johnstone to give her one of her twins. She becomes increasingly worried about Mrs Johnstone coming between her and Edward, and fires Mrs Johnstone. Her mental health deteriorates and she attacks Mrs Johnstone. She tells Mickey about Edward and Linda's meetings, leading to the deaths of the two men.

## Edward

Edward is the twin raised by the Lyons. At seven, he is well-spoken and friendly, eager to make new friends. At 14, he has been to boarding school. His friendship with Mickey gives him freedom and adventure, as well as introducing him to Linda. On return from university, his new friends and interests are very different from the problems facing Mickey. He becomes a local councillor, and begins a relationship with Linda.

## Mr Lyons

At first, a kindly, if absent, husband. He is reluctant to fire Mrs Johnstone and he plays affectionately with Edward. To help his family, particularly his wife, he agrees to move to the countryside. However, he is shown firing his employees with little feeling, saying it is 'just another sign of the times'.

## Narrator

A mysterious figure. He comments on the action and reminds the audience that there are 'debts to pay' and there will be a 'reckoning day'.

### TASK 3.7

Choose a key line from the play for each character. Explain its importance in understanding the character and how it could be delivered by the actor. What physical and vocal skills would be most effective?

**KEY TERM:**

**Received Pronunciation (also called RP):** A way of speaking that is considered the 'standard' form of British Pronunciation. It is not specific to a certain location, but is associated with education and formality.

# Use of vocal skills

*Blood Brothers* makes particular demands on its performers. Mickey, Edward and Linda, for example, age from seven years old to their 20s, and their voices should reflect these different ages. The Johnstones and the Lyons represent different social classes, with the Johnstones speaking in a Liverpool dialect, whereas the Lyons might speak **Received Pronunciation** or perhaps another dialect associated with the middle class of that area.

The actors might use their vocal skills to highlight the play's comedy or to underline the drama of a scene. As the play develops, Mrs Lyons shows signs of mental instability, which could be reflected in her use of her voice, as could Mickey's later depression.

Vocal skills that actors might consider include:

**Accent and dialect** **Pace** **Volume** **Pitch**

**Pauses and timing** **Intonation** **Phrasing** **Emotional range**

## TASK 3.8

With a partner, experiment with vocal skills to interpret the lines on the right. Note down the choices you make, including reasons.

> Mrs Johnstone: OK. All right. All right, Mrs Lyons, right. If I'm goin' I'm takin' my son with me, I'm takin'…' (page 22)

> Edward: Fantastic. When I get home I'll look it up in the dictionary. (page 29)

> Sammy: Shut it. I'm fourteen. I wanna fourpenny scholar. (page 64)

> Mickey: Now give me the tablets… I need them. (page 100)

## TASK 3.9

For each character listed below, give three examples of different vocal skills that the actor playing the role could use. Justify each of your choices by explaining why it is appropriate. (Examples have been given for Mr Lyons.)

- **Mrs Johnstone**
- **Mickey**
- **Linda**
- **Sammy**.

| Character | Vocal skill | When vocal skill could be displayed | Justification |
|---|---|---|---|
| Mr Lyons | Using **Received Pronunciation**. | Throughout the play. | This would reflect his educational background and important position in the company. |
| | • **Volume:** Increasing.<br>• **Emotional range:** Anger. | Page 44. | It is clear that he grows frustrated with Mrs Lyons when she wants them to move. He swears and calls her 'woman' instead of her name, so he could shout at her in an attempt to stop what he sees as her unreasonable worrying. |
| | **Pause.** | Page 48. | Mr Lyons doesn't want to move, but after the policeman's visit, he reluctantly asks Edward his opinion. The pause after he says 'Edward' indicates his hesitation – this is a difficult decision to make. |

# Use of physical skills

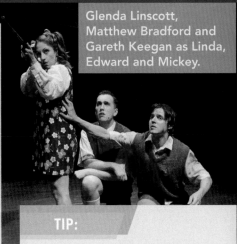

Glenda Linscott, Matthew Bradford and Gareth Keegan as Linda, Edward and Mickey.

Although the action of *Blood Brothers* spans more than 20 years, in most productions the same actors play the characters at every age. This is particularly noticeable with Mickey, Edward and Linda who grow from seven year olds to young adults, which would be demonstrated by their posture, gestures and facial expressions.

Actors could also use their physical skills to highlight the comedy of certain scenes, such as the children shooting the airgun, or the teenage Mickey's awkwardness around Linda. There are also moments of high drama, such as Mrs Lyons attacking Mrs Johnstone with a knife and the final scene, which would require physical choices to bring out the power and shock of these events.

Physical skills that actors might consider include:

**Posture** **Movement** **Pace** **Gestures**
**Facial expressions** **Proxemics** **Eye contact**

**TIP:**

Stage fights must be carefully rehearsed and any physical danger avoided. You should mime the knife or use a safe alternative. What the audience should register are the characters' intentions and reactions.

## TASK 3.10

**A** In a pair, experiment with the physical skills needed for the knife scene between Mrs Lyons and Mrs Johnstone, from Mrs Lyons' line 'How much?' to Mrs Johnstone screaming, 'Go!' (pages 78–79).

Try to perform the scene in three different ways, using a range of gestures, expressions and speeds of movement. Which were the most successful?

**B** Afterwards, answer the following questions:

1 How near is Mrs Lyons to Mrs Johnstone when she takes out the knife?

2 How quickly does Mrs Lyons lunge at Mrs Johnstone?

3 What facial expression does Mrs Lyons have when she attacks Mrs Johnstone?

4 What physical actions might Mrs Johnstone make to express her shock?

5 What gesture might Mrs Lyons make when she curses Mrs Johnstone?

6 What expression does Mrs Johnstone have on the final line?

## TASK 3.11

For each key character below, give at least three examples of how they could use their physical skills in the play. Justify your choices. (Examples are given for Edward.)

- **Narrator**
- **Mrs Lyons**
- **Mickey**
- **Linda**.

| Character | Physical skill | When physical skill could be displayed | Details and justification |
|---|---|---|---|
| Edward | A very upright **posture**. | As a seven year old. | One interpretation is that Edward has been raised to be a little man, so his posture and movements will seem mature for his age. |
| | Use of **body language and choreography**. | As a 14 year old, when he is playfully dancing with Linda's friend. | He has been taught how to dance by his mother, so he would be putting those skills to use, but in a comic, silly way to express how excited he is to be out with his friends. |
| | **Proxemics** and **eye contact**. | The scene with Linda when Edward declares his love for her. | He would stand close to Linda so he can speak softly, but finds it difficult to make eye contact, until he finally says he loves her. Then he looks into her eyes, searching for her response. |

In this design by Ted Roberts, for Vancouver's Arts Club Theatre, the Narrator can watch and comment on the action from a high level.

# Stage directions

In addition to dialogue, a way for the playwright to convey what a character is doing, thinking and feeling is through stage directions. For example:

Page 15: Mrs Lyons shows the Bible to Mrs Johnstone, who is at first reluctant and then lays her hand on it.

Page 47: Edward laughs until through the laughter he senses that all is not well. He sees that he alone is laughing. The laughter turns to tears which sets the other two off.

Page 95: We see Mickey, nervously keeping lookout, as behind him, as if inside a filling station office, we see Sammy, his back to us, talking to an offstage character.

## TASK 3.12

**A** In a small group, perform each of the stage directions above.

**B** Discuss and write down what you believe each character is thinking and feeling. For example, on page 15, is Mrs Johnstone happy to swear on the Bible, or nervous or frightened? Why do you think she agrees to do it?

**C** Talk about what the audience learns about the character from the stage directions. From the stage direction on page 15, for example, what might we discover about Mrs Lyons and her understanding of Mrs Johnstone?

## LOOK HERE

See pages 200–202 for rehearsal techniques suited to exploring characterisation and practising performance skills.

## TASK 3.13

**A** Read the extract below from a candidate-style response about the stage directions on pages 82–83, describing the teenage Linda, Mickey and Edward. Highlight three details that show how the stage directions reveal aspects of the characters and their relationships.

The stage directions demonstrate the close relationship between Linda, Mickey and Edward. As teenagers, they are shown taking part in a number of playful, light-hearted activities: going to a fairground, buying chips, taking photos. Linda's closeness to both boys is communicated to the audience by her posing for photos with each of them. Edward hides his attraction to Linda by exaggerating a romantic pose, going down on one knee and kissing her hand. Mickey shows his mischievous nature by pulling silly faces, adding to the playful tone of the scene.

The audience might interpret the final section as being ominous, however, as the Narrator, who has been warning that the play will end tragically, is brought on to take a photo which captures a final image of three happy teenagers together. The characters happily waving to him contrasts with the dark events which are to follow.

**B** Choose other stage directions involving Mrs Johnstone and Mrs Lyons, and answer the following question: 'How do the stage directions communicate the characters of Mrs Johnstone and Mrs Lyons and their relationship to the audience?'

## TIP:

Remember that communication is at the heart of drama. Always consider what the performance and staging choices you make are communicating to the audience. Do they create…

- Sympathy?
- Fear?
- Excitement?
- Suspense?
- Pity?
- Comedy?
- Greater understanding?

# Use of space

As part of their characterisation, actors might use the stage space in many different ways, including:

**Levels** **Proxemics** **Positioning on stage**

**Entrances and exits** **Use of the 'fourth wall'**

In addition, the type of staging configuration and the set design could influence the actors' use of space.

Below is a candidate-style response about how a performer playing the Narrator could use a traverse stage space, and some benefits and challenges of this space.

The Narrator needs to have a strong presence in the play, while not detracting from the scenes in which he is an observer. [1] An advantage of a traverse stage is that it often creates an intimacy with the audience. [2] With the audience on both sides, the Narrator could treat them like they are a jury, making eye contact when he invites them to 'judge' Mrs Johnstone. Another advantage is that there is the opportunity to have platforms at the extreme ends. The Narrator could stand on these, surveying the action, without blocking the audience's view. [3]

A disadvantage of a traverse stage is that different sides of the audience view the piece from different angles, so it might be difficult to provoke a united reaction from the audience. [4] Blocking has to be done very carefully, or half of the audience will miss characters' expressions or key events. Another disadvantage is that scenery would need to be limited, so domestic scenes could be difficult to block and might have to be conveyed in a minimalistic way. [5]

As the Narrator is a more symbolic character, however, he could use the traverse stage to his advantage. [6] At the beginning and ending of the play, I would have the Narrator centre stage as if he is conducting the other actors. In the final scene, he could motion to the ensemble to begin moving through the audience as they sing the final song. [7] This would show the dominance of his character while making the audience more closely involved in the tragedy of the ending. [8]

[1] Opens with some understanding of the role of the Narrator.

[2] Explains an advantage of traverse staging.

[3] Identifies a second advantage of traverse staging.

[4] Identifies a disadvantage of traverse staging.

[5] Uses correct terminology, such as 'to block' and 'minimalistic'.

[6] Interprets the Narrator as a non-naturalistic character ('symbolic').

[7] Suggests creative advantages of how the ending could be staged.

[8] Considers the impact on the audience.

## TASK 3.14

**A** Working in a small group, write notes and/or draw sketches showing how the following scenes could be produced in different staging configurations:

- When Edward and Mickey first meet (pages 26–30)
- The school scenes (pages 65–67)
- Mrs Lyons attacking Mrs Johnstone (pages 77–79)
- The death of the twins (pages 105–107).

**B** Choose one of the scenes above and write down at least two advantages and two disadvantages of performing it in each staging configuration described on pages 8–11.

**TIP:**

If an exam question asks for advantages and disadvantages, you need to discuss at least two of each. Similarly, if a question asks for examples, you must offer more than one.

Learners must know and understand:

- How meaning is communicated through:
  - The use of performance space and spatial relationships on stage
  - The relationship between performers and audience
  - The design of: set, props, costume, lighting and sound
  - An actor's vocal and physical interpretation of character
  - The use of performance conventions
- How performance styles affect the direction, acting and design of a performance.

### TIP:

There is no one right way of interpreting this or any other scene. The choices you make, however, must be rooted in your understanding of the play and how theatre works.

# Directorial choices

A director of *Blood Brothers* needs to consider:

- How to guide the actors' physical and vocal choices
- How to use design to reinforce the play's meaning and impact
- How key moments of the play might be staged
- The style of the play and potential use of performance conventions
- The effect the play should have on the audience.

## TASK 3.15

**A** Working in a small group, read the filling station robbery scene (pages 95–96), from the Narrator's 'There's a full moon…' to Linda's 'But I've ironed him a shirt.'

Discuss the impact you want this scene to have for the audience. Do you want it to be tense, for example? Frightening? Surprising? Alarming? Sad? A combination of these?

**B** Experiment with using:

- Changes in pace and volume to increase the tension
- Performance conventions, such as slow motion or still images, to highlight key moments
- The Narrator's proxemics to create certain effects, such as standing apart from the action as an observer, sitting among the audience or being in the middle of the action during the robbery
- Sound effects to create surprise or alarm
- Mickey's physical and vocal skills to show his distress.

**C** Now write a paragraph in response to the following question: 'As a director, how would you stage the robbery scene in order to create a specific impact on the audience?'

## TASK 3.16

Below are two candidate-style responses about staging the opening of the play.
Decide how well you believe the writers explained and justified their ideas. Highlight:

- Clear ideas about what they want to achieve
- Specific examples from the play
- Correct use of theatrical terminology
- The effect on the audience.

I want the opening of the play to be sad, so I will have all the actors all looking very sad. That way the audience knows the play will end badly. The Narrator will be dressed all in black, like he is at a funeral. When Mrs Johnstone begins to sing, she will move around the stage, flirting with the audience, just like she is Marilyn Monroe. The narrator will hold a large book, as if he is reading from it. He will call up members of the cast, and direct them into still images to match his narration.

In order to grab the audience's attention from the beginning, I will open with a sound effect of babies crying. This reinforces the idea of the narrative following the twins throughout their lives. The Narrator will climb to the top of a scaffold and look down on the audience and characters to show he is in charge of the play's actions. He will control a series of projections that show key moments from the characters' lives. On the line about their deaths, the actors playing the twins will step in front of the projections and, in slow motion, re-enact their deaths. I want this to be done in a stylised way to emphasis the tragedy of ending. When Mrs Johnstone is introduced, I will use a recorded sound effect of crowds booing, encouraging the audience to judge her as being responsible for the tragedy.

# Design choices

Costume, set, lighting and sound design all contribute to the impact of *Blood Brothers*. They are vital in presenting the play's setting, meaning and director's interpretation. For example, the way Mickey and Edward are costumed at seven contrasts their different upbringings. The way Linda is costumed at 14 will be very different from her costume at seven, showing how she has changed over the years.

Setting and props are important for establishing the context of the play and the contrasts between different groups of characters. Sound can be used to establish location and create atmosphere or tension. Lighting can focus attention on certain characters and suggest a certain mood or location.

## Costume design

When writing about costume, it is important to consider what the costume tells the audience about the character's role and personality. It is useful to consider:

**Period and context**   **Colour**   **Fabric**
**Silhouette**   **Fit**   **Condition**
**Headwear and footwear**   **Make-up and hair**

Below is an excerpt from a candidate-style response about Linda's costume at age 14, demonstrating one possible approach to her costume. Note the references to the play's context.

Linda has changed significantly from the tomboyish seven year old of the first act. **[1]** At 14, for the field scene, I would dress Linda in a short, tight skirt. **[2]** This would emphasise how attractive and flirtatious she is and makes sense of Edward's reaction of 'Wow' when he sees her. **[3]** Although she is in her school uniform, which I imagine to be a grey wool skirt, white cotton blouse and green knit pullover, she will have adjusted them, suiting her rebellious personality. **[4]** She will have taken off her pullover and the blouse will be partially unbuttoned. Although her school would probably want her to wear her skirt to her knees, in the late 1960s and early 1970s, it was fashionable to wear shorter skirts, so Linda would roll her skirt at the waistband to achieve this. **[5]** Instead of regulation school shoes, she will wear heels, which will add to the comedy of her walking through a muddy field. **[6]** She would have applied make-up, such as blue eye shadow, peach blush and pink lipstick, which she would probably have seen in magazines of the time. **[7]**

### TASK 3.17

Draw sketches for your own costume design ideas for the following characters:

- Sammy aged 16.
- Mickey at age seven.
- Mr Lyons in Act One.
- Edward at the end of the play.

## WHAT THE SPECIFICATION SAYS...

Learners must know and understand:
- How meaning is communicated through:
  - The design of: set, props, costume, lighting and sound.

Costumes for Linda and Mickey include brown corduroy and beige polyester (Astoria Performing Arts Center).

**[1]** Understanding of character and how she has changed.

**[2]** Describes silhouette/fit.

**[3]** Justifies choices with specific reference to the text.

**[4]** Describes colours and fabrics and justifies these.

**[5]** Appropriate to the period.

**[6]** Considers footwear and explains the effect of the choice on the specific scene.

**[7]** Explains and justifies the period make-up style.

## LOOK HERE

Page 179 has useful vocabulary for writing about costumes.

# Set design

The set designer of *Blood Brothers* could help to convey the play's meaning through some of the following:

- Focusing on the theme of social class by showing the differences between the Lyons and Johnstone homes and schools
- Emphasising naturalistic aspects of the play by providing realistic props and set furnishings
- Emphasising non-naturalistic aspects of the play by symbolically suggesting themes such as violence, love, injustice or fate
- Establishing a particular relationship between the audience and the performers, by use of proxemics or levels
- Establishing the period of the play and the passage of time through the use of particular props or set furnishings.

## TASK 3.18

**A** Below is a sketch of a street outside the Johnstone house in Act One. After studying it:

- Add two more details that you think would improve the design
- Consider specific moments in the play when this setting would be appropriate and how the actors could use it.
- Answer the question: 'How does this set help to convey the ideas and themes of *Blood Brothers*?'

**B** Then draw a contrasting set sketch of the inside of the Lyons' house.

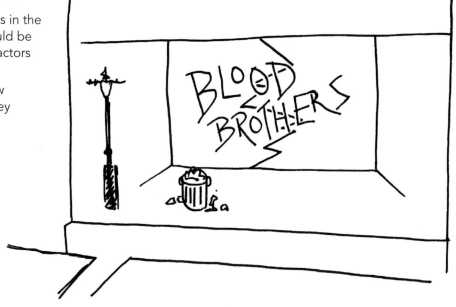

## TASK 3.19

At 14, Mickey and Edward attend very different schools. At Edward's school, he is 'confronted by a teacher... looking down his nose at Edward' (page 65). At Mickey's school, the atmosphere is described as 'all boredom and futility' (page 66). Draw and annotate a set design in which the differences between the two schools could be quickly established and understood by the audience. Remember to consider:

- Colours and textures
- The scale of the set
- Positioning of the set dressings on stage
- Levels
- Materials
- Props and stage furnishings.

# Lighting design

The lighting in *Blood Brothers* has many functions, including:

- Establishing the time of day and location
- Focusing the audience's attention on certain characters and events
- Highlighting and increasing the intensity of certain moments
- Creating an atmosphere or mood
- Suggesting a transition from one time or location to another.

## TASK 3.20

**A** Read this candidate-style response that describes how to create a lighting design for the end of the first act. Highlight the technical terminology used.

At the end of the first act, the Johnstones believe they are heading for a 'bright new day'. I would use my lighting design to emphasise both the change in their location and their new optimism. The previous lighting, based in a city environment, would have been harsher and greyer, so I want to show they are moving away from this world. I would use rosy gels on the followspot that tracks Mrs Johnstone as she sings. On the upstage wall, I would have green floodlights suggesting the light, fresh countryside, and bright, golden down-lighting to create the effect of sunlight pouring onto a field. Gobos could create a leafy pattern on the back wall and floor of the stage.

**B** With a partner, create a lighting design for the play's ending, from Mickey's entrance to the death of the twins (pages 105–107). Consider:

- Changes to the type, direction, colour and so on of the lighting
- How the lighting will contribute to the mood or atmosphere
- How you will achieve technically the lighting effects you want.
- What effect you want your final lighting to have on the audience.

**LOOK HERE**

More ideas about lighting design can be found on pages 224–226. Useful lighting vocabulary is on page 185.

In Encore Theatre Company's production there is a clear contrast between the cool lighting and calm detachment of the Narrator and the hot temper, violent action and sense of danger indicated by the red light on Sammy. (Lighting design by Daniel Jow.)

# Sound design

Sound can be used to establish location or a transition, and is also useful in creating an atmosphere or reflecting the **psychological** state of a character. Sound design can also add to the romance, comedy or tension of a scene, often having a significant impact on the audience's experience of the play. When writing about sound design, you might consider:

- Volume: How amplified will the sound be? Will it grow louder or quieter?
- Recorded or live: Will sound effects and music be pre-recorded or performed live?
- Type of sound: Will the sound be naturalistic or abstract?
- Special effects: Will you use distorting effects such as reverb?
- How the sound or music begins and ends: Should it gradually become louder or will there be a sudden burst of sound? Will it end abruptly or fade out?

## TASK 3.21

Look at the following ideas and note at least one occasion in *Blood Brothers* when each sound effect might be appropriate:

| An exaggeratedly loud school bell | A recording of children playing |
|---|---|

| A sudden silence | An echoing reverb | Fairground music |
|---|---|---|

| A recorded sound of a cow mooing | A screeching high violin sound |
|---|---|

## TASK 3.22

Working with a partner, look closely at the scene in which Mickey is told by Mrs Lyons that Edward and Linda are seeing each other (pages 103–104). Consider when and how you could use sound for each of the following effects:

- Creating tension
- Showing Mickey's mental state
- Emphasising the physical actions of the characters
- Making use of a realistic sound effect
- Creating an abstract sound effect.

## KEY TERM:

Psychological: Referring to a mental or emotional state and the reasons behind it.

**LOOK HERE**

For more information on sound design, including vocabulary, see pages 186 and 227–229.

## CHECK YOUR LEARNING *Blood Brothers*

### Do you know…?

- ✓ When *Blood Brothers* was written.
- ✓ The years in which it is set.
- ✓ Where it takes place.
- ✓ The genre of the play.
- ✓ How its contexts might affect choices of costumes, sets and props.
- ✓ How the relationships between the characters, and the changes to these relationships, could be shown.
- ✓ Advantages and disadvantages of producing the play in different staging configurations.
- ✓ How key scenes might be staged.
- ✓ The performance style (or styles) of the play.
- ✓ How the performers could use their physical and vocal skills to convey characters' motivations, thoughts and feelings and to impart meaning to the action.
- ✓ The role of the director and how they influence the way an audience responds to and understands the play.
- ✓ Key moments a director could use to convey their concept of the play.
- ✓ Different design choices to be made, why they are important and how they can be effective.
- ✓ What impact the play should have on the audience and what messages they should be left with.

# DEATH OF A SALESMAN
## by Arthur Miller

The OCR specification identifies editions of the texts that are used to set questions in the 'Drama: Performance and response' (Component 04) examination paper. It is not required that centres use these editions for teaching this component.

Page numbers given here refer to the Penguin Modern Classics edition of *Death of a Salesman*, ISBN-13: 978-0-141-18274-2, one of those used by OCR for question setting.

### KEY TERM:

**Flashback:** A scene from an earlier period of a character's life than that shown in the play's main timeline.

# Plot synopsis

## Act One

Willy Loman, a 63-year-old travelling salesman, returns exhausted from an unsuccessful sales trip. His wife, Linda, encourages him to ask his boss, Howard, for a job in New York. Linda and Willy discuss their son, Biff, whom Linda describes as 'lost'. Upstairs, Biff and his younger brother, Happy, discuss their frustrations with their lives: Biff's rootless life working on farms and Happy's more financially steady but unsatisfying and lonely life. In the kitchen, Willy imagines he is speaking to Biff.

In a **flashback** to a happier time, a young Biff and Happy appear. Young Bernard, their neighbour, reminds Biff that he needs to study. Linda and Willy discuss his commissions on his sales and that the family is struggling to pay their bills.

Willy remembers an affair in which the Woman thanks him for giving her a pair of stockings. Willy shouts at Linda for mending stockings. Bernard and Linda tell Willy they are worried about the teenage Biff's behaviour.

Adult Happy speaks to his father. Willy regrets he didn't go to Alaska with his brother Ben. Bernard's father, Charley, visits and he and Willy play cards. Uncle Ben appears to Willy. Willy reveals that Ben died a couple of weeks before. Willy's conversation veers back and forth between his dream of Ben and the present with Charley. Ben explains that instead of going to Alaska he went to Africa to make his fortune. He beats young Biff in a fight saying, 'Never fight fair with a stranger, boy.'

Linda comes down to the kitchen to get Willy to come to bed. Biff and Happy discuss their father's behaviour. Linda tells Biff that he must treat Willy with respect. She describes Willy's struggles with his job and money. She calls Happy a 'philandering bum' and asks Biff why he no longer loves his father. Biff says Willy is a 'fake', but also says he will live at home, get a job and contribute to the finances. Linda reveals that Willy might be thinking of suicide. She has found a rubber pipe with which she fears he will gas himself. Willy enters and argues with Biff. Biff says he is going to meet with Bill Oliver about staking him in a business. The family becomes excited by the idea of Happy and Biff going into a sporting goods business together. Willy tells Biff he has 'a greatness' in him and Happy tells his mother that he is going to get married. Biff goes downstairs and pulls out the rubber pipe, while, upstairs, Linda hums Willy to sleep.

death of a Salesman

*The* **PLAYBILL** *for the Morosco Theatre*

The cover of the programme for the original Broadway production, 1949.

# Act Two

Willy and Linda discuss their hopes for Biff's meeting with Oliver. They imagine getting a little place in the country. Willy plans to speak to Howard about getting a job in New York. Linda tells Willy that the boys are going to take him out to dinner that evening.

In his meeting with Willy, Howard refuses to give Willy a job in New York, despite Willy's desperate pleading. Instead, he fires Willy and tells him that his sons should help him.

A distressed Willy appeals to a vision of Ben, who advises him to get out of the city. This leads to a memory of Ben and Willy discussing with Linda a possibility of going to Alaska. Willy chooses to remain in the city. A teenage Biff, along with his family and Bernard, head off to an important football game.

The adult Bernard is at his father's office when a secretary tells him that Mr Loman is causing a commotion. Willy contrasts Bernard's success with Biff's failure. Bernard wonders why Biff never took summer school classes to make up for the maths he failed in high school. After visiting Willy in Boston, Biff seemed to give up on life. Willy asks Charley for a loan. Charley offers him an office job, but Willy refuses it. Charley gives him the loan. Willy tells him that he's the only friend he's got.

In a restaurant, Happy flirts with a pretty girl, Miss Forsythe, and asks her to find another girl to join them and Biff, who has just arrived. Biff tells Happy about waiting all day to see Oliver only to realise that Oliver didn't remember him. Biff stole Oliver's pen and ran out of the office. Biff wants to tell his father the truth, but Happy doesn't. When Willy arrives, Biff tells him that he was only a shipping clerk for Oliver not a salesman and that they need to hold onto facts. Willy tells them he was fired. Willy's memory of Young Bernard saying that Biff failed mathes combines with Biff telling Willy that his meeting with Oliver was unsuccessful. However, seeing Willy's distress, Biff lies and says that Oliver will speak to his partner about investing in him.

Miss Forsythe returns with her friend Letta. Willy becomes confused, remembering Biff finding him in a hotel room with the Woman, which caused Biff to lose respect for Willy. Lost in his memory and unaware that the boys and their dates have gone, Willy shouts at the waiter and goes out to buy some flower seeds.

When Biff and Happy return home, Linda is angry at them for deserting Willy. She orders them out of the house. Biff insists on going to talk to Willy, who is in the garden planting the seeds. Willy imagines he is getting advice from Ben on the insurance payment if he dies. Biff says goodbye to Willy and that he won't be back. Linda tries to get them to shake hands but Willy refuses. Willy says Biff is ruining his life for spite. Biff confronts Willy with the rubber pipe. Biff cries and says that he realises he will never bring home 'any prizes' and that they need to face their limitations. When Biff goes upstairs, Willy is astonished, saying 'Biff – he likes me!' After the others go to bed, Willy rushes out of the house. There is the sound of a car moving away at full speed.

Happy, Biff, Linda, Charley and Bernard enter dressed sombrely. Linda lays flowers at a grave.

## Requiem

Linda wonders why nobody came to Willy's funeral. Biff is still angry that Willy didn't know himself, but Charley says that a salesman has to dream. Linda cries at his grave, saying that she doesn't understand why he did it. She has made the last payment on their house and they are finally free.

**TIP:**

You might want to consider the playwright's original intentions. For example, what might Arthur Miller be saying about families, money and dreams?

**TASK 3.1**

A Working in a small group, create a two-minute version of the play, making sure that you cover what you all agree are the most significant events in the plot.

B Given your understanding of the play's plot, answer the following questions:

1 Why doesn't Willy want to travel for his job any more?

2 What evidence does Linda have that Willy might try to kill himself?

3 How does Charley try to help the Lomans? Is he successful?

4 What effect did Biff discovering his father's affair have on his life?

# Genre

*Death of a Salesman* is a modern tragedy. A tragedy follows a **protagonist** – the **tragic hero** – who, through a combination of factors, such as a **tragic flaw** or fate, experiences a downfall. There is a tragic ending, usually resulting in one or more deaths. Although classic tragedies, such as Greek or Shakespearean ones, feature high-status characters, such as kings or generals, modern tragedies usually follow a more ordinary protagonist. Willy Loman does not have power or status, but some believe that his dreams, for himself and his boys, give him a certain heroic height, from which he falls. His relationship with society, including the importance of money, and the distance between his dreams and reality, contribute to his defeat.

## KEY TERMS:

**Protagonist:** The main character of a narrative.

**Tragic hero:** The main character in a tragedy.

**Tragic flaw:** A defect, failing or weakness in the tragic protagonist, such as jealousy, ambition or pride, that brings about their downfall.

**Foreboding:** A feeling that something bad will happen. It is often associated with **foreshadowing:** A warning or hint of something that is going to happen.

**Catharsis:** When a tragedy comes to a climax and there is a moment of emotional release.

---

### TASK 3.2

Look at these elements of a modern tragedy and find at least one example of each from *Death of a Salesman*. (A suggested answer has been given to start you off.)

- The hero is admired by others. *The teenage Biff and Happy admire the hard-working, big-dreaming Willy, as does his wife, Linda.*
- The hero has personal weaknesses.
- Fate or other outside forces work against the hero.
- There is a sense of **foreboding** that events will unfold badly for the hero.
- The action takes place over a limited amount of time.
- The play has a tragic ending.
- The audience experiences **catharsis**.

---

### TASK 3.3

**A** Read the Act One scene between Linda, Happy and Biff in which she reveals Willy's suspected attempts to kill himself (pages 46–47). In a small group, experiment with how this could be performed to emphasise the sense of fear, urgency and danger. Consider:

- The movements and interactions between the characters
- The pace of the scene, for example when the dialogue and action might speed up or slow down
- The reactions of the characters – such as facial expressions and gestures – to Linda's revelations
- How the actors might use vocal skills, such as volume, phrasing and emphasis.

**B** Look closely at the end of Act Two (page 108) and discuss how design could be used to heighten the tragedy of the ending. Think about:

- The use of sound, including music and sound effects
- If characters change costumes, how these will be different from the previous scene
- How lighting could create a change in mood
- How the set could show the move to the funeral scene.

**C** Choose one of these two scenes and write a paragraph, or create a series of images for a storyboard, to explain how it could be performed and staged. Look especially to highlight the importance of these features in establishing the relationship between the characters and the mood of the scene.

# Structure

The play is divided into two acts, plus a short 'requiem'. The main action of the play takes place over, roughly, the final 24 hours of Willy's life, with the first act occurring during one night and the second act starting with a hopeful morning and ending with Willy's death that night.
The requiem takes place at Willy's funeral.

Miller uses time in a fluid way, however, so, in addition to the main timeline, there are both flashbacks to earlier periods and episodes where dreams and memories are confused with the present.

The requiem, with Charley's compassionate speech, resolves the final aspects of the plot. Linda, Willy's faithful wife, speaks the play's final lines.

This stark, pared-back set by Georgia Lowe has naturalistic elements, such as the homely bedding, but is dominated by the neon banner and its ironic comment on one of the play's main themes.

# Style

The play is usually performed naturalistically, with the actors creating believable, three-dimensional characters. Miller does also suggest stylised aspects to the play, such as the dream-like quality of some of the memories and the changes of locations and time periods. Some set designs are realistic, while others create a more fluid, abstract, stylised quality.

## TASK 3.4

**A** From your knowledge and understanding of *Death of a Salesman*, identify examples of each of these structural and stylistic features:

- An example of conflict (this could be between characters or between a character and their situation)
- An example of foreshadowing
- A flashback to an earlier period in the characters' lives
- An example when the present and past are shown at the same time
- The climax of the play
- The **resolution** of the play.

**B** Read the statements below about the play. Then work with a partner to put them in order, with the one you agree with most as 1, and the one you agree with least as 5.

- ☐ The play is about the common man, represented by Willy Loman.
- ☐ The play criticises the **American dream** and highlights its flaws.
- ☐ It is about the delusions of an unimportant man.
- ☐ It is concerned with families and the lies they tell each other.
- ☐ The play is about ageing and lost dreams.

### KEY TERMS:

**Resolution:** The solution or bringing together of loose elements of a plot; an ending or conclusion.

**American dream:** The concept that anyone in the US, with enough hard work, can achieve success and prosperity.

### TIP:

Remember: There are many ways in which the play and Willy can be interpreted.

Downtown New York seen from Brooklyn docks.

# Context

*Death of a Salesman* was first produced in 1949, two years after Miller's first successful play, *All My Sons*. *Death of a Salesman* was an immediate success and went on to win the Pulitzer Prize for Drama and the Tony Award for Best Play. It continues to be considered a masterpiece, performed around the world, and is a classic example of an American tragedy.

## Historical context

*Death of a Salesman* is set in New York. The Lomans' house is in Brooklyn, from where many people would commute to their jobs in the more metropolitan New York City. During this period, areas like Brooklyn were becoming more urban and this is reflected in the Lomans' complaints about the buildings around them and the lack of sunlight in their garden. Willy's job requires him to travel throughout New England, a collection of states in the north-east of the country. The teenage Biff finds his father in a hotel in Boston, Massachusetts: one of Willy's sales areas.

Although Miller does not mention particular dates, the main action of the play is thought to take place in the late 1940s. After the Second World War, America was in a stronger position economically than it had been during the Depression of the 1930s. For many, there was greater prosperity and **upward mobility**. This is true for Bernard, who represents the American dream, with hard work leading to success as a lawyer. Bernard and Biff are neighbours and attend the same school, but Biff, who was a star athlete in high school, is unable to find success. Throughout the play, how much characters earn and what they owe are itemised and used to measure their success.

## Cultural context

The play was written when there was a great interest in **psychologically** realistic and insightful portrayal of characters. Playwrights of the 1940s, including Arthur Miller, and Tennessee Williams, who wrote *The Glass Menagerie* and *A Streetcar Named Desire*, were aware of how a character's past influenced their present behaviour.

Throughout *Death of a Salesman*, there are clues about Willy's psychology, including his yearning for a father figure. We also see that characters are influenced by advertising and famous brands. A car was an important symbol of wealth and freedom and there was a particular pride in owning American cars, such as Chevrolets and Studebakers. Willy knows that it will be the end of his career as a salesman when he can no longer drive.

**KEY TERMS:**

**Upward mobility:** A movement where a person's status, power and/or wealth are improved.

**Psychological:** Referring to a mental or emotional state and the reasons behind it.

Celebrations for the 25 millionth car to come off a General Motors production line, 1940.

It was also an age of increasing technology, represented in the play by items such as Howard's dictation machine. Sports were also a great American obsession, which is reflected in Biff's status as a high-school football star and in Happy's dream of running a sporting-goods business with his brother. There is poignancy in Biff's sporting dreams, however, as the afternoon when he was captain of the football team competing for the All-Scholastic Championship remains the high point of his life.

ENJOY FOOD

A college football game.

A vending machine at a radio station in Chicopee, Massachusetts.

## Social context

In the 1940s, it was conventional for the man to be the breadwinner and his wife to stay at home and look after the family, as is the case with the Lomans. Willy travels on sales trips in order to support the family, while Linda looks after the house, doing chores such as the shopping or sewing. In order to purchase a house, families would usually take out a mortgage. Big purchases such as cars, refrigerators, washing-machines or boilers could also be paid for in instalments.

Marriage and family were considered essential to the country's social fabric, and that neither Biff nor Happy (who are in their 30s) has married is a source of unhappiness for the family. Biff says, 'I'm not married, I'm not in business, I just – I'm like a boy' (page 17), while Happy continually reassures his mother he will get married, but without having anyone in mind. Instead, he takes pleasure in dating women engaged to other men. As women were expected to stay pure for their husbands, he claims he has 'ruined' them (page 19). He is also critical of women he can easily pick up, like the girls in the restaurant, whom he accuses of being 'on call' (page 81). Linda, however, is held up as an unobtainable ideal. Happy says he wants 'somebody with character' who is 'like mom' (page 19).

A travelling salesman rests on the stoop of a potential client's home.

### EXTENSION

Research the USA in the 1940s to gain a better understanding of the context. There are many audio-visual resources online. Useful areas to explore include:

- Social context: Families, schools, housing, roles of women, employment
- Cultural context: Fashion, music, architecture, advertising
- Historical context: New York, economics.

Make a note of anything that helps your understanding of the play and how it could be staged or designed.

A prosperous 1940s family packing for a picnic.

## TASK 3.5

Look at the following list of key moments from the play and write a few sentences about each to explain what it tells you about the context of the play. (An example has been given for you.)

**1** Willy complains that he has worked a lifetime to pay off the house and now there's no one to live in it. Home ownership was important in 1940s America and this shows the many years and sacrifices Willy has made to pay off his mortgage. Instead of feeling pleasure, however, it makes him aware how empty the house is and how little he has to show for a lifetime of work. This makes him question how he has spent his life.

**2** Willy doesn't understand why Biff, 'in the greatest country in the world' (page 11), can't make a success of his life.

**3** Willy loses his job.

**4** Willy complains about being boxed in, as too many people have moved into Brooklyn.

---

**TIP:**

In your exam questions, alternative wording might be used instead of 'context', such as 'reflect the time in which the play was written' or 'show when and where the play is set'.

When depicting the context of the play, there are a number of factors you can consider, such as:

- How much money a character might have
- Fashions of the 1940s
- The influence of the culture of the time, such as advertised brands and sports figures
- The occupation of the character
- The age of the character
- Props a character might use, such as food and kitchen items or sports equipment
- Types of houses and furnishings available for a family like the Lomans.

## TASK 3.6

**A** Look at the list of costume items and props on the right and choose which character each would be most suitable for.

**B** Choose one of the costume items or props and research what a 1940s version of the item would look like. Sketch a design for it.

Tennis racket    Umbrella    Fur stole    'Letter' sweater

Sharp three-piece suit    Black slip    Flowered bathrobe

Gold fountain pen    Worn, grey suit    Slippers

---

**KEY TERMS:**

**Stole:** A strip of fabric or fur that is draped over the shoulders.

**'Letter' sweater:** A knitted cardigan or jumper decorated with a large capital letter, awarded to high school or varsity athletes.

**Slip:** A thin, sleeveless, undergarment worn under skirts or dresses.

## TASK 3.7

**A** Some productions of *Death of a Salesman* depict the Loman house in great detail. From Miller's description and your research into the period, draw a sketch of the set at the opening of play. Consider:

- The materials from which the homes would be made (brick, wood, concrete and so on)
- The styles and colours of this 20th-century home (windows, doors, flooring, decorations)
- Anything visible outside the home (view from windows, doorways, the yard…).

**B** Write two paragraphs in response to the following question: 'Describe how you could show the social or historical context of the play by your design choices for the opening set of the play.'

# Interpretations of key characters

You must demonstrate that you understand the main characters in the play, including different ways in which they could be interpreted.

**WHAT THE SPECIFICATION SAYS...**

Learners must know and understand:
- How meaning is communicated through:
  - An actor's vocal and physical interpretation of character.

## The Lomans

### Willy Loman

A 63-year-old travelling salesman. He has worked for the same firm for over 30 years, but is now exhausted and doesn't earn enough to pay his bills. He is married to Linda and they have two grown sons. His sense of failure as a father and as a salesman is at the heart of the play.

### Linda

Willy's loyal wife, who is 'not even sixty'. She 'more than loves' Willy and supports him through his doubts and disappointments. She speaks frankly to her sons about how they treat their father and demands that they respect him.

### Biff

The Lomans' 34-year-old son. After his early promise in high school, he has found it difficult to settle down or stay in a job. He is unable to live up to his father's high expectations, realising he can only earn 'one dollar an hour' despite having tried in 'seven states'.

### Happy

The younger brother, 32, who has a job and an apartment. He exaggerates how well he is doing, however, and clings to the idea of becoming 'number-one man'. In the family, he is often in Biff's shadow and Linda judges him harshly.

## Their neighbours

### Charley

A successful businessman. Although he and Willy argue, he is frequently kind to him. He lends him money and offers him a job. His son is Bernard.

### Bernard

High-school friend of Biff, now a successful lawyer. When young, he encourages Biff to study, and hero-worships him, for example wanting to carry his helmet before the big football game. He doesn't understand why Biff gave up on his studies.

## Other key characters

### Uncle Ben

Willy's older brother, 'a great man', seen only in Willy's memories and dreams, as he has died several weeks before the beginning of the play. He claims that, at 17, he 'walked into the jungle' and was rich by the time he was 21. He represents the choices that Willy did not make and the success he never achieved.

### Howard Wagner

Unlike the self-made men whom Willy admires, Howard has inherited his business from his father. Despite being much younger than Willy, he is his boss. He treats him insensitively and ultimately, despite Willy's pleas, fires him.

### The Woman

'Quite proper-looking' and roughly Willy's age, Willy has an affair with her when he travels to Boston. She works at one of the businesses where Willy makes sales calls.

TASK 3.8

Choose one important line from the play for each character. Write one sentence explaining its importance in understanding the character and another one or two on how it could be delivered by the actor. What physical and vocal skills would be most effective?

## Use of vocal skills

Typically in *Death of a Salesman*, the characters have American accents. Their accents might suggest geographical areas, particularly New York.

The characters' voices might change during the flashback sequences, where, for example, the boys' voices might become lighter and more youthful, and Linda and Willy's might be more energetic and hopeful. The characters' voices will also be influenced by the situations they are in and the emotions they are either expressing or **repressing**.

Vocal skills that actors should consider include:

**KEY TERM:**

Repressing: Hiding, pushing down, controlling or preventing something, such as a thought or emotion.

| Accent and dialect | Pace | Volume | Pitch |

| Pauses and timing | Intonation | Phrasing | Emotional range |

TASK 3.9

With a partner, experiment with vocal skills to interpret the following lines. Note down the choices you make, including reasons.

Happy: I gotta show some of those pompous, self-important executives over there that Happy Loman can make the grade. (page 18)

Willy: Chevrolet, Linda, is the greatest car ever built. (page 26)

The Woman: I'll put you right through to the buyers. (page 30)

Ben: Never fight fair with a stranger, boy. (page 38)

Bernard: Just the two of us, punching each other down the cellar, and crying right through it. (page 74)

Charley: Now, look, kid, enough is enough. I'm no genius but I know when I'm being insulted. (page 76)

Linda: Don't you care whether he lives or dies? (page 97)

Biff: I stole myself out of every good job since high school! (page 104)

Robin Moseley as Linda answers a phone call from Biff at the Old Globe, San Diego.

## TASK 3.10

For each key character listed below, give three examples of different vocal skills that the actor playing the role could use. Justify each of your choices by explaining why it is appropriate. (Examples have been given for Willy.)

- Linda
- Biff
- Bernard
- Charley.

**KEY TERM:**

Nostalgia: Remembering an earlier time with longing or affection.

| Character | Vocal skills | When vocal skill could be displayed | Details and justification |
|---|---|---|---|
| Willy | **Volume** | Act One, in the restaurant | Willy shouts 'I gave you an order' first at Biff, then at the waiter. When he realises the boys have left, he says softly, 'But we were supposed to have dinner together.' This will show, first, how lost he is in his memories, which causes him to act irrationally, and then, second, the realisation of how little his boys care for him. |
| | **Emotional range**, **volume** and **emphasis** | Act Two, with Howard | Willy expresses a range of emotions in this scene, including desperation, **nostalgia** and anger. His tone is soft and dreamy when he remembers the old salesman. He speaks loudly and stresses the word 'got' when he is pleading to go to Boston. |
| | **Pauses** | Act Three, when Biff discovers his affair | Willy pauses when the Woman leaves the room. He knows his affair has been discovered by Biff and he can't think what to say. He babbles out a lie, but stops himself and pauses again, attempting to assume his former high status. |

# Use of physical skills

Physical skills can help to present the high emotion of the play as well as the intricate relationships between the characters. There are also particular physical demands in the flashback scenes where the characters' energy and bearing will contrast with their later movements. The actor playing Biff, for example, needs to show the change from teenage football star to defeated man in his 30s.

All of the characters might move naturalistically, but actors playing the dream/memory characters such as Ben might choose to exaggerate or heighten movements to demonstrate what they represent to Willy.

Physical skills that actors might consider include:

Posture   Movement   Pace   Gestures

Facial expressions   Proxemics   Eye contact

Matthew Linhardt and Joneal Joplin as Biff and Ben, with John Contini and Susie Wall, Insight Theatre Company.

## TASK 3.11

**A** With a partner, read page 15, when the older Biff and Happy are discussing Willy. How can you use your physical skills to show…?

- It is late at night and they are tired.
- They are upset by Willy's behaviour.
- Biff is embarrassed by his lack of success.
- Happy is trying to find out what is wrong with Biff.

Make a note of the physical skills required, for example, when and how they might move, physical contact they have, gestures they make and what their facial expressions might be.

**B** Then read pages 22–23, noting in particular the actions of the teenage Biff and Happy. Consider how the actors could use their physical skills to clearly portray these characters as teenagers.

**C** Now compare Biff's and Happy's use of the following physical skills in these two scenes (and at the two ages). Give precise examples to explain your choices.

- Posture, including sitting or standing
- Movements and ways of walking
- Pace of movement and actions
- Gestures (Are they slight and subtle or bold and exaggerated?)
- Facial expressions
- Proxemics, particularly in relation to each other
- Eye contact with each other.

## TASK 3.12

For each key character listed below, give at least three examples of how they could use their physical skills in the play. Justify each of your choices. (Examples have been given for Willy.)

- **Linda**
- **Bernard**
- **Ben.**
- **Charley**
- **The Woman**

| Character | Physical skill | When physical skill could be displayed | Details and justification |
|---|---|---|---|
| Willy | His **posture** shows he is exhausted. | Willy's first entrance | Willy's trip was tiring and disappointing. He carries two large sample cases, and his shoulders are slumped with the effort and disappointment. He is at his physical limits at the age of 63 and does not think he can drive any more. |
| | Willy uses **gestures** to try to force Howard into paying attention to him. | In his scene with Howard | He pounds on the desk and points at Howard when he discusses Howard's father. Willy is tired of being ignored, but is also on the verge of a breakdown, so is behaving in a more aggressive way than usual. |
| | **Proxemics** and **eye contact** | The scene with the Woman in Act One | He pulls her close and stares intently at her when he says, 'Why do you have to go now?' The sensuous nature of their relationship contrasts with his more respectful actions towards his wife. |

 **LOOK HERE**

See pages 200–202 for rehearsal techniques for exploring characterisation and practising performance skills.

# Stage directions

In addition to the play's dialogue, a way for the playwright to convey what a character is doing, thinking and feeling is through stage directions. For example:

Page 47: [Linda] is bent over in the chair, weeping, her face in her hands.

Page 67: Happy carries Biff's shoulder guards, gold helmet, and football pants.

Page 83: Biff takes a breath, then reaches out and grasps Willy's hand.

## TASK 3.13

**A** In a small group, perform each of the stage directions above.

**B** Discuss and write down what you believe each character is thinking and feeling. For example, what might Biff be thinking or feeling when he takes a breath before shaking hands with Willy (page 83)?

**C** Talk about what the audience learns about the character from the stage directions. From the stage direction on page 67, for example, what do we learn about the relationship between Happy and Biff?

## TASK 3.14

**A** Read the candidate-style response below about the stage directions on page 54. Highlight three details that show how stage directions help the actors to put across the characters and their relationships.

These stage directions demonstrate both Biff and Linda's concern for Willy's well-being and mental state. Biff is described as moving 'slowly', which heightens the suspense and perhaps shows his reluctance to take action. When he 'stops' and 'stares' at the heater, the audience will see that he is thinking about what he has learned about Willy and his possible attempts to kill himself. Linda's 'desperate' humming upstairs shows how hard she is trying to soothe and help Willy and adds to the dramatic atmosphere when Biff pulls out the rubber tubing. His 'horrified' expression shows his shock at the confirmation of Willy's actions. When he takes the tubing away, it suggests that he is trying to protect Willy from himself. The act ends with the audience feeling great sympathy for Biff, Linda and Willy and an understanding of how fragile their futures are.

**B** Focusing on the stage directions involving Linda, Happy and Biff on page 97, starting with 'Happy appears at the door of the house...', answer the following question: 'How do the stage directions communicate the characters of Linda, Happy and Biff and their relationship to the audience?'

TIP:

Remember that communication is at the heart of drama. Always consider what the performance and staging choices you make are communicating to the audience. Do they create…

- Sympathy?
- Fear?
- Excitement?
- Suspense?
- Pity?
- Comedy?
- Greater understanding?

Tim Pigott-Smith as the exhausted, despairing Willy.

Jo Mielziner's set for the original production starring Lee J. Cobb.

Note the use of proxemics, posture and expression by Joseph Mydell as Ben and Wendell Pierce as Willy at the Young Vic.

# Use of space

As part of their characterisation, actors might use the stage space in many different ways, including:

**Levels** **Proxemics** **Positioning on stage**
**Entrances and exits** **Use of the 'fourth wall'**

In this scene from South Coast Repertory's production, the actors use close contact, relaxed posture, lifted heads and smiling expressions to present a happy time for Willy and his boys.

In addition, the type of staging configuration and the set design could influence the actors' use of space.

Below is a candidate-style response about how a performer playing Willy Loman could use a traverse stage space, and the benefits and challenges of this space.

---

[1] Opens with some understanding of the role of Willy Loman.

[2] Explains an advantage of traverse staging.

[3] Identifies a second advantage of traverse staging.

[4] Notes a disadvantage of traverse staging and uses correct terminology ('blocking').

[5] Identifies a second disadvantage and uses correct terminology ('sightlines').

[6] Interprets how Willy's thoughts could be shown in a minimalistic/symbolic way.

[7] Suggests a positive effect created by the use of traverse staging and considers the impact on the audience.

Willy Loman is the central character in the play and the audience must be able to connect with him and read his emotions through his use of facial expressions and movements. [1] An advantage of a traverse stage is that it creates an intimacy with the audience, so they will be close to Willy Loman and therefore aware of subtle changes in his expressions and movements. [2] The traverse space could also be used to symbolise the journeys that Willy makes with the image of him slowly trudging, sighing and struggling, along the walkway, for example, at the play's opening. [3] A difficulty with a traverse stage is enabling the two sides of the audience to see the same 'stage picture' at the same time. The blocking would have to be done carefully so that all the audience can see Willy Loman and his facial expressions at important moments, such as his realisation that he has let Biff down, or his decision to kill himself. [4] Another disadvantage is that the scenery would have to be positioned in such a way that any large items, such as the refrigerator, would be placed at one of the far end platforms to avoid obscuring the audience's sightlines. [5] A production of *Death of a Salesman* on a traverse stage might use more minimalistic, symbolic sets to reinforce what is happening is in Willy's mind, rather than a naturalistic representation of the Loman house and other locations. [6] This configuration would keep the audience close to Willy, with the feeling they are sitting in judgement on him. [7]

## TASK 3.15

**A** Working in a small group, make notes and/or draw sketches showing how the following scenes could be produced in different staging configurations:

- Flashback of Willy with the teenage Biff and Happy (pages 22–23)
- Charley and Willy playing cards, Ben's entrance (pages 33–36)
- The restaurant (pages 80–86)
- Requiem (pages 110–112).

**B** Choose one of the scenes above and write down at least two advantages and two disadvantages of performing it in each staging configuration described on pages 8–11.

**TIP:**

If an exam question asks for advantages and disadvantages, you need to discuss at least two of each. Similarly, if a question asks for examples, you must offer more than one.

# Directorial choices

A director of *Death of a Salesman*, needs to consider:

- How to guide the actors' physical and vocal choices
- How to use design to reinforce the play's meaning and impact
- How key moments of the play might be staged
- The style of the play and potential use of performance conventions
- The effect the play should have on the audience.

## TASK 3.16

**A** Working in a small group, read the scene in the hotel in the second act (pages 92–95), from 'Willy: I'm so lonely' to 'I'll whip you.'

Discuss the impact you want this scene to have for the audience. Do you want it to be tense, for example? Frightening? Surprising? Alarming? Sad? A combination of these?

**B** Experiment with using:

- Changes in pace and volume to increase the tension
- Performance conventions, such as slow motion or still images to highlight key moments
- Design elements such as changes in the lighting, or sound effects, to emphasise that this is happening in the past
- Different ways of using the stage space, including where the Woman will enter and exit
- Using sound and/or lighting to heighten a mood or underscore a key moment
- Willy and Biff's physical and vocal skills to show their distress.

**C** Now write a paragraph in response to the following question: 'As a director, how would you stage the hotel scene in Act Two in order to create a specific impact on the audience?'

**WHAT THE SPECIFICATION SAYS...**

Learners must know and understand:

- How meaning is communicated through:
  - The use of performance space and spatial relationships on stage
  - The relationship between performers and audience
  - The design of: set, props, costume, lighting and sound
  - An actor's vocal and physical interpretation of character
  - The use of performance conventions
- How performance styles affect the direction, acting and design of a performance.

A physical and emotional moment in an RSC production, with Sam Marks, Anthony Sher and Alex Hassell.

## TASK 3.17

Below are excerpts from two candidate-style responses about staging the opening of Act Two. Decide how well you believe the writers explained and justified their ideas. Look for and highlight the following:

- Clear ideas about what they want to achieve
- Specific examples from the play
- Correct use of theatrical terminology
- Understanding of how a certain impact on the audience can be achieved.

In order to show the relationship between Linda and Willy, she will appear to anticipate his every need in this scene. Willy will sit in a chair at a table centre stage, surrounded by props suggesting his morning routine, such as a newspaper, a cup and a briefcase. Linda will move around him, pouring coffee and offering food. This will show how her life revolves around him. The pace will be quick and the mood upbeat, a significant change from the beginning of the play when Willy seemed so defeated. When Willy stands up, Linda will automatically try to put his jacket on him and straighten his tie, making sure he looks his best. Willy will accept her fussing over him. My goal is to present a naturalistic version of a long marriage, with the deep understanding Linda has of Willy.

I want to establish the context of the play and the mood of the scene, so will start the scene brightly lit and with a popular 1940s song playing as Linda moves around the kitchen in time to the music. The scene will be stylised, with the appearance of an advertisement showing a perfect household, which will contrast with the darkness at the end of Act One. Willy will also seem transformed; more powerful and positive than in the previous act. There will be a hint of comedy as Linda tries to put Willy's coat on him as he, excitedly talking about the boys, walks downstage out of her reach and it takes her several attempts to get it on him. However, the mood will turn darker when Linda brings up the topic of money and that they are 'a little short again'.

> **TIP:**
>
> There is no one right way of interpreting this or any other scene. The choices you make, however, must be rooted in your understanding of the play and how theatre works.

**WHAT THE SPECIFICATION SAYS...**

Learners must know and understand:

- How meaning is communicated through:
  - The design of: set, props, costume, lighting and sound.

# Design choices

Costume, set, lighting and sound design all contribute to the impact of *Death of a Salesman*. They are vital in presenting the play's setting, meaning and director's interpretation. For example, the way Biff and Happy are costumed as teenagers will contrast with their clothing in their 30s, showing how they have changed over the years. The way Miss Forsythe or the Woman are dressed will contrast with Linda's clothes in order to show the different roles they play.

Setting and props are important for establishing the context of the play and the contrasts between characters, such as Willy and Biff compared with Charley and Bernard. Sound can establish location or create atmosphere. Lighting can focus attention on certain characters and suggest a mood or location.

## Costume design

When writing about costume, it is important to consider what the costume tells the audience about the character's role and personality. It is useful to consider:

Period and context / Colour / Fabric / Silhouette

Fit / Condition / Headwear and footwear / Make-up and hair

Below is an excerpt from a candidate-style response about Miss Forsythe's outfit, demonstrating one possible approach to her costume.

Miss Forsythe should be dressed in an eye-catching outfit as she immediately attracts Happy's attention. She claims that she has been on a magazine cover, so she is aware of her appearance and takes pride in it. **[1]** I would have her wearing a bright red, satin dress, fitted at the waist, with its hemline just below her knees, a fashionable silhouette for the 1940s. **[2]** It would have a **sweetheart neckline** and a **boned bodice**. **[3]** She would wear tan seamed stockings and black kitten-heeled shoes, which would be very noticeable as she crosses her legs. **[4]** She is described as 'lavishly dressed' and 'furred'. As she has come in from outside, she would enter wearing a small brown fur stole around her shoulders — not an expensive fur, but one that would have immediate visual impact — perhaps a gift from an admirer. **[5]** She would wear a black and red hat, decorated with feathers, suggesting that she is aiming at a sophistication that she doesn't quite possess yet. She would carry a small black clutch bag from which she would remove accessories, such as a compact and lipstick. **[6]** Her hair would be shoulder-length and curled. Her make-up would be carefully applied, with dark arched brows and bright red lipstick. **[7]** Her overall appearance would suggest that she is somewhat over-dressed for the restaurant and looking forward to a night on the town. **[8]**

**[1]** Understanding of character and makes reference to the text.

**[2]** Describes colour, fabric and silhouette/fit, including why it is appropriate for the context.

**[3]** Precise details, using correct terminology.

**[4]** Describes colours/fabrics and justifies choices.

**[5]** Justifies choices with clear reference to text.

**[6]** Considers accessories and how they add to an interpretation of the character.

**[7]** Explains period make-up.

**[8]** Considers the effect of the costume.

**KEY TERMS:**

**Sweetheart neckline:** A heart-shaped neckline that emphasises the neckline and upper chest.

**Boned:** A garment stiffened with strips of material, such as plastic or bone, in order to give it a particular shape.

**Bodice:** The upper part of a dress.

**TIP:**

These are just some ideas for costumes for Miss Forsythe and Linda. Other designers will make different choices.

 **LOOK HERE**

For examples of technical vocabulary useful for describing costumes, see page 179.

## TASK 3.18

Shown here is a sketch of one possible interpretation of a costume design for Linda at the beginning of Act Two.

Draw your own sketches for costume designs for the following characters:

- Biff at 17
- Bernard as an adult
- Willy in Act Two.

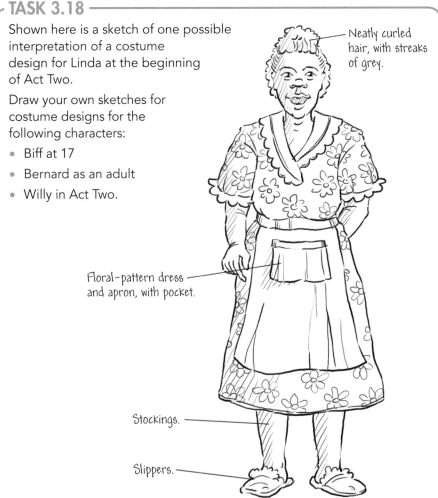

Neatly curled hair, with streaks of grey.

Floral-pattern dress and apron, with pocket.

Stockings.

Slippers.

# Set design

The set designer of *Death of a Salesman* could help to convey the play's meaning through some of the following:

- Emphasising naturalistic aspects of the play by providing realistic props and set furnishings
- Emphasising non-naturalistic aspects of the play by symbolically suggesting themes such as memory, dreams, money or family
- Establishing a particular relationship between the audience and the performers, by use of proxemics or levels
- Establishing the period of the play and the passage of time through the use of particular props or set furnishings.

## TASK 3.19

**A** Below is a sketch of the Loman house in Act One, for a thrust stage. After studying it:

- Add two more details that you think would improve the design.
- Answer the question: 'How does this set help to convey the ideas and themes of *Death of a Salesman*?'

**B** Then sketch a contrasting set for the locations in Act Two, including the offices of Howard and Charley. Consider if these would all be visible at the same time, or if one area could be used to represent all the different locations.

Painted city skyline backdrop.

Biff and Happy's bedroom.

Willy and Linda's bedroom.

The garden.

## TASK 3.20

Draw and annotate a set design showing how the scenes that switch rapidly between the restaurant and the Boston hotel could be established and understood by the audience. You will need to consider:

- Colours and textures
- The scale of the set
- Positioning/placement of set items on the stage
- Levels
- Materials
- Props and stage furnishings.

# Lighting design

The lighting in *Death of a Salesman* has many functions, including:

- Establishing the time of day and location
- Focusing the audience's attention on certain characters and events
- Highlighting and increasing the intensity of certain moments
- Creating an atmosphere or mood
- Suggesting a transition from one time or location to another.

## TASK 3.21

**A** Read this candidate-style response that describes a lighting design for the end of the first act. Highlight the technical terminology.

*I want to establish that it is late at night, in an urban location, and also that the family members are desperate and alienated from each other. I will use three separate spotlights on the multi-levelled set, in order to pick out Linda and Willy in one, Happy in his room and Biff downstairs. Upstage, I will have a neon light flashing on one of the buildings behind the Loman house, increasing the feeling of the world encroaching on their lives and hemming them in. The spotlights will gradually fade on Willy and Happy, while the spotlight on Biff will increase in intensity as he approaches the heater. I will use an LED light to create a small, blue flame effect on the heater and will increase the eeriness by having a blue-filtered light shining over the kitchen. The final image of the act will be Willy lit by the moonlight in his bedroom window, created by a fresnel lantern angled downwards to reflect its pearly white light onto his face, and Biff, in a blue spotlight holding the tubing. The lights will gradually fade down as Biff hurries back to his room.*

**B** With a partner, create a lighting design for the play's ending, from Ben's exit (page 108) to the end of the Requiem. Consider:

- Changes to the type, direction, colour and so on of the lighting
- How the lighting will contribute to the mood or atmosphere
- How you will achieve technically the lighting effects you want.
- What effect you want your final lighting to have on the audience.

**LOOK HERE**

For useful lighting vocabulary, see page 185.

This lighting design by Maya Michele Fein is true to the naturalistic style of the Williams Street Rep production, using the rooms' 'real-life' key lights. These also indicate the time of day of the scene. In addition, the effects emphasise the sense of separation between the characters.

# Sound design

Sound can be used to establish location or a transition, and is also useful in creating an atmosphere or reflecting the psychological state of a character. Sound design can also add to the romance, comedy or tension of a scene, often having a significant impact on the audience's experience of the play. When writing about sound design, you might consider:

- Volume: How amplified will the sound be? Will it grow louder or quieter?
- Recorded or live: Will sound effects and music be pre-recorded or performed live?
- Type of sound: Will the sound be naturalistic or abstract?
- Special effects: Will you use distorting effects such as reverb?
- How the sound or music begins and ends: Should it gradually become louder or will there be a burst of sound? Will it end abruptly or fade out?

## TASK 3.22

Look at the following ideas and note at least one occasion in *Death of a Salesman* when each sound effect might be appropriate:

> Flute music   A recorded voice   Sad music
>
> Offstage laughter   Banging on a door   Joyful music
>
> Traffic sounds   A car driving off

## TASK 3.23

Working with a partner, look closely at the scene when young Bernard announces that Biff has failed his maths course (pages 86–87). Consider when and how you could use sound for each of the following effects:

- Creating tension and excitement
- Showing Willy's mental state
- Emphasising the physical actions of the characters
- Recreating a realistic sound effect
- Creating an abstract sound effect.

**LOOK HERE**

For more advice on sound design, see pages 227–229.

## CHECK YOUR LEARNING *Death of a Salesman*

### Do you know...?

- ✓ When *Death of a Salesman* was written.
- ✓ In which decade it is set.
- ✓ Where it takes place, including different specific locations.
- ✓ The genre of the play.
- ✓ How its context might affect choices of costumes, sets and props.
- ✓ How the relationships between the characters, and the changes to these relationships, could be shown.
- ✓ Advantages and disadvantages of producing the play in different staging configurations.
- ✓ How key scenes might be staged.
- ✓ The performance style (or styles) of the play.
- ✓ How performers could use their physical and vocal skills to convey characters' motivations, thoughts and feelings and to impart meaning to the action.
- ✓ The role of the director and how they influence the way an audience responds to and understands the play.
- ✓ Key moments a director could use to highlight their concept of the play.
- ✓ Different design choices to be made, why they are important and how they can be effective.
- ✓ What impact the play should have on the audience and what messages they should be left with.

This bronze statue in Budapest of Hungarian actor Timár József shows how the weight of the sales bags represent the weight of worries, disappointments and sense of failure pulling Willy down.

# FIND ME
## by Olwen Wymark

The OCR specification identifies editions of the texts that are used to set questions in the 'Drama: Performance and response' (Component 04) examination paper. It is not required that centres use these editions for teaching this component.

Page numbers in this chapter refer to the Samuel French edition of *Find Me*, ISBN-13: 978-0-573-11136-5, one of the editions used by OCR for question setting.

# Plot synopsis

Based on a real story, *Find Me* explores the life of a troubled young girl, Verity, and the effects of her behaviour on her family, as well as their struggles to find help for her. The character of Verity is divided into Verity I, II, III, IV and V, and each is played by a different actor.

The play begins with the Narrator explaining that, in November 1975, Verity Taylor, age 20, is charged with 'damaging a chair by fire'. She is convicted in 1976 and admitted to Broadmoor for an indefinite period of time.

**Flashback** to several years earlier. Verity's family – Edward, her father; Jean, her mother and her brothers, Mark and Nicky – attempt to take photographs, while Verity, age 16, disrupts. Younger brother, Nicky, doesn't know her well as she was sent away as an in-patient when he was only a few months old and then sent to Broadmoor when he was ten.

An Interviewer from the Child Guidance Clinic asks Edward about Verity's childhood. Verity is nine and they are seeking help. He explains their worries about her behaviour, such as her wandering off, and their inability to change or control her behaviour. She is an intelligent child, being treated for mild epilepsy. She doesn't have any friends.

Flashback to a younger Verity who is playing intently with a village she has made out of blocks. She throws a tantrum when asked to move them. Jean feels that Verity's behaviour is worse around her than with her father.

The Teacher reads out a report about nine-year-old Verity. Verity is rude to her mother in the playground ('you old cow') and pretends to drink out of her Wellingtons, to her mother's embarrassment. Jean hears other children saying that nobody likes Verity and that she is a 'mad woman'.

Mark expresses his frustration at living with Verity and explains how she had ruined their holiday in France. Verity becomes over-excited in the restaurant and embarrasses the family. Mark and Jean leave, but Verity refuses to leave with her father.

The Taylor family and neighbours begin making a bonfire. Eleven-year-old Verity is noisy and Jean is afraid she will wake her baby brother, Nicky. In her excitement, Verity knocks over one of the neighbourhood children. Her father and the neighbours encourage Verity to recite a poem she wrote in school, which she does, receiving appreciative reactions.

A teacher announces preparations for the swimming gala. All five Veritys explain how much they love swimming and their hopes for the future. They hope to win all the prizes in the swimming gala and that everyone will be proud of them. However, when it is discovered Verity has left her swimming cap at home, she isn't allowed to take part in the gala. When she returns home, she has a breakdown during which she tears up photographs and letters, floods the bathroom and cuts off half of her hair. With strange hair and make-up, she declares that she is a bomb and runs through the auditorium screaming.

## Optional interval.

Edward and Jean speak to a Nurse to have 11-year-old Verity II admitted to a hospital. At the same time, Verity I is describing Broadmoor Hospital. Speaking to a Registrar, Jean and Edward describe Verity's actions after the swimming gala. They are then sent to a psychiatric doctor. They must repeat their reports of Verity's behaviour to Doctors, a Registrar and a Clerk, who finally agrees to admit Verity to the children's ward.

A year later, Jean and Edward discuss whether they think Verity is making progress. A flashback to six months earlier when Verity came home for Christmas. Verity claims that she destroyed her Christmas presents and threw them in a bin. She is jealous that she wasn't allowed to go to the zoo. When Jean and the boys return, Verity cuts her arms. She tries to change clothes with her mother, saying that they should exchange places. Then she runs off.

Miss Everitt, a social worker, delivers the news that they have been unable to find a suitable residential place at a boarding school for Verity. Jean explains that, for the past two years, Verity has twice been hospitalised due to breakdowns and that all attempts at other arrangements have been unsuccessful. She says that Verity is disruptive at home and runs away. After Miss Everitt leaves, Jean's monologue expresses her guilt and her frustration at the lack of help.

Edward writes letters trying to get help for Verity, but is turned away by everyone. Jean decides to leave the family home with Nicky.

Verity (V) is in a half-way house. A staff member, Dottie, and the warden, Tom, disagree on whether it is right for Verity to be there, but Tom advocates compassion. Verity helps Tom with some gardening. Jean, now back home, and Edward are happy to receive a letter from Tom saying that Verity seems 'contented'. Then Tom calls to say that Verity has either jumped or fallen from her first-floor window and broken the bones in her feet.

Two years later, a consultant psychiatrist says that Verity cannot return to the half-way house. They tried a trial weekend and it was a 'disaster'. Verity, at 19, is kept in a geriatric ward of a mental hospital. The Consultant explains how her behaviour is increasingly destructive, but no one has been able to make a 'definite diagnosis' for her. The only option they are offered is bringing her home, which the Taylors decline.

Verity (I) is on the ward jotting in a notebook about a play she would like to write. Verity (IV) is in the garden of a couple, Ted and Dora, who are watching TV. Her odd behaviour attracts their attention and Ted invites her in, thinking she is lost. She claims to have been raped. Dora calls the police. The Consultant writes to Mr Taylor to say that Verity is now in a locked ward for geriatric patients.

Verity (II) is in the dayroom with the other patients for an exercise session. Her behaviour is very disruptive and she is angry with Sister Moses. She decides to set fire to a chair in order to 'burn her backside'. The fire service arrives and Verity is taken to Holloway Prison.

At the trial, an order is made for Verity to be admitted to Broadmoor, a maximum security hospital. The play ends with all five Veritys calling out, 'Find me!'

KEY TERM:

Flashback: A scene from an earlier period of a character's life than that shown in the play's main timeline.

TIP:

You might want to consider the playwright's original intentions in writing the play. For example, what is Olwen Wymark saying about care and support for the mentally ill and the stresses on a family caring for someone like Verity?

## TASK 3.1

A Working in a small group, create a two-minute version of the play, making sure that you cover what you all agree are the most significant events in the plot.

B Given your understanding of the play's plot, answer the following questions:

1 What is Verity's relationship with her mother like?

2 How does Verity's brother, Mark, feel about her?

3 What evidence is there that Verity finds it difficult to make friends?

4 What are the occasions when Verity seems to be happy?

## KEY TERMS:

**Social drama:** A genre of plays that deal with the interactions between different social groups, an exploration of a social group, or the place of an individual within a society.

**Documentary theatre:** Theatre based on real people and events and using documentary material, such as interviews, letters, reports and newspaper articles, often without changing the actual words, in order to create a play.

# Genre

*Find Me* is an example of **social drama**, which uses dramatic forms and conventions to explore social issues. In this case, it highlights the lack of understanding and help for those suffering from mental health issues and how this impacts on family life. Using information gathered from interviews with Verity's parents, the play demonstrates failures in various institutions, including schools, hospitals and the court system. As the play is based on a real case (and is dedicated to the person on whom the character of Verity is based), it also has features of **documentary theatre**, where actual events are brought to life on stage.

### TASK 3.2

**A** Read the section of the play after the optional interval (pages 26–33), when Edward and Jean meet with a series of medical professionals in an attempt to get help for Verity. In a small group, experiment with how this could be performed to emphasise how Verity and her family are being treated. Consider how:

- The constant repetition of questions could be highlighted
- Jean and Edward's facial expressions, postures and body language might change as they are repeatedly asked the same questions
- The various professionals might speak to the parents
- The pace and staging of the scene could be used to emphasise the impersonal treatment they are experiencing.

**B** Either create a storyboard or write a paragraph explaining how this scene could be staged in order to show the difficulties that the family is experiencing.

### TASK 3.3

**A** Look closely at Jean's monologue after Miss Everitt's exit (page 39), starting with 'What are we going to do?' Discuss in a group:

- What has happened to Jean leading up to this moment?
- What is Jean trying to work out in this speech?
- How might the actor move and use facial expression and eye contact in order to show that she is speaking her most private thoughts?
- What lines do you believe are the most important and should be emphasised?
- In order to convey her character's emotional state, how could she use particular vocal skills, such as volume, diction and pace?

**B** Imagine you have been asked to advise an actor on how to perform Jean's speech. Write five bullet points explaining what you believe are the most important notes you could give them to guide their performance of this monologue.

# Structure

The play has an **episodic** structure, covering Verity's life from childhood to her being charged by the police at age 20 and admitted to Broadmoor, a high-security psychiatric hospital, just after her 21st birthday. The play is **bookended** with a Narrator repeating the same speech about Verity's legal situation at both the play's beginning and its conclusion.

Although much of the play is **chronological**, there are flashbacks and other time jumps, so the overall structure is **non-linear**. The playwright has suggested that the play may have an interval, with the first half ending with Verity's episode in the bathroom and the second half beginning with her parents' seeking help the next day.

# Style

The play uses a number of non-naturalistic styles, such as narration, multi-rolling and the sharing of the role of Verity between five performers. The original production was staged in a minimalistic style, without special costumes or props. The tone of the piece is serious and dramatic. Throughout the play, characters step out of the play's main action and use **direct address** to speak their thoughts to the audience.

## TASK 3.4

**A** From your knowledge and understanding of the play, identify examples of the following structural or stylistic features:

- Narration
- Conflict
- A passage of a substantial amount of time
- A flashback to an earlier time
- A character speaking directly to the audience.

**B** Read the statements below about Verity in *Find Me*. Then work with a partner to put them in order, with the one you agree with most as 1, and the one you agree with least as 5.

- [ ] As most of the play is seen from Verity's parents' points of view, it is difficult to fully understand what Verity is really thinking and feeling.

- [ ] Verity is played by more than one actor to show the many different aspects and complexity of the character.

- [ ] The audience receives a fractured picture of Verity constructed from letters, reports and interviews, leading them to feel pity for both Verity and her family.

- [ ] Verity is failed by every institution that should be helping her.

- [ ] Verity is a fascinating, changeable character whose actions might be better understood and treated today than they were when the play was written.

---

**KEY TERMS:**

**Episodic:** A structure involving a series of scenes, or episodes, which are usually short and might take place in many different locations. They often 'stand alone' without relying upon a previous scene to explain their meaning. This is in contrast to traditional dramatic narratives, which usually have scenes or acts covering a restricted period of time, taking place in a limited number of locations and ultimately building to a climax.

**Bookended:** A structural device in which the beginning and ending of a play are similar and, like bookends, appear at either side of the main action of the play.

**Chronological:** Presenting events in the order in which they occur.

**Non-linear:** A sequence that is not arranged in a straightforward or chronological way.

**Direct address:** Speaking directly to the audience.

---

**TIP:**

Remember that there are many ways in which Verity and *Find Me* can be interpreted.

---

# Context

Olwen Wymark (1932–2013), was an American playwright who lived and studied in England. She wrote a number of plays for the stage and radio. She was approached to write the play that became *Find Me* for a group of students at Kingston Polytechnic. Their production of the play was performed at the Edinburgh Festival in 1977. She then created the published version of the play, which was first performed by a professional cast at the Orange Tree Theatre, in Richmond, Surrey in October 1977. The play remains a favourite text for study and performance in schools.

## Historical context

Wymark was writing about actual events that occurred in the mid-20th century. She set the play in 'the present', but there is now a historical aspect to it. The character of Verity Taylor (her real name is never revealed) was born on 13th February 1955 and the action of the play ends in February 1976, with most of the play taking place in the mid-1960s to mid-1970s.

The play ends with Verity being sentenced under the Mental Health Act of 1959, provision 65, which allows people to be imprisoned without time limit if there is a 'risk' of their 'committing further offenses' and 'it is necessary for the protection of the public…' The Mental Health Act of 2007, which replaced it, provides more rights and alternatives for patients, including the right to an advocate and provision of Supervised Community Treatment. This suggests that the treatment someone like Verity would receive today is different from that in the 1970s. There are still patients today, however, who find themselves sectioned under the Mental Health Act in cases that are difficult to diagnose or treat, where they are considered a risk to others.

## EXTENSION

Research England in the 1960s to 1970s to gain a better understanding of the context. There are many audio-visual resources online. Some possible topics include:

- Social context: families, schools, roles of women, mental health and healthcare provision
- Cultural context: fashion and uniforms, music, architecture
- Historical context: England in the 1960s and 1970s, politics, socio-economics.

Make a note of anything that helps your understanding of the play and how it could be staged or designed.

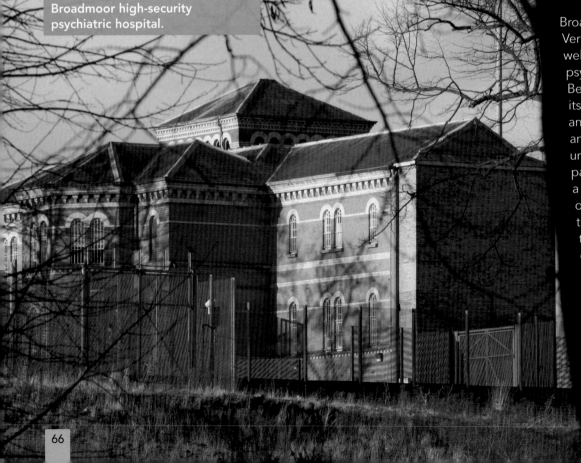

**Broadmoor high-security psychiatric hospital.**

Broadmoor Hospital, where Verity was admitted, is a well-known high-security psychiatric hospital in Berkshire. It accepted its first patient in 1863 and it housed both men and women patients until 2007, when female patients were moved to a different centre. Many of the patients are sent to Broadmoor through the court system after committing crimes and most have been diagnosed with severe mental illness.

# Cultural context

The 1960s are associated with youth, pop music and fashions such as mini-skirts. Men generally wore their hair longer and facial hair was popular. Bold prints, such as paisley or floral, and bright colours were fashionable. 1960–70s fashion trends included clothing influenced by other cultures, such as India and Mexico. Bell-bottomed or flared trousers became popular. Many people who were not particularly fashion-conscious, however, might only subtly alter their clothing. For example, a mother might wear a knee-length skirt or tailored woollen trousers or a man might wear a suit with slightly flared trousers. British students would usually wear a school uniform.

Films of the 1970s were often gritty and realistic. In 1975, *One Flew Over the Cuckoo's Nest*, an award-winning film starring Jack Nicholson (adapted from Ken Kesey's novel), presented a critical view of an American psychiatric hospital in which the patients were treated inhumanely. It shares themes with *Find Me*, such as inadequate diagnosis and treatments and poor care and lack of understanding of those with mental illness.

There was much experimentation in British theatre in the 1970s, with many theatre makers moving away from conventional dramatic structures. The ground-breaking British playwright, Caryl Churchill, famous for plays including *Top Girls* (1982), is a near contemporary of Wymark's. In 1975, a Women's Theatre Festival hosted works by both playwrights.

# Social context

The Taylors are depicted as a middle-class family, who are typical of the 1970s in many ways. Jean is in charge of domestic tasks and activities such as the school run. The school has clear rules and structures, which a non-conforming student like Verity does not obey. Her teacher reports that 'her social behaviour' is 'unreliable' (page 9). One mother in the play suggests that Verity should be in a 'special school' (page 12), that is, one for children who cannot cope in mainstream education. At one stage, the teenage Verity is inappropriately placed in a ward for geriatric patients.

Although it is impossible to know from the script of a play exactly why Verity behaves the way she does, the real Verity today might have received different treatment and care. There is also greater openness and awareness of mental health issues now, so her family might have been treated with more sympathy and understanding.

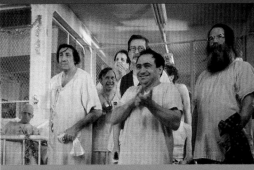

A Christmas scene from *One Flew Over the Cuckoo's Nest*, in which patients are neglected, abandoned or abused and have experimental treatments forced upon them. They are ruled over, with a distinct lack of compassion, by the cold-hearted Nurse Ratched.

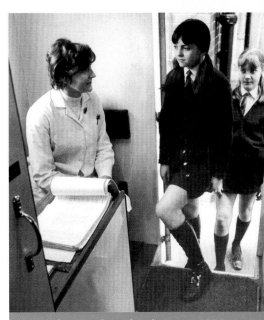

Two girls visit the school nurse, 1970s.

A swimming gala at Binley Park Comprehensive School, 1962.

**TIP:**

In your exam questions, alternative wording might be used instead of 'context', such as 'reflect the time in which the play was written' or 'show when and where the play is set'.

## TASK 3.5

Look at the following list of key moments from the play and write about each one to explain what it tells you about the social or historical context of the play. (The first one has been completed for you.)

1 Edward describes Verity's behaviour to the Interviewer.

*This shows Edward's reluctance to think of Verity as 'abnormal' and how her behaviour has not led to a clear diagnosis. On one hand, she is 'very intelligent', but, on the other, 'bizarre' and 'anti-social'. At this time, many people with misunderstood conditions were mislabelled or untreated.*

2 The family is embarrassed by Verity's behaviour in a restaurant in France.

3 Angry that she wasn't taken to the zoo, Verity cuts herself and tries to put on her mother's clothes.

4 Nicky begins experiencing distress and Jean decides to leave home, taking Nicky with her.

When depicting the context of the play, there are a number of factors you can consider, such as:

- How much money a character might have
- Fashions of the 1960s and 1970s
- The occupations of the characters
- Homes, schools and hospitals of the 1960s and 1970s
- The ages of the characters
- Props a character might use, such as toys or books from the period.

## TASK 3.6

A Look at the list of costume items and props below and decide which characters they might be suitable for:

Gardening equipment    Building blocks

Swimming goggles    Wellington boots    Umbrella    School uniform.    Writing paper

Briefcase    White coat    Spectacles    Cape    Scarf    Apron

B Then choose one character and draw a detailed sketch showing how you think they could be costumed and any props they might use.

## TASK 3.7

A Due to the many scene changes, *Find Me* is usually produced in a stylised or minimalistic way. There are, however, opportunities to show the context with details of costume and set design. You might choose certain colours, pieces of furniture or other set dressings, or projections in order to convey the 1970s. Draw sketches of the set and costumes for the first two pages of the script. Make sure your designs reflects the period in which the play was written.

B Write two paragraphs in response to the following question: 'Describe how you could show the social or historical context of the play by your design choices for the costumes and sets for Jean and Edward and their home.'

# Interpretations of key characters

You must demonstrate that you understand the main characters in the play, including different ways that they could be interpreted.

**WHAT THE SPECIFICATION SAYS...**
Learners must know and understand:
• How meaning is communicated through:
  • An actor's vocal and physical interpretation of character.

## The family

### Jean
Married to Edward, and mother of Mark, Verity and Nicky. She has a difficult relationship with Verity and is frustrated and embarrassed by her. Worn down by psychological and physical demands, at one point, she leaves the family home with Nicky. When Verity is at the half-way house, she comes home.

### Edward
Jean's husband, and the children's father. He attempts to look for positives and is slow to accept the severity of Verity's problems. He frequently takes Verity's side. Jean and he seek professional help from a number of sources.

### Mark
Verity's brother, three years older and 'very different' from her. He is upset and embarrased by Verity's behaviour. She spoils things, and Jean worries that there is no 'peace' for him while he prepares for his exams.

### Verity
The Taylors' middle child. She suffers from mild epilepsy and displays worrying unconventional behaviours. Edward describes her as very private and quite emotional and says that she can be 'very imaginative, very witty'. She loves swimming and dreams of winning at the gala. She is frequently in conflict with Jean and says she is the 'underdog female' in the family. Except for a brief 'contented' interlude at a half-way house, her behaviour becomes increasingly destructive.

### Nicky
Verity's much younger brother, only a few months old when she was first an in-patient and ten when she was sent to Broadmoor. He feels he 'hardly knew her'.

## The half-way house

### Tom
The kindly warden. In a rare scene of contentment for Verity, Tom gently coaxes her to help with some gardening. This period of peace ends when Verity jumps from a window. Despite Tom's willingness to have Verity back at the house, a consultant explains that it isn't worth 'the gamble'.

### Dottie
A staff member at the half-way house. She doesn't think it is the right place for Verity because her mental health issues put a strain on the other residents. She is shown coaxing the others to their jobs while Tom focuses on Verity.

## The professionals

### Miss Everitt
A busy social worker who arrives in response to Edward's letter about 14-year-old Verity. She tells Jean that there are 'much worse cases'. She doesn't offer any help, or sympathy, reminding Jean shat 'she is your child'.

### Teacher
In her report, the Teacher suggests that nine-year-old Verity is fair or good in most subjects and has made progress, but her social behaviour is 'unreliable'.

### Sister Moses
A nurse in the geriatric ward in which Verity is placed. She and Verity are shown in conflict, including Moses 'bundling' Verity towards a door 'fairly roughly'. Verity takes revenge by burning Moses' chair.

### Miss Blake
A hospital physiotherapist. She tries to lead the patients in a set of exercises, which Verity interrupts.

### Consultant
A doctor in charge of Verity's medical care. He writes, 'Verity continues to be a disappointment to us all.'

## Others

### Ted and Dora
A couple whose garden Verity sits in after she escapes from the hospital. Thinking she is lost, they invite her in and she says she has been raped. Dora phones the police.

**TASK 3.8**

Choose one important line from the play for each character. Write one sentence explaining its importance in understanding the character and another one or two on how it could be delivered by the actor. What physical and vocal skills would be most effective?

# Use of vocal skills

**KEY TERM:**

Received Pronunciation (also called RP): A way of speaking that is considered the 'standard' form of British Pronunciation. It is not specific to a certain location, but is associated with education and formality.

Performers in *Find Me* could use their voices in a variety of ways. The Taylors' dialect could indicate where they live and their social class. For example, they might speak with **Received Pronunciation**, often heard in middle-class families in England, or use a regional dialect. The family are often shown in emotional situations, so their voices will reflect what they are undergoing. The performers playing the five Veritys should decide if they will attempt similar tones, volumes or pitches of voice, or if they will be individual. Most productions of *Find Me* involve multi-rolling, so performers need to find ways of differentiating vocally between the characters they play.

Vocal skills that actors might consider include:

Accent and dialect   Pace   Volume   Pitch

Pauses and timing   Intonation   Phrasing   Emotional range

**TASK 3.9**

With a partner, experiment with vocal skills to interpret the following lines. Note down the choices you make, including reasons.

Verity: 'They're all dead now. They're killed. That's what you wanted. You wanted them killed.' (page 7)

Mark: 'I wish I didn't have to live at home.' (page 13)

Edward: 'Verity, come out! Stop that! Come out of there!' (page 24)

Jean: 'Imagine your own child driving you to drink. Your own child that you love.' (page 40)

**TASK 3.10**

For each key character listed below, give three examples of different vocal skills that the actor playing the role could use. Justify each of your choices by explaining why it is appropriate. (Examples have been given for Jean.)

- **Edward**
- **Verity**
- **Mark**
- **Tom**.

| Character | Vocal skill | When vocal skill could be displayed | Details and justification |
|---|---|---|---|
| Jean | Speaking with **Received Pronunciation**. | Throughout the play. | This reflects the formality and use of standard English in Jean's dialogue and would suit this largely conventional middle-class family. It would make Verity's non-conforming and sometimes shocking behaviour stand out more. |
| | Use of **pause** – to show hesitation and uncertainty about how much to reveal. | Pages 9–10. | In the conversation with the other mothers, Jean pauses to hide her feelings. For example, she would pause when a mother says children are 'daft' because the mother doesn't understand how extreme Verity is. She is trying to pretend that everything is ordinary, but she is uncomfortable. |
| | **Emotional range** and **volume**: Upset, despairing, angry. | Page 24. | When Verity tears up her things, Jean cries out in despair 'Oh God, stop her.' She speaks through sobs. This shows how shattered she is by Verity's actions and brings the end of the first act to a dramatic climax. |

# Use of physical skills

Actors may use a combination of naturalistic and stylised movement in the play. Scenes such as those in the school playground, the half-way house or the Taylor home might be performed with realistic gestures and movements, while other scenes, for example the swimming gala, could use stylised or choreographed movement. Due to the minimalistic approach of most productions, mime might be employed in many scenes.

The audience sees characters at a range of ages, so the performers should consider how they could use posture, movement and gestures to show their age. The demands of multi-rolling would also require physical skills, for example when the actor playing the Waitress changes to Verity, or Sister Moses becomes Jean.

Physical skills that actors might consider include:

| Posture | Movement | Pace | Gestures |

| Facial expressions | Proxemics | Eye contact |

**TIP:**

All stage falls must be carefully prepared and any actual danger avoided. The person falling controls the movement, not the person pushing. What the audience should register are the characters' intentions and reactions.

## TASK 3.11

A Focus on the bonfire-night scene (pages 17–21). Explore physical skills you could use to achieve the following:

- The actors transforming from the characters in the French restaurant to the characters in the bonfire-night scene (for example, the French child to Jean).

- How the performers' use of proxemics might indicate their relationships to each other, such as family groups.

- How Verity's movements and gestures could show how excited she is.

- How the child physically reacts to Verity pushing her over.

- What gestures or movements Edward might make in an attempt to calm Verity.

- How Verity's movement and facial expressions might change when she recites her poem.

B Try to perform the scene in three different ways, using a range of gestures, facial expressions and speeds of movement. Which were the most successful?

## TASK 3.12

For each key character listed below, give at least three examples of how they could use their physical skills in the play. Justify each of your choices. (Examples have been given for Verity.)

- **Jean**
- **Edward**
- **Mark**
- **Sister Moses**.

| Character | Physical skill | When physical skill could be displayed | Details and justification |
|---|---|---|---|
| Verity | **Posture** and **body language** to show how young she is. | Pages 5–6. | Verity is 'very small'. She sits cross-legged on the floor, leaning far over, concentrating hard on her building blocks, handling them very precisely. This will emphasise her youth and how important her game is to her. |
| | **Movement** and **gesture**, to show her extreme distress. | Page 25. | Verity is acting in wild, violent despair after not being allowed to take part in the swimming gala. She makes large swinging gestures towards her family to keep them away from her. Then she throws her arms out and spreads her fingers when she says 'I'm a bomb.' Finally she runs zig-zag through the audience to show how chaotic and out of control she is. |
| | Facial **expression** and **eye contact**, to show how odd her behaviour seems to Ted and Dora. | Page 50. | Verity has escaped from the hospital and is dancing on Ted and Dora's wall. When Ted first comes out, Verity does not make eye contact with him but looks down with a furrowed brow as she concentrates on her gyrating movements. When he first speaks to her, she makes only momentary eye contact and gives an odd, tight, little smile, before resuming her dance. This makes her seem strange to Ted, but not dangerous. |

# Stage directions

In addition to the play's dialogue, a way for the playwright to convey what a character is doing, thinking and feeling is through stage directions. For example:

> Page 1: The light stays on Verity I, who remains throughout the following, kneeling and hugging herself in her arms. The lights come up in another area on Verity II, who is waving hands, smiling, hopping, dancing, walking in a curious duck-like way.

> Page 47: They [Jean and Edward] smile at each other. Black-out. In the darkness each of the five Veritys screams one after another. The lights come up on Tom with a phone.

> Page 45: Tom gets two windowboxes and a bag of bulbs. He sets them down a little distance from Verity and begins planting the bulbs. She watches. Then, very slowly, she stands and leaves her circle, takes a step or two toward Tom, stops, and watches him for a bit.

## TASK 3.13

A In a small group, perform each of the stage directions above.

B Discuss and write down what you believe each character is thinking and feeling. For example, what is Verity thinking when she approaches Tom? What are Jean and Edward feeling when they smile at each other?

C Talk about what the audience learns about the characters and their situations from the stage directions. For example, what do we learn about Tom and how he relates to Verity? What does the screaming from the Veritys tell the audience about how Jean and Edward's situation is going to change?

**LOOK HERE**

See pages 200–202 for more rehearsal techniques for exploring characterisation and practising performance skills.

## TASK 3.14

A Read the extract below from a candidate-style response about the stage directions on pages 11–12 (describing nine-year-old Verity, Jean and others in the playground). Highlight three details that show how the stage directions reveal aspects of the characters and their relationships.

The stage directions show how Verity behaves differently from the other children. While the rest of the children 'scramble' to leave, Verity stays behind, unnoticed by her teacher, holding pencils. The actions of the other mothers and children show their friendly routine of doing up coats and chatting, whereas Verity is slow to acknowledge her mother and then insults her. The embarrassment of this is heightened by the stage direction 'The mothers look up and then look away.' Verity's odd behaviour escalates with her pretending to drink from a Wellington boot and stamping in a puddle. To add to her humiliation, Jean has to chase after Verity when she runs away.

These stage directions highlight for the audience the contrast of Jean and Verity's relationship with that of the other mothers and their children. At the end, Jean is shown to be isolated as she waves 'forlornly' as the other mothers leave, which will make the audience pity her.

B Choose a stage direction involving Edward and Jean and answer the question: 'How do the stage directions communicate the characters of Edward and Jean and their relationship to the audience?'

**TIP:**

Remember that communication is at the heart of drama. Always consider what the performance and staging choices you make are communicating to the audience. Do they create…

- Sympathy?
- Fear?
- Excitement?
- Suspense?
- Pity?
- Comedy?
- Greater understanding?

# Use of space

Actors might use the stage space in many different ways including:

**Levels** | **Proxemics** | **Positioning on stage**
**Entrances and exits** | **Use of the 'fourth wall'**

In addition, the type of staging configuration and the set design could influence the actors' use of space.

Below is a candidate-style sample response about how the performers playing Verity could use theatre in the round, and the benefits and challenges of this space.

**[1]** Opens with some understanding of the role of Verity and the staging configuration.

**[2]** Explains an advantage of theatre in the round.

**[3]** Identifies a creative example of how Verity could use this staging.

**[4]** Identifies another advantage of this staging and uses correct terminology ('breaking the fourth wall').

**[5]** Uses correct terminology and identifies a disadvantage.

**[6]** Gives a precise example of a disadvantage.

**[7]** Suggests creative advantages of theatre in the round and the impact on the audience.

Although in some ways a mystery to the audience, Verity remains at the centre of the play and the audience must attempt to 'find' her. A theatre in the round is a good choice for this play as the audience will surround the performance space, enclosing and trapping Verity, as she is so often restricted or imprisoned in the play. **[1]** The play is usually staged in a minimalistic style, so the intimate theatre in the round setting suits the needs of the play as it creates a closeness and will focus the audience on the acting. **[2]** Some scenes, such as the swimming gala scene where the five Veritys speak about their love of swimming, could be performed with all the Veritys in a circle, replicating the circular configuration of the stage to great effect and, at other points, Verity could be positioned centre stage while the characters speaking about her surround her. **[3]** It will also be easy using this configuration to have Verity breaking the fourth wall and exiting through the audience, such as at the end of the first act. **[4]**

A disadvantage of this configuration is the difficulty of using technology so that all the audience can see them, such as projections, which could otherwise aid a portrayal of Verity's context. **[5]** Additionally, key scenes will have to be staged very carefully so that the audience can clearly see facial expressions. For example, the performer playing Verity will have to move during the 'Dear Reader' speech in the second act so that no section of the audience is looking at her back for large portions. **[6]** Ultimately, theatre in the round could be a highly effective configuration, drawing the audience into Verity's world and helping to place her at the centre of it, as well as serving the stylised aspects of the production. **[7]**

### TIP:

If an exam question asks for advantages and disadvantages, you need to discuss at least two of each. Similarly, if a question asks for examples, you must offer more than one.

 **LOOK HERE**

See pages 8–11 for reminders of the advantages and disadvantages of different staging configurations.

## TASK 3.15

**A** Work in a small group to discuss – and describe using sketches, for example – how the following scenes could be produced in different staging configurations:

- The school playground
- The French restaurant
- The swimming gala
- Miss Blake's hospital exercise group.

**B** Choose one of the scenes and write down at least two advantages and two disadvantages of performing it in each staging configuration described on pages 8–11.

# Directorial choices

A director of *Find Me* needs to consider:

- How to guide the actors' physical and vocal choices
- How to use design to reinforce the play's meaning and impact
- How key moments of the play might be staged
- The style of the play and potential use of performance conventions
- The effect the play should have on the audience.

## TASK 3.16

**A** Working in a small group, read the hospital scene with Sister Moses and Miss Blake (pages 54–56), from 'Sister Moses: Into the day-room, everyone…' to 'I smell smoke!'

Discuss the impact you want this scene to have for the audience. Do you want it to be tense, for example? Frightening? Surprising? Alarming? Sad? A combination of these?

**B** Experiment with using:

- Changes in and volume to increase the tension
- Performance conventions, such as slow motion or still images, to highlight key moments
- Conflict between Sister Moses and Verity
- Sound effects to cause surprise or alarm
- Props, such as the ball, basket or the matches to create certain effects.

**C** Now write a paragraph in response to the following question: 'As a director, how would you stage the hospital scene in order to create a specific impact on the audience?'

WHAT THE SPECIFICATION SAYS…

- How meaning is communicated through:
  - The use of performance space and spatial relationships on stage
  - The relationship between performers and audience
  - The design of: set, props, costume, lighting and sound
  - An actor's vocal and physical interpretation of character
  - The use of performance conventions
- How performance styles affect the direction, acting and design of a performance.

The Veritys from Youth Action Theatre have identical costumes and similar hairstyles.

Verity contemplates revenge on Sister Moses in this Footscray City College production.

The Veritys perform exaggerated swimming strokes in this production by Caterham School.

## TASK 3.17

Below are excerpts from two candidate-style responses about the staging of the swimming gala scene. Decide how well you believe the writers explained and justified their ideas. Look for and highlight the following:

- Clear ideas about what they want to achieve
- Specific examples from the play
- Correct use of theatrical terminology
- Understanding of how to make an impact on the audience.

This begins as a high point for Verity. To capture her excited and happy mood, I will use some non-naturalistic staging techniques. I will have the five Veritys enter backwards, as if they are swimming backstroke. During the dialogue, they will stand in an outward facing circle, with each Verity doing a different exaggerated swimming stroke, except for the Verity who is speaking. I want this to have a dream-like effect, with graceful movements underscored with music. At the end of this section, each Verity will be frozen in a triumphant, celebratory still image on the line 'The winner!' with Verity V ultimately being lifted up by two of the others. This use of levels will create a powerful image, showing Verity succeeding for once. The subsequent blackout will change the mood, and the offstage voice will sound harsh and inhuman, breaking Verity's dream.

My concept for the play is a promenade production in which the audience can follow the Veritys. For the swimming gala, the audience will be divided up to follow one of the five Veritys. The Veritys will use microphones so that they can whisper their thoughts as if confiding their most private dreams. The teacher will not appear but simply be a voice projected through a speaker. The audience would then be guided into an end on position in order to witness the family's reaction to Verity's cries of 'No! No! No!' I think the unpredictability of promenade staging will engage the audience.

## WHAT THE SPECIFICATION SAYS...

Learners must know and understand:

- How meaning is communicated through:
  - The design of: set, props, costume, lighting and sound.

# Design choices

Costume, set, lighting and sound design all contribute to the impact of *Find Me*. They are vital in presenting the play's setting, meaning and director's interpretation. For example, costumes might set the Veritys apart from the other characters or establish the professions of multi-rolling characters.

Setting and props are important for establishing the context of the play and the contrasts between different groups of characters. Sound can be used to establish location and create atmosphere or tension. Lighting can focus attention on certain characters and suggest a certain mood or location.

## Costume design

When writing about costume, it is important to consider what the costume tells the audience about the character's role and personality. It is useful to consider:

| Period and context | Colour | Fabric | Silhouette |

| Fit | Condition | Headwear and footwear | Make-up and hair |

Below is an excerpt from a candidate-style response about Jean, demonstrating one possible approach to her costume.

As the actor playing Jean is seen in a number of situations, as well as playing other characters, I will aim for a versatile costume that gives an indication of her personality and social class, but which can also be quickly altered. **[1]** I think of Jean as a character who has high standards and, while not at the forefront of fashion, will make an effort to look attractive and appropriate for the situation. **[2]** For her basic costume, upon which other items may be layered, I will have brown tartan trousers that are slightly flared and a brown wool turtleneck, in keeping with the 1970s context. These will look conservative. **[3]** The script refers to Jean wearing a 'cape and scarf' when she returns from the zoo. **[4]** I interpret this as being a stylish woollen dark-brown cape with a gold fastener at the neck, and a floral scarf. These should appear attractive and important to Jean, which will make it all the more powerful when Verity tries to take them from her. **[5]** Her hair will be in a neat bob and she will wear small gold earrings and a wedding ring. Her make-up will be understated, with subtle lipstick and a pale foundation. I want to project that she is a neat, orderly person, in contrast to Verity's chaos. **[6]** In the playground scene, she will wear a trench coat. At interviews, she will wear a smart blazer, showing the care she takes about her appearance. All of her clothes will be in pristine condition, well-fitting and pressed. **[7]** When playing the French child, the actress might wear a sweatshirt and then when, changing for the bonfire scene, wear a trench coat over it to show she is Jean again. **[8]**

**[1]** Demonstrates understanding of practical demands of the costume.

**[2]** Shows understanding of the character.

**[3]** Detailed costume suggestions and reference to context.

**[4]** Direct reference to the script.

**[5]** Detailed description of costume and its effect.

**[6]** Hair and make-up described and the effect considered.

**[7]** Condition of costume described ('pristine', 'well-fitting', 'pressed').

**[8]** Considers practical demands of multi-rolling.

Some productions make stylised choices to highlight the minimalistic or abstract aspects of the play. For example, all the performers might wear basic garments, such as overalls, hospital uniforms or black trousers and tops, upon which other costume details can be added. Colour-coding might be used to connect all the Veritys, with them dressed identically or in different costumes of the same colour.

## TASK 3.18

Here is a sketch of one possible costume design for Tom. It uses a standard costume – hospital porter's – for all characters, over which details are added for Tom. It helps to give the effect that the story is being retold in a hospital setting.

Draw your own sketches for costume designs for the following characters:

- Verity at the beginning of the play.
- Edward at the beginning of the second act.
- Miss Blake near the end of the play.

Wool cap.

Short-sleeved, V-neck top.

Bright, patterned, knitted waistcoat.

Blue drawstring trousers.

White, Velcro sneaker-shoes.

# Set design

The set designer of *Find Me* could help to convey the play's meaning through some of the following:

- Focusing on the theme of family, with a set to represent the family home
- Emphasising naturalistic aspects of the play by providing realistic props and set furnishings
- Emphasising non-naturalistic aspects of the play by symbolically suggesting themes such as mental health, institutionalisation and safety versus danger

- Establishing a particular relationship between the audience and the performers, by use of proxemics or levels
- Establishing the period of the play and the passage of time through the use of particular props or set furnishings.

## TASK 3.19

**A** Here is a sketch for a traverse stage of a hospital setting for Act Two. After studying it:

- Add two more details that you think would improve the design.
- Answer the question: 'How does this set help to convey the ideas and themes of *Find Me*?'

**B** Then draw a contrasting set sketch for the school scene.

## TASK 3.20

Some sets for *Find Me* are entirely non-naturalistic. Productions might use only blocks or chairs for the set, for example. Other set designers make symbolic choices, such as creating cages, restraints or padded walls.

Imagine you want to create a non-naturalistic set that emphasises the theme of imprisonment. Draw a sketch or write a list of how you could create this set and what materials you would need.

# Lighting design

The lighting in *Find Me* has many functions, including:

- Establishing the time of day and location
- Focusing the audience's attention on certain characters and events
- Highlighting and increasing the intensity of certain moments
- Creating an atmosphere or mood
- Suggesting a transition from one time or location to another.

## TASK 3.21

**A** Read this candidate-style response about a lighting design for the firework scene. Highlight technical terminology used.

To establish that it is night-time in the Taylors' neighbourhood, I will cross fade the lights from the restaurant scene to a downstage area, where there will be a few profile lanterns in the fly space used to illuminate the Taylors and their neighbours, with much of the stage in darkness. On the upstage wall, I will use low level lanterns, with pink and purple filters, projecting upwards. A gobo in a profile lantern will break up the colours and give the effect of movement. A strobe could also be employed to give bright flashes of light. There could also be handheld torches or glow-in-the-dark tubes for the 'children' to wave.

**B** With a partner, create a lighting design for the play's ending, from 'A red light comes up on her' (page 56) to the play's end. Consider:

- Changes in the lighting, such as hospital lighting, the fire or the court
- How the lighting will contribute to the mood or atmosphere
- How you will achieve technically the lighting effects you want
- What effects you want your final lighting to have on the audience.

# Sound design

Sound design can be used to establish location or a transition, and is also useful in creating an atmosphere or reflecting the **psychological** state of a character. Sound design can also add to the tension, comedy or mood of a scene, often having a significant impact on the audience's experience of the play. When writing about sound design, you might consider:

- Volume: How amplified will the sound be? Will it grow louder or quieter?
- Recorded or live: Will sound effects and music be pre-recorded or performed live?
- Type of sound: Will the sound be naturalistic or abstract?
- Special effects: Will you use distorting effects such as reverb?
- How the sound or music begins and ends: Should it gradually get louder or will there be a burst of sound? Will it end abruptly or fade out?

## TASK 3.22

Look at the following ideas and note at least one occasion in *Find Me* when each sound effect might be appropriate:

- Children playing
- The bang of fireworks
- Water running
- A few bars of a David Bowie song
- A television programme
- An offstage voice.

## TASK 3.23

Working with a partner, read Verity I's 'Dear Reader' speech (page 50). Consider how you could use sound design to:

- Show Verity's mental state
- Establish the location
- Emphasise Verity's words
- Suggest the period in which the play takes place
- Reproduce a realistic sound effect
- Create an abstract sound effect.

**KEY TERM:**

Psychological: Referring to a mental or emotional state and the reasons behind it.

 **LOOK HERE**

For more ideas about how to achieve lighting and sound effects, see pages 224–229.

## CHECK YOUR LEARNING *Find Me*

### Do you know…?

- ✓ When *Find Me* was written.
- ✓ In which decades it is set.
- ✓ The different locations and settings in which it takes place.
- ✓ The genre of the play.
- ✓ How its context might affect choices of costumes, sets and props.
- ✓ How the relationships between the characters, and the changes to those relationships, might be shown.
- ✓ Advantages and disadvantages of producing the play in different staging configurations.
- ✓ How key scenes might be staged.

- ✓ The performance style (or styles) of the play.
- ✓ How the performers could use their physical and vocal skills to convey characters' motivations, thoughts and feelings and to impart meaning to the action.
- ✓ The role of the director and how they influence how an audience responds to and understands the play.
- ✓ Key moments a director could use to convey their concept of the play.
- ✓ Different design choices to be made, why they are important and how they can be effective.
- ✓ What impact the play should have on the audience and what messages they should be left with.

# GIZMO
## by Alan Ayckbourn

The OCR specification identifies editions of the texts that are used to set questions in the 'Drama: Performance and response' (Component 04) examination paper. It is not required that centres use these editions for teaching this component.

For this chapter, page numbers provided refer to the Samuel French edition of *Gizmo*, ISBN-13: 978-0-573-15206-1, one of those used by OCR for question setting.

Alan Ayckbourn at the Stephen Joseph Theatre.

# Plot synopsis

## Scene One

A hospital lecture theatre. Professor Raymond Barth and Dr Bernice Mallow introduce Ben Mason, their patient, and David Best, a neurologist, to an audience of doctors and other professionals. David explains that Ben is paralysed and in a wheelchair due to post-traumatic stress disorder ('he literally froze with fear') after witnessing a double murder in a bar where he worked as a cocktail barman. The GIZMO team have developed an experimental device, PMRS (positive movement replication synchronicity) in order to help paralysed patients like Ben. After receiving an implant, Ben's movements are controlled by whoever is wearing the special PMRS 'watch' and he replicates their movements. The team demonstrate the effectiveness of the PMRS by undertaking some basic movements for the audience.

## Scene Two

Ben's hospital bedroom. Ben is annoyed that his nurse, Ted, who is wearing the PMRS, won't turn it on and let him move around. Nerys, a physiotherapist, enters and, wearing the PMRS gadget, makes Ben undertake a number of vigorous exercises. David enters and says he is disappointed with Ben's progress, as he should be able to make some movements independently by now.

## Scene Three

Ben's hospital bedroom. Ben is increasingly annoyed by the limitations of the hospital. He convinces Ted, despite it being against the rules, to take him for a walk in the park ('I'm a patient, not a prisoner').

## Scene Four

The park. Ted and Ben are in the park, with Ben's movements controlled by Ted. Ben describes the murders he witnessed and explains that he would recognise the murderer if he saw him again. As they begin to walk away, they are blocked by a female gang (Hezza, Tiz and Dart), who try to get Ted to give them some money. When he refuses, their friends, a boy gang (Rust, Dazer and Fritzo), appear and beat and rob Ted. They haven't seen Ben, who reacts to all of Ted's movements a short distance away. Both Ted and Ben end up on the ground, Ted beaten and Ben unable to move. Rust takes the PRMS 'watch' and Ben's movements now mirror Rust's actions. They fight, until gang leader Manny Rice appears with his two bodyguards, Rudi and Keith. Rust is forced to handover everything he has stolen from Ted, including the watch, which causes Ben to collapse. Manny orders Keith to look after Ben and bring him back to his place.

# Scene Five

Manny's apartment. Cevril, an attractive young woman, is in the apartment. Keith places Ben on a sofa in the apartment. Manny tells Cevril to look after Ben while he recovers. After the others leave, Ben tries to explain to Cevril about his condition and the PMRS 'watch'. Cevril puts it on. Ben teaches Cevril how to mix a drink. Lando, a hit man, enters and Ben recognises him as the killer of the two people in the bar. After Lando leaves, Ben tells Cevril and she decides to help him, but says she needs to change first. During this, a glitch in the system means that Cevril and Ben become out of sync and they find it difficult to leave the apartment. Cevril turns off the device and Ben collapses. She tries to pull him out of the apartment, but Manny enters and stops them. Cevril and Manny fight, with Ben mimicking Cevril's movements, knocking Manny out. Cevril reveals she is an undercover Detective Sergeant. Lando enters and throws Cevril out a window. Ben manages to control his own movements and he and Lando fight for a gun. During a blackout, a single gunshot is heard.

# Scene Six

The same hospital lecture room as Scene One. Professor Barth introduces the Chief Constable, Sir Trevor Perkins, to present two awards. Perkins presents an award to Ben, who is now moving normally. Cevril is pushed on in a wheelchair. She is given the second award. Ben reveals that he is wearing a PMRS 'watch'. He turns it on and controls Cevril's movements. They bow to the audience and kiss.

## TASK 3.1

A Working in a small group, create a two-minute version of the play, making sure that you cover what you all agree are the most significant events in the plot.

B Given your understanding of the play's plot, answer the following questions:

1 What has caused Ben to be paralysed?

2 What treatment have the medical professionals agreed for him and how successful is it?

3 Why is Cevril in Manny's apartment?

4 In your opinion, how successful is the PMRS gadget?

## TASK 3.2

A The story of what happened in the bar might be referred to as the 'backstory', and it is important in understanding the play and Ben's character. In a small group, read pages 18–20, when Ben describes the events to Ted. Then create a series of still images showing the key moments of that evening at the bar, including portraying the young couple, the gunman and Ben.

B Decide what moment in particular caused Ben to freeze and discuss how this event affects Ben for the rest of the play.

> **TIP:**
>
> You might want to consider the playwright's original intentions in writing the play. For example, what is Alan Ayckbourn saying about technology, science and violence?

# Genre
## Children and young people's theatre

*Gizmo* was written as one of the 1999 Connections plays commissioned by the National Theatre. Connections plays are designed to be performed by a wide variety of schools, youth groups and drama clubs across the country. Some common features of the plays tend to be substantial roles for young people, themes of interest to teenagers and relatively large casts. Ayckbourn specifies in the script that the sets should be 'as simple as possible' and that the play is written with a 'flexible cast' in mind. With actors multi-rolling, he suggests it could be performed with as few as 11 actors. However, if a company wants more roles for the actors, it could be produced with 18 speaking roles and others with non-speaking roles.

## Science fiction

The play has a science fiction element in the sense that the 'gizmo' of the play is a technological device that doesn't yet exist. The opening of the play uses doctors and scientists to introduce the audience to this new technology, which is a straightforward way of conveying **exposition**. Tension is created by the dramatic question of whether the new device will be a force for good or evil.

It has been said that the best science fiction is all about the human condition. *Gizmo* could be seen to be exploring what makes a person finally take action, or it could be making a comment about how we are controlled by others, including our dependency on technology. It also questions the ethics of technology companies and their drive to make a profit.

Ayckbourn's play *Henceforward* (1987) is a comedy which also uses elements of science fiction. In it, a robot is programmed to be the perfect female companion. His 2012 play *Surprises* is a science fiction play that explores time-travelling, androids and holograms. These plays have the challenge of predicting a future which can, within years, seem obsolete or old-fashioned. They also make significant demands on the actors' physical skills when they represent the effect of technology on their movements.

> **KEY TERM:**
>
> Exposition: A literary device in which background information is explained to the audience.

## Comedy

Ayckbourn is most famous for his many successful comedies, which are both funny and poignant. Some of his well-loved comedies include *Season's Greetings* (1980), about an uncomfortable family gathering at Christmas, and *The Norman Conquests* (1977), a trilogy about the complicated romantic relationships of six characters over a weekend in a suburban home.

Oliver Chris, Jenna Russell and Neil Stuke in *Season's Greetings*.

At first glance, *Gizmo* seems unlikely material for comedy as it is about a man who has witnessed a horrible crime and become paralysed, but Ayckbourn discovers the comic potential of this situation. In the very first scene, Ben helplessly plants a kiss on Bernice's nose, alerting the audience to the surprising humour that could follow. In the next scene, Nerys takes revenge on Ben for calling her a 'stupid woman' by forcing him to exercise over-vigorously. In the scenes with Cevril, their enforced physical cooperation leads to romantic comedy.

Throughout the play, Ben's inability to control his body creates opportunities for humorous misunderstandings and physical comedy, as well as allowing Ayckbourn to demonstrate his inventiveness in the different ways Ben's condition can be explored. A director would need to decide how to balance the more serious aspects of the play with its comic elements.

# Identifying genre features in *Gizmo*

## TASK 3.3

**A** Look at the following elements of science fiction and explain their relevance to *Gizmo*. (An example has been given for you.)

- It has technology that does not currently exist. *The PMRS device that helps someone move by connecting their movements to another's is not technology that exists at present.*
- Technology and/or scientific advances are explained.
- Technology is used to solve a problem.
- Technology and/or scientific advances do not solve all problems and instead create new ones.

**B** Now look at these elements of children and young people's theatre and see if you can find examples of the following in *Gizmo*:

- Topics appropriate for and of interest to young people.
- A large cast of mainly younger characters.
- Staging elements that are relatively easy and fairly inexpensive to produce.
- Theatrical style and conventions that will engage young people.

Comedy is an important aspect of Ayckbourn's work. Some ways that humour can be created include:

- **Irony** and **dramatic irony**
- Physical slapstick, such as trips, falling down, unexpected violence
- Word play, for example, playing on the sound of words
- Exaggerated, over-the-top characters
- Misunderstandings
- Characters in disguise or mistaken for another character
- Unexpected changes in mood or actions
- Words or actions that are **incongruous** or absurd given the situation or characters.

**KEY TERMS:**

**Irony:** Using language to suggest one thing but meaning another.

**Dramatic irony:** When the audience know something that one or more characters on stage do not.

**Incongruous:** Out of place; appearing wrong in a certain location or situation.

## TASK 3.4

**A** Look at the following moments from the play and decide what makes them humorous.

- Ben's reactions to being controlled by Nerys (pages 8–10)
- Ben suddenly collapsing in the hospital (page 12)
- The gang characters and Manny speaking in a formal way (pages 21 and 29)
- Cevril and Ben making the cocktail (pages 39–40).

**B** Choose one of the sections in part A of this task, or another appropriate moment in the play, and either write a paragraph or draw a storyboard explaining how you would create comedy through performance choices for that section.

In this Philippine play, *3 Stars and a Sun*, a metallic, scaffold-type set, plain white uniforms and blue lighting are familiar stylistic features of science fiction.

TASK 3.5

Consider how you could use design to highlight one of the genres of *Gizmo*. You could consider, for example:

- Science fiction: How the set and sound design could emphasise a future period and a dependency on technology
- Young people's theatre: How costumes could be designed to appeal to and engage a youthful audience
- Comedy: How set and sound design could contribute to making moments comical.

## KEY TERMS:

**Linear:** A sequence arranged in a straightforward or chronological way.

**Chronological:** Presenting events in the order in which they occur.

**Circular:** A literary structure in which the ending returns the action to the beginning, perhaps in the use of setting, wording or content. In some cases, it suggests that the same or a similar story will be repeated.

# Structure

The play consists of six scenes, with no interval or break for acts. Ayckbourn suggests that the scenes should be played with a 'minimum of hold-up between them'. The plot is **linear**, with the events occurring **chronologically** in four locations:

- Lecture room
- Hospital room
- Park
- Manny's flat.

Scene One, the presentation, takes place in the morning, approximately 14 months after Ben's paralysis. Although the time between Scene One and Scene Two is not specified, there has been some passing of time as David is annoyed that Ben is not able to move more 'by now' (page 11). However, the actions of Scene Three (the hospital room), Scene Four (the park) and Scene Five (Manny's flat) all occur on the same day. Scene Six, several months later, brings the action full circle, by returning to the lecture room of Scene One with a fresh presentation. In this way, the structure could be considered **circular**. Barth says that their story has come 'more or less full circle' (page 51), with Cevril now the patient instead of Ben.

# Style

Ayckbourn's play are usually performed naturalistically with the actors believably conveying the characters' feelings, thoughts and motivations. There can also be a heightened or stylised aspect to the performances, especially if a character needs to be exaggerated for comic effect and when there are technical requirements such as physical comedy or mime.

TASK 3.6

**A** In a small group, read the stage directions at the end of Scene One (page 6), then experiment with performing them with the following style choices:

- A slow, sombre way. Try having the performer playing Ben show how difficult and humiliating he finds the experience through his use of his facial expressions.
- Emphasising the physical comedy. Aim for a strong contrast between Ben's facial expressions and his movements. Make sure his movements are a perfect imitation of David's.
- A very mechanical way, as if all of the characters are robotic, with forced artificial expressions and jerky, puppet-like movements.

**B** Then discuss what style choices were most effective and why.

## TASK 3.7

Read the statements below about *Gizmo*. Then work with a partner to put them in order, with the one you agree with most as 1, and the one you agree with least as 5.

- ☐ It is about how technology can help those with medical or psychological problems.
- ☐ It shows the limits of technology.
- ☐ It is about confronting fears.
- ☐ It is about good versus evil.
- ☐ It is about the power of love.

**TIP:**

There is no 'right' answer to what *Gizmo* is about, but, as you study the play, you should consider what aspects of it you find the most compelling and how an interpretation of the play could emphasise those.

# Context

Alan Ayckbourn was born in 1939 and wrote his first play at the age of ten. He is one of Britain's most successful and productive playwrights having written over 80 full-length plays. His experience as a director also informs his playwriting, as he is aware of the need to engage an audience at all times and of innovative ways in which plays can be staged.

## Historical context

Written in 1999, Ayckbourn does not specify when *Gizmo* is set but, since it is dealing with an invention that does not yet exist, it might be presumed that it is set in the future. The future that Ayckbourn presents is rooted in the 1990s, but with some futuristic touches. In this way, the play is comparable to *Henceforward*, which is set in London, 'sometime quite soon'. That play presents a bleak future where law and order has started to break down and the streets are unsafe. One of the central characters in *Henceforward* is a female robot, and much of the play's humour is derived from technological malfunctions as the robot reacts inappropriately to trigger words or pours tea when there is no cup. The limits of future technology are also apparent in *Gizmo*.

The specific location of *Gizmo* is not specified. The scenes take place in a research hospital and the park of what is, presumably, a city, as Sir Trevor Perkins rails against the gangs who 'terrorise' 'our cities'. As the play was written for youth drama groups around the UK, it might have been desirable to keep the location 'universal', rather than a particular city.

The 1990s were a time of change in the UK, with the Conservative government losing the 1997 general election to Tony Blair's 'New Labour'. In London, there was rapid building expansion, with an increase in office buildings and tower blocks. Alongside economic growth and the image of 'Cool Britannia', were worrying trends, such as knife crime and gang culture. *Gizmo*'s plot reflects this concern with its portrayal of gangs and violence.

*Henceforward* makes use of physical comedy when, for example, the 'perfect' android is unable – or refuses – to perform basic tasks.

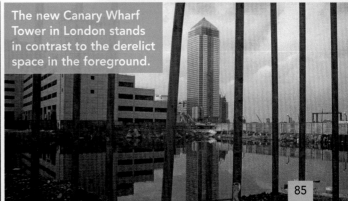

The new Canary Wharf Tower in London stands in contrast to the derelict space in the foreground.

Keanu Reeves, as Neo, fends off a hail of bullets in *The Matrix*.

## Cultural context

The National Theatre, which commissions Connections plays like *Gizmo*, is a large, publicly supported theatre. It has three main performance spaces in its London complex, but also tours and promotes educational outreach, such as the Connections programme, which started in 1995. Each year, a select group of the youth theatre productions of the Connections plays from across the UK are invited to perform in the National Theatre. The Connections plays are written by respected professional playwrights. Popular Connections dramas include *Chatroom* by Enda Walsh and *Citizenship* by Mark Ravenhill.

Science fiction films were popular in the 1990s, with many posing questions about ethics and the dangers of technology, such as *Total Recall* (1990), which involved memory implants, and *The Matrix* (1999), in which a battle is waged against controlling machines.

## Social context

The 1980s and 1990s saw an increase of women in the workplace. Margaret Thatcher was the first female British Prime Minister, from 1979 to 1990, and there were more women in leadership positions in industry and technology. *Gizmo* reflects this with the prominence in the first scene given to Dr Bernice Mallow, who leads much of the discussion of the project. At first, Cevril appears to be a stereotypical 'attractive young woman' playing on her physical appeal, but she is revealed to be a brave Detective Sergeant, who can 'give as good as she takes' (page 48). In contrast, Ben is shown to be at the mercy of women such as Nerys and Cevril who, at times, literally control his movements.

At this time, many women in business favoured 'power dressing', such as jackets with shoulder pads and high heels, to assert their status in the work place. In casual wear, there was a greater emphasis on unisex looks, including tracksuits and other sportswear.

The 1990s saw many new gadgets in entertainment, security, education and communications. Mobile phones became popular, although they were large and basic compared with smartphones. *Street Fighter*, *Tomb Raider* and *Super Mario* increased the popularity of video gaming.

### EXTENSION

Research medical and technological developments from the late 1990s to the present day that could be relevant to the set, costumes, characterisation and themes of the play, for example:

- Watches that have multiple functions
- Computer miniaturisation and microchips
- Advances in technology to help people with paralysis and other disabilities.

Make a note of anything that helps your understanding of the play and how it could be staged or designed.

## TASK 3.8

Look at the following list of key moments from the play and write one or two sentences about each to explain what it tells you about the context of the play. (The first one has been completed for you.)

1 Bernice describes the cost of the GIZMO project to an audience. *Her speech emphasises the connection between medical and technological developments and the need to make a profit. She is shown to be an intelligent, powerful woman, but also one who is aware of the 'impatience' for results.*

2 Ted is approached by three girl gang members.

3 Manny expects people to do what he says.

4 The Chief Constable believes that they are making progress 'against the gangs that terrorise and presume to own our cities'.

**TIP:**

In your exam questions, alternative wording might be used instead of 'context', such as 'reflect the time in which the play was written' or 'show when and where the play is set'.

When depicting the context of the play, there are a number of factors to consider, such as:

- How much money a character might have
- Fashions of the time (such as the 1990s or an idea of what futuristic fashions might be)
- The influence of the culture of the time, such as literature, music, art, television, sport and films
- The backgrounds and occupations of the characters
- The ages of the characters
- Props that characters might use, such as phones or weapons
- Furnishings that might be seen in a hospital or apartment.

## TASK 3.9

A Look at the costume, make-up and hair ideas on the right and decide which character they would suit best.

B Using those ideas as inspiration, or others from your research, draw costume sketches for Cevril and Dr Bernice Mallow. Consider how your designs would emphasise the differences between the two characters.

Pink velour tracksuit    Dangling earrings    Pink lipstick

Sharp pin-striped suit    Sweat pants and a T-shirt

White doctor's coat    Spiky, dyed hair    Black mascara

Navy-blue skirt suit    Long hair pulled into a ponytail

Colourful silk scarf    Low-cut jersey dress    Tattoos

**TIP:**

There is no one set way the characters could be costumed, but it is worth thinking about how you could differentiate between them.

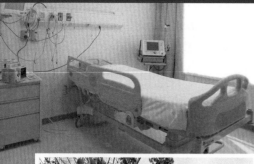

## Ideas for different locations

If a designer were asked to create a set to convey the period in which the play was written or a vision of the near future, some points to consider would be:

- How to create a cityscape that suggests the violence and fears mentioned by Sir Trevor Perkins. Would it have looming skyscrapers or abandoned parks? How could you suggest an atmosphere?

- How could the set for the hospital show that it is at the forefront of medical and technological developments? Would the props include any medical equipment or other devices? What colour palette would suggest the institutional setting?

- How could you differentiate between the scenes set inside and those in the park? How could you quickly and efficiently create these different environments?

- How realistic or abstract would the set be? Could a few pieces of set suggest a number of different settings? Or will each set be unique and realistic? Will something in the design suggest that the play is set in an unknown future rather than the present?

### TASK 3.10

**A** After considering the points above, make some notes and/or sketches of ideas for at least two of the settings of the play.

**B** Write two paragraphs in response to the following question: 'Describe how you could show the social, cultural or historical context of the play by your design choices for the set of the play.'

---

### WHAT THE SPECIFICATION SAYS...

Learners must know and understand:

- How meaning is communicated through:
  - An actor's vocal and physical interpretation of character.

# Interpretations of key characters

You must demonstrate that you understand the main characters in the play, including different ways that they could be interpreted.

### Ben Mason

A young man. While working as a cocktail barman he has witnessed an appalling double murder and only just escaped being killed himself. The shock has left him without physical injuries but unable to move. When we meet him, he has been paralysed for 14 months. He is frustrated and longs to escape the hospital.

## Hospital

### Ted Wilkins

A long-time nurse at the research hospital. Rather cynical and lazy. Ben thinks the park looks beautiful but Ted says, 'Might look beautiful. It's full of perverts and muggers.' When he reluctantly agrees to go to the park, his fears come true when he is overpowered by a gang.

### Nerys Potter

The hospital physiotherapist. Described as 'fit, young and hearty'. She barges into Ben's hospital room and puts him through a series of vigorous exercises. She is unsympathetic to Ben's condition, claiming that he is 'perfectly healthy'. When he calls her a 'stupid woman' for this remark, she increases the intensity of the exercise as a punishment.

## David Best

A neurologist (specialist in the nervous system, brain and spinal cord). He presents Ben's case to the audience in the lecture theatre of the hospital, demonstrating the PMRS for the first time. He is under pressure to show that Ben is making progress.

## Professor Raymond Barth

The chief administrator of the GIZMO project, in charge of the development of this ground-breaking technology. He introduces the demonstration of the PMRS. He also appears at the end of the play introducing the award ceremony.

## Dr Bernice Mallow

One of the key scientists on the GIZMO project. She plays a role in the presentation. The dialogue in this scene seems prepared and staged to show off the PMRS's capabilities as strikingly as possible. She asks questions leading up to a dramatic presentation of what the PMRS can do.

# Gangs and gangsters

## Manny Rice

The 'Mr Big of the neighbourhood'. Described as 'a well dressed, well groomed thug', he intimidates Rust and his gang and controls his girlfriend Cevril, insisting, for instance, that she dresses the way he wants. He is concerned with his reputation.

## Lando

A cold-hearted hit man. He killed the couple in the cocktail bar and intended to kill Ben. He fights with Cevril and throws her out of a window. Ben then fights him for the gun.

## Hezza, Dart and Tiz

The girl gang members. Confident and streetwise. There is humorous interaction with the boys. The girls lie about Ted's behaviour, accusing him of 'flashing' and terrifying them. Dart claims Ted broke her arm. However, Tiz gives Ben a knife to 'even things up a bit' when he is fighting with Rust.

## Rudi and Keith

Manny's henchmen. They have little dialogue, but are likely to have a forbidding presence, as people tend to do as they tell them.

## Rust

The leader of the gang in the park. A violent boy, he taunts Ted and is involved with his beating. When Manny appears, Rust is frightened and respectful of him.

## Dazer and Fritzo

The boy members of the gang. Dazer claims Dart is his fiancée. Fritzo speaks little, but might be physically intimidating as he offers to hit Ben.

## Cevril Teese

She appears to be a gangster's girlfriend, but is later revealed as an undercover police officer. As Manny's girlfriend, she is described as 'an attractive young woman in a low-cut dress'. Although she obeys Manny's commands, she also shows that she can speak up for herself. Later she is shown to be a capable and brave police officer. In the final scene, when she appears in a wheelchair, she is 'for once lost for words'. Ben now 'controls' her with the PMRS and the play ends with their kiss.

# Law enforcement

## Sir Trevor Perkins

The Chief Constable. Appears at the award ceremony. He confirms that Ben and Cevril have helped to strike a 'strong blow' against the gangs.

## TASK 3.11

**A** In a group, read Scene Four. Then decide which of the following characters have the most status, on a scale of 1 to 10, with 1 for the least status and 10 for the most: Ted, Ben, Hezza, Tiz, Dart, Rust, Dazer, Fritzo, Manny, Keith, Rudi.

**B** Create a still image to indicate how each character could show their status in relation to each other. A character who is 10, for example, will easily dominate a character who is 5, who in turn might bully a character who is 2. Think about how their posture, gestures and proxemics might show who has high or low status.

**C** Focus on Manny's entrance on page 28 and explore how the scene could be staged to emphasise his power and effect on other characters.

## TASK 3.12

Choose one line that you think is important for each character below. Write a few sentences explaining its importance in helping to understand the character and how the actor might deliver the line. What physical and vocal skills would be most effective? (An example has been provided for Ben.)

- **Ted**
- **Cevril**
- **David**
- **Manny.**

Ben: 'You can't imagine what it's like. Just being able to look out of the window again' (page 15). This line shows the frustration that Ben feels with his lack of independence and movement. He is yearning to move, while Ted is trying to do as little as possible. In this line, I would have Ben standing stiffly looking wistfully out of the window. His voice will have an edge of anger, accusing Ted of being unsympathetic. He will lower his volume, almost as if speaking to himself, when he says 'Just to be able...'

# Use of vocal skills

**KEY TERM:**

**Register:** How formal or informal language is, or language used for a particular purpose or in a certain setting, such as the language of medicine or law. Informal language tends to use less precise pronunciation and might include more slang.

The characters in *Gizmo* speak in different **registers** that reflect their occupations and backgrounds. Barth, Bernice and David give a scientific presentation and comfortably use words to suit this situation such as 'disassociate' or 'atrophying'. They are also trying to give a positive impression of a project that has had limited success. This could affect their tone, as they try to convey an optimism that they might not feel.

The gangster characters, however, employ a different vocabulary and would have a different manner of speaking that would affect their tone, volume and pace. They are likely to be more informal and perhaps use a specific dialect.

Ben undergoes a number of distressing events in the course of the play, which would be reflected in the emotional range he uses.

Vocal skills that actors might consider include:

**Accent and dialect** **Pace** **Volume** **Pitch**

**Pauses and timing** **Intonation** **Phrasing** **Emotional range**

## TASK 3.13

With a partner, experiment with vocal skills to interpret the following lines. Note down the choices you make, including reasons.

Bernice: Sounds good in theory, David. Can we give it a try? (page 5)

Nerys: No, you're not, you're perfectly fit. There's nothing wrong with you at all. (page 9)

Ben: No, no stay! Please stay, this woman's trying to kill me! (page 10)

Ted: Wish I could sit down for fourteen months. (page 15)

Manny: We can't have my park getting a bad name, can we? (page 32)

Cevril: You touch me and Manny'll tear you apart. (page 41)

## TASK 3.14

For each key character below, give three different examples of vocal skills that the actor playing the role could use. Justify each of your choices by explaining why it is appropriate. (Examples have been given for Rust.)

- Ben
- Cevril
- Manny
- Ted.

| Character | Vocal skill | When vocal skill could be displayed | Details and justification |
|---|---|---|---|
| Rust | **Dialect/ intonation**. | Scene Four, first speech with Ted. | I think Rust would speak with an urban youth dialect, possibly London. His words appear oddly formal, so I will have him speak this first line ('Pardon me…') with an exaggeratedly polite way. |
| | **Volume**. | Scene Four, commands group. | Rust raises his voice and speaks sharply to the gang to control them. When he shouts, 'That's enough,' they all obey him. |
| | **Pace** and **pause**. | Scene Four, confrontation with Ben. | Rust will pause when he sees Ben, puzzled by his odd behaviour. However, when Ben begins moving (controlled by Rust's wearing the PMRS) the pace will increase as Rust gets agitated and exclaims 'What you playing at?' |

## Use of physical skills

*Gizmo* makes a number of physical demands on the actors. Most plays require the actors to use their movement, gestures and expressions to present their characters and this is particularly the case with *Gizmo*, where the gang members or medical staff might have certain ways of moving to convey their occupations, personalities and relationships.

There are also the physical challenges of the characters who control Ben's movements, and Ben, whose movements are controlled. In these cases, the actors' actions need to be synchronised, while their facial expressions will reveal that they are experiencing the shared movement in different ways. This is played for comic effect in Scene Five, when Cevril is offstage changing, but the audience sees Ben replicating her motions, miming putting on a bra and struggling into tight jeans, possibly confused or embarrassed by doing actions that come naturally to Cevril. In addition, there are demanding stage fights in Scenes Four and Five.

Physical skills that actors might consider include:

Posture / Movement / Pace / Gestures

Facial expressions / Proxemics / Eye contact

**TIP:**

Stage fights must be carefully rehearsed and any physical danger avoided. What the audience should register are the characters' intentions and reactions.

The cast from Artists Theatre School rehearse a fight scene from *Gizmo*.

## TASK 3.15

**A** With a partner, experiment with the physical skills required for Ben on page 43, from 'Cevril closes the door' to 'Ben does likewise.' Consider:

- How realistic or stylised you want the movement to be
- The pace of movement
- Facial expressions Ben should use
- The effect to be created for the audience.

**B** Agree the series of movements that Ben will need to make, such as unzipping a dress, stepping out of it, throwing it to one side and so on. Practise the movements until you can both do them identically. As you experiment with different physical skills, note which, in your opinion, are most effective and when. For example, is there a certain section when the pace of the actions might speed up or slow down or when a particular gesture might be used? Do Ben's facial expressions add to the comedy of the scene?

## TASK 3.16

**A** In a group, read Scene Four, page 21. Then experiment with physical skills to establish the following:

- Ben must do everything that Ted does, although they are very different people.
- The three girls are gang members who want something from Ted.
- Ted is nervous of the girls.

**B** Rehearse the scene in different ways, and make particular notes on how:

- The girls relate to each other, such as standing close together, making eye contact, making secret signs
- The girls use eye contact, facial expressions and gestures to intimidate Ted
- Ted uses gesture, posture and movement in response.
- Ted and the girls react when the gang of boys enters.

## TASK 3.17

In a small group, read pages 8–10 in Scene Two. Discuss how the performers playing Ben and Nerys could use their physical skills to show their characters and situation. Remember to consider when the PMRS is turned on and how that affects Ben's movements. Experiment with:

- Posture and levels
- Movement
- Pace and pauses
- Gestures
- Facial expressions
- Proxemics.
- Eye contact, or lack of

## TASK 3.18

For each key character below, give at least three examples of how they could use their physical skills in the play. Justify your choices. (An example has been given for Manny.)

- **Ben**
- **Cevril**
- **Rust**
- **David.**

| Character | Physical skill | When physical skill could be displayed | Details and justification |
|---|---|---|---|
| Manny | **Posture:** He stands tall with his chest puffed out and his chin high. | Throughout the play. | Manny is the 'Mr Big' of the play and should occupy a large amount of space. He has a high status, which others acknowledge. Even when he is standing still, he appears frightening and powerful. |
| | **Gesture:** Flicking his hand at Cevril. | 'Shift yourself' (page 33). | Manny expects to be obeyed immediately. It is a simple, elegant flick of the wrist. All his gestures are surprisingly elegant, to fit the heightened way he speaks. |
| | Facial **expression:** scowling, frowning at Cevril. | Page 46. | When he says he has had to 'punish' Cevril, he looks annoyed and disappointed in her. His facial expression is not pure anger, but shows that he finds it unfortunate to have to discipline her again. The audience might be worried by the implied threat in his words, backed up by his annoyed expression. |

# Stage directions

In addition to the play's dialogue, a way for the playwright to convey what a character is doing, thinking and feeling is through stage directions. For example:

> Page 5: Ben's body convulses slightly. From now on both men move almost exactly together. David grips the arms of his chair; Ben involuntarily grips the arms of his wheelchair. David rises slowly from his chair: Ben does likewise.

> Page 30: Meanwhile, Keith kicks Rust's legs apart and forces his arms above his head. Ben follows suit.

> Page 49: Lando appears in the doorway. His face is covered in blood from a deep cut in his head.

## TASK 3.19

**A** In a small group, perform each of the stage directions above.

**B** Discuss and write down what you believe each character is thinking and feeling. For example, what might Rust be thinking when Keith searches him? How does David feel when he begins to rise from the chair in front of the audience?

**C** Talk about what the audience learns about the character from the stage directions. For example, how do they feel about their jobs or the situation in which they find themselves?

**LOOK HERE**

See pages 200–202 for rehearsal techniques for exploring characterisation and practising performance skills.

## TASK 3.20

**A** Read the extract below from a candidate-style response about the stage directions on pages 51 to the end of the play. Highlight three details that show how the stage directions reveal to the audience aspects of the characters and their relationships.

At the end of the play, the stage directions show a very different Ben. Previously he has been controlled by others, but now he is the one wearing the PMRS. The stage directions remind the audience of the opening scene of the play, but now it is Ben controlling Cevril, rather than David controlling Ben. This shows the audience a more confident Ben who 'switches it on', 'rises slowly' and 'steps forward', whereas Cevril 'twitches' and is forced to follow. Cevril is described as looking 'slightly startled', which makes her reaction to the situation **ambivalent**.

Instead of the comic kiss that Ben plants on Bernice at the end of the first scene, Ayckbourn suggests that this kiss between Ben and Cevril is a more romantic one, as the stage directions indicate that 'one rather gathers' that Cevril likes the kiss and responds. However, the audience might also have a somewhat uncomfortable feeling about a previously independent character like Cevril being controlled by a possible love interest. The actor playing Cevril would have to choose how her facial expressions would indicate how happy this occasion is for her.

**B** Focusing on the stage directions at the end of Scene One (page 6), make notes about what the audience learns about the characters and the play's themes. What effect do you think this scene, including its stage directions, would have on an audience?

**KEY TERM:**

Ambivalent: With mixed feelings; unsure or unconcerned.

**TIP:**

Remember that communication is at the heart of drama. Always consider what the performance and staging choices you make are communicating to the audience. Do they create…

- Sympathy?
- Fear?
- Excitement?
- Suspense?
- Pity?
- Comedy?
- Greater understanding?

The Stephen Joseph Theatre.

# Use of space

As part of their characterisation, actors might use the stage space in many different ways, including:

**Levels** **Proxemics** **Positioning on stage** **Entrances and exits** **Use of the 'fourth wall'**

In addition, the type of staging configuration and the set design could influence the actors' use of space. *Gizmo* could be performed on any one of a number of staging configurations. Ayckbourn is famous for his use of theatre in the round, particularly at the Stephen Joseph Theatre in Scarborough for which he was many years the artistic director. That theatre was designed to be in the round, but his plays have also been performed in virtually every type of space from the main stages of the National Theatre to tiny black box theatres.

Below is a candidate-style response about how performers could stage Scene Four in a theatre in the round, and benefits and challenges of this space.

[1] Opens with some understanding of the requirements of the scene.

[2] Explains an advantage of theatre in the round and gives a precise example of when it would benefit this scene.

[3] Identifies a second advantage of theatre in the round, with precise example.

[4] Identifies a general disadvantage of theatre in the round and uses some correct theatre terminology ('projections'), but could connect more to performance and scene.

[5] Identifies a second disadvantage related to a requirement of the script.

[6] Suggests a positive effect created by theatre in the round and the impact on the audience.

Scene Four could work well in a theatre in the round, as it would be relatively easy to convey the open outdoor space with minimal scenery. **[1]** Ben and Ted will enter through the audience, adding interest as they watch Ben following Ted down the aisle and onto the playing area. Theatre in the round is a very dynamic space and this entrance would make the audience feel very close to the action. **[2]**

The girl gang's arrival from another section of the audience will cause surprise and the gang can quickly circle Ted and move around him. Their movements would mean that all sections of the audience have something interesting to view. **[3]**

A disadvantage of the space for this scene is that it could limit scenery. There could be no projections or backdrops, and any stage furniture like park benches would have to be carefully chosen so they didn't block the view. **[4]** Another disadvantage is that it is possible for an actor to have their back to part of the audience for an extended period. This would especially be an issue during Ben's long speech about what caused his paralysis. I would suggest that the actors playing Ted and Ben find reasons to change their positions occasionally during this section. Ted's use of the cigarette, for example, could give him reasons to move and for Ben to follow. **[5]**

Overall, theatre in the round would create an exciting space, particularly for the group scenes, but the actors would need to be very aware of the audience and that key moments can be seen by all. When used well, the audience should find the interactions and fights in this scene exciting in this configuration as they will be so near to the action. **[6]**

## TIP:

If an exam question asks for advantages and disadvantages, you need to discuss at least two of each. Similarly, if a question asks for examples, you must offer more than one.

## TASK 3.21

**A** Working in a small group, experiment with staging these scenes in different staging configurations:

- Play's opening (pages 1–3)
- Cevril and Ben (pages 39–41)
- Nerys and Ben (pages 8–9)
- End of Scene Five (pages 47–49).

**B** Choose one of the scenes and write down at least two advantages and two disadvantages of performing it in each staging configuration described on pages 8–11.

# Directorial choices

A director of *Gizmo* will need to consider:

- How to guide the actors' physical and vocal choices
- How to use design to reinforce the play's meaning and impact
- How key moments of the play might be staged
- The style of the play and potential use of performance conventions
- The effect the play should have on the audience.

## TASK 3.22

**A** Working in a small group, read Scene Five, from Cevril's entrance on page 43 to the end of the scene. List what you think are the five main plot points that the audience must understand from this section. For example, that Ben and Cevril have become out of sync.

**B** Discuss the impact you want this scene to have on the audience. Think about, for example:

- When does the mood of the scene change?
- What moments are humorous and which are more serious, tense or frightening?
- How do the relationships between the characters change during the scene?

**C** Experiment with the following:

- The positioning and proxemics of the actors
- Creating effective entrances for Manny and Lando
- Generating suspense through the characters' movements, handling of props and sound effects
- Changing pace and volume to increase interest in the scene
- Using the stage space to create comedy in some sections and tension in others
- Helping the audience to focus on and understand key moments
- Playing the scene in different styles, such as realistically, exaggeratedly or melodramatically, in slow motion or highly choreographed, in order to see which is most effective.

**D** Now write a paragraph in response to the following question: 'As a director, how would you stage the ending of Scene Five in order to create a specific impact on the audience?'

## WHAT THE SPECIFICATION SAYS...

Learners must know and understand:

- How meaning is communicated through:
  - The use of performance space and spatial relationships on stage
  - The relationship between performers and audience
  - The design of: set, props, costume, lighting and sound
  - An actor's vocal and physical interpretation of character
  - The use of performance conventions
- How performance styles affect the direction, acting and design of a performance.

## TASK 3.23

Below are excerpts from two candidate-style responses about the gang's mugging of Ted on page 23. Decide how well you believe the writers have explained and justified their ideas for performance. Look for and highlight the following:

- Clear ideas about what they want to achieve
- Specific examples from the play
- Correct use of theatrical terminology
- Understanding of how impact on the audience can be achieved.

Although much of the play has been comic, and Ted might be seen as lazy and not particularly bright, I want to create tension and surprise in this section. The audience might laugh at Dart's ridiculous claim that Ted broke her arm, but I want the mood to change when Dazer says 'Right you, I'm having you.' Instead of naturalistic acting, I will have the two gangs behave as a unit. While electronic music plays, they will surround Ted, centre stage, and create a wave of synchronised movement around him. Ted will be totally hidden from the audience with only an arm shooting up at one point, before he falls to ground. As the music fades out, the group will all take two steps back to reveal Ted curled in a ball, with Ben in a similar position upstage left.

My theme for the play is the danger of technology. Although this scene takes place outside, I will emphasise society's dependence on technology by having the gangs all carrying props such as electronic equipment and wearing costumes advertising media productions. When Ben's movements and gestures are controlled by Ted, they will seem stiff and odd, to show that the PMRS has not solved his problems. Before the fight begins, I will have the gang ready themselves for action by attaching speakers to a phone to amplify some fighting music and doing a few warm-up movements to show that this is something they have done before. One gang member will stand on a park bench downstage left to film the event. This footage will be projected onto a large screen upstage to give the audience the sensation of watching a viral video. To create tension and excitement, I will have the camera zoom in on Ted's face, showing his pain at the beating.

### TIP:

There is no one right way of interpreting this or any other scene. However, whatever choices you make must be rooted in your understanding of the play and how theatre works.

### WHAT THE SPECIFICATION SAYS...

Learners must know and understand:

- How meaning is communicated through:
  - The design of: set, props, costume, lighting and sound.

# Design choices

Costume, set, lighting and sound design all contribute to the impact of *Gizmo*. They are vital in presenting the play's setting, meaning and director's interpretation. For example, the way the characters are costumed will communicate whether you are setting the play in the very near present or some time in a far-off imagined future. Costume is also helpful to indicate a character's occupation or social standing. Cevril, for example, will dress differently when she is undercover as a gangster's girlfriend than in last scene when she would probably be dressed in uniform or her own civilian clothes.

Setting and props are important for establishing the context of the play and the contrasts between different characters, such as items in Manny's apartment and Ben's hospital room. Sound can be used to establish location and create atmosphere or tension. Lighting can focus attention on certain characters and suggest a certain mood or location.

# Costume design

When writing about costume, it is important to consider what the costume tells the audience about the character's role and personality. It is useful to consider:

**Period and context** | **Colour** | **Fabric** | **Silhouette**

**Fit** | **Condition** | **Headwear and footwear** | **Make-up and hair**

Below is an excerpt from a candidate-style response about Hezza's outfit in Scene Four, demonstrating one possible approach to her costume.

Hezza is the first of the girl gang to speak, so might be the leader of the gang and the bravest. In order to show that she is both part of a gang and a leader, I will make a costume that matches the other girls', but with a few individual features. **[1]** In my concept, the girls will wear matching, close-fitting velour tracksuits. **[2]** Tracksuits like this were popular in the 1990s when the play was written, but I will have them in a grey tone, to make them appear more modern and less stereotypically 'feminine'. **[3]** Hezza will have black and silver glittery trainers and silver highlights in her spiky hair to give her an edgy, slightly futuristic appearance. She will wear a large silver medallion with Rust's name on it, as he is her 'fiancé'. She will use very dark eye liner and mascara, silver eye shadow and silver lipstick. **[4]** The use of silver and grey will go well with the theme of technology in the play, as these colours are common in laptops and other electronic equipment. **[5]** The effect I am aiming for is a combination of recognisable teenage gang outfits and eerie, futuristic touches. **[6]**

**[1]** Understanding of the character and situation.

**[2]** Describes basic costume, including fit and fabric.

**[3]** Justifies choice, describes colour and discusses effect.

**[4]** Describes footwear, make-up and hair and discusses effect.

**[5]** Justifies choices with reference to the play's themes.

**[6]** Considers the effect of the costume.

## TASK 3.24

On the right is a sketch of one possible interpretation of a costume design for Manny.

Draw your own sketches for costume designs for the following characters:

- **Ben**
- **Cevril** (Scene Five and a contrasting costume for Scene Six)
- **Ted**.

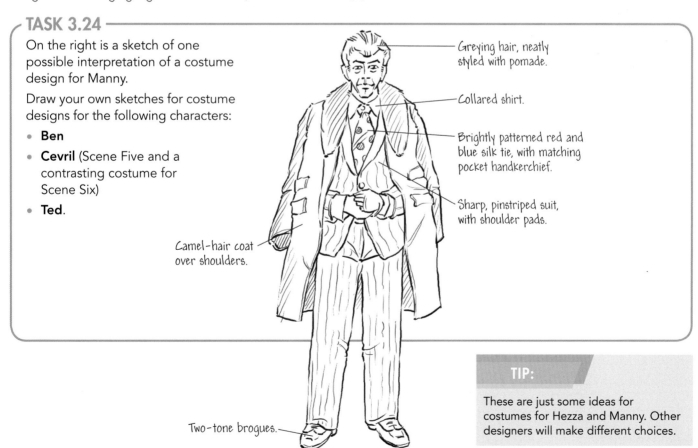

Greying hair, neatly styled with pomade.

Collared shirt.

Brightly patterned red and blue silk tie, with matching pocket handkerchief.

Sharp, pinstriped suit, with shoulder pads.

Camel-hair coat over shoulders.

Two-tone brogues.

**TIP:**

These are just some ideas for costumes for Hezza and Manny. Other designers will make different choices.

# Set design

The set designer of *Gizmo* could help to convey the play's meaning through some of the following:

- Emphasising naturalistic aspects of the play by providing realistic props and set furnishings
- Emphasising non-naturalistic aspects of the play by symbolically suggesting themes such as the future, technology and violence
- Establishing a particular relationship between the audience and the performers, by use of proxemics or levels
- Establishing the period and style of the play through the use of technology, colour and how transitions are handled.

## TASK 3.25

**A** On the right is a sketch of the lecture room in the hospital in Scene One.

- Add two more details that you think would improve the design.
- Answer the question: 'How does this set help to convey the ideas and themes of *Gizmo*?'

**B** Then sketch a contrasting set for the same scene suitable for a theatre in the round, thrust or traverse configuration. What do you want to emphasise in your design and how can it be used at key moments in the play? Consider:

- Colours and textures
- The scale of the set
- Positioning/placement of set items on the stage
- Levels
- Materials
- Props and stage furnishings.

Multimedia display screen.

THE GIZMO PROJECT

Ramp for Ben's wheelchair.

Lectern.

## TASK 3.26

Imagine that you want to create a set for the play that is highly stylised or abstract. You want it to convey the themes of the play and the mental state of the characters rather than focusing on realistic depictions of the different locations.

Consider what you would like to emphasise and how you could use design to create your set. For example, you might highlight technology by giving each location the appearance of coming from a video game, or you could emphasise the threat of violence by having a dark, eerie urban setting created with black and splashes of red.

Once you have made your decisions, draw and annotate your design.

# Lighting design

The lighting in *Gizmo* has many functions, including:

- Establishing the time of day and location
- Focusing the audience's attention on certain characters and events
- Highlighting and increasing the intensity of certain moments
- Creating an atmosphere or mood
- Suggesting a transition from one time or location to another.

**LOOK HERE**

For more ideas about lighting, including technical terminology see pages 185 and 224–226.

## TASK 3.27

**A** Read the candidate-style response below that describes how to create a lighting design for Scene Four. Highlight the technical terminology used.

*I want to establish two basic lighting states for this scene. The first will create the park, and will look pleasant and bright. The second will be a more abstract, stylised design for the fight scene. Through my lighting, I want to show how quickly a situation can change from ordinary to frightening. To create the first state, I will have a wash of yellow and white light created by the fresnel lanterns in the flies and wings. In addition, I will place some gobos with leaf designs into profile spots to create two areas with leaf patterns, one upstage left and the other downstage right. When the fight begins, I will fade up an intense profile spot centre stage to create the area in which the violence will occur. During the fight, I will use a strobe, so key moments of the fight are frozen and others are not entirely seen. At one moment, the strobe will flash brightly and Ted's arm will be visible above the gang. In the next, he will have disappeared down to the ground. At the end of the fight, the group will step back, the strobe will stop and Ted will be lying in a pool of blue light.*

**B** With a partner, create a lighting design for Scene Five, from page 46 to the end of the scene. Consider:

- Changes in the lighting, such as when a character enters, or during the fights
- How the lighting will contribute to the mood or atmosphere
- How you will achieve technically the lighting effects you want
- What impact you want your lighting to have on the audience at the end of the scene.

In this scene from *Harmony Park* by Detroit Repertory Company, the lighting designer has considered the time of day, the effect of the sky, the use of shadows and how the acting area could be illuminated in the outside setting.

# Sound design

Sound design can be used to establish location or a transition, and is also useful in creating an atmosphere or reflecting the **psychological** state of a character. Sound design can also add to the tension, humour or other mood of a scene, often having a significant impact on the audience's experience of the play. When writing about sound design, you might consider:

- Volume: How amplified will the sound be? Will it grow louder or quieter?
- Recorded or live: Will sound effects and music be pre-recorded or performed live?
- Type of sound: Will the sound be naturalistic or abstract?
- Special effects: Will you use distorting effects such as reverb?
- How the sound or music begins and ends: Should it gradually get louder or will there be a sudden burst of sound? Will it end abruptly or fade out?

## TASK 3.28

Look at the following ideas and note at least one occasion in the play when each sound effect might be appropriate:

Applause    Birdsong    The beeping of hospital equipment

Music    A gunshot    Broken glass

Sounds of an audience settling down

A sound designer might wish to create a symbolic or abstract sound design for *Gizmo*. Some ideas that a designer might consider are:

- Electronic noise to signal when the PMRS is turned on or off
- Music to accompany the fight scenes
- Light, comical music to accompany the cocktail scene
- Music to underscore Ben's story of the murders in the bar
- Music to accompany various characters entrances, such as the gangs or Manny
- Electronic sound effects during transitions
- Humorous sound effects when Ben collapses.

## TASK 3.29

Note any possibilities in the play for the abstract sound choices above and what effect they would have on the audience.

## LOOK HERE

For more ideas about sound design, including technical terminology see pages 186 and 227–229.

## KEY TERM:

**Psychological:** Referring to a mental or emotional state and the reasons behind it.

## EXTENSION

One of the important choices a sound designer might make is whether or not to create 'futuristic' music or sound effects to establish the setting though sound. Use the internet to research different types of music and locate some possible music and sound choices. Decide the following:

- Do you want it to be recorded or performed live?
- Should it to be a single repeated piece of music or sound effect, or several?
- What volume do you want it to be? Will this change?
- What effect should it have on the audience?

## CHECK YOUR LEARNING *Gizmo*

**Do you know…?**

✓ When *Gizmo* was written.

✓ When it is set.

✓ Where it takes place, including the different locations within the overall setting.

✓ The genre of the play.

✓ How its context might affect choices of costumes, sets and props.

✓ How the relationships between the characters, and the changes to these relationships, could be shown.

✓ Advantages and disadvantages of producing the play in different staging configurations.

✓ How key scenes might be staged.

✓ The performance style (or styles) of the play.

✓ How the performers could use their physical and vocal skills to convey characters' motivations, thoughts and feelings and to impart meaning to the action.

✓ The role of the director and how they influence the way an audience responds to and understands the play.

✓ Key moments a director could use to convey their concept of the play.

✓ Different design choices to be made, why they are important and how they can be effective.

✓ What impact the play should have on the audience and what messages they should be left with.

# KINDERTRANSPORT
## by Diane Samuels

The OCR specification identifies editions of the texts that are used to set questions in the 'Drama: Performance and response' (Component 04) examination paper. It is not required that centres use these editions for teaching this component.

Page numbers given here refer to the Nick Hern Books edition of *Kindertransport*, ISBN-13: 978-1-85459-527-0, one of those used by OCR for question setting.

# Plot synopsis
## Act One
### Scene One

*Set in an attic, the action switches between the late 1930s to 1940s to decades later.*

Eva, a nine-year-old Jewish German girl is reading a book about the Ratcatcher. Her mother, Helga, interrupts her to teach her how to sew on a button on her coat. When she succeeds, Helga says 'See. You don't need me. It's good.'

Evelyn, the adult Eva, now in her 50s, enters the attic with her daughter, Faith (in her 20s). Faith is moving into a flat and they go through the boxes to see if anything stored in the attic would be useful to her.

Eva and Helga discuss the journey Eva is making to England. Helga says that she and 'Vati' plan to join Eva in England once their permits arrive.

Faith decides she doesn't want to move into a flat. As Evelyn was planning to sell her house, she says she will now have to call the estate agent. Evelyn exits. Faith finds pieces of a toy train and sings 'Runaway Train'.

Helga finds that Eva has packed a mouth organ in her suitcase and tells her to remove it as she is only allowed to take clothes.

Faith begins to lay out dolls that she has found in the attic.

Helga tells Eva that she has stored some of her precious jewellery in the heels of her shoes as a 'travelling gift'.

Lil, Evelyn's English foster mother (in her 80s) enters and tells Faith that Evelyn has begun cleaning. She advises Faith not to make a mess. Faith finds *The Ratcatcher* book.

Eva asks for a bedtime story, *Der Rattenfänger*. Reluctantly, Helga agrees to read it. As Faith is looking and commenting on the book, Helga reads the story of the frightening Ratcatcher who seeks out 'the ungrateful one'.

At a railway station, Eva calls out to her parents from the train carriage. A Nazi border official interrogates Eva and inspects her suitcase. He draws a Star of David on her label; allows her to keep her mouth organ; takes the few coins she has and gives her a toffee. She arrives in England. Helga reads the ending of the Ratcatcher story. Faith plays a tune on the mouth organ she has found.

The cold, imperious Border Official commands the distressed Eva in Charlotte Westenra's production for the LAMDA Linbury Studio.

## Scene Two

Faith reads a letter from Helga dated 6 March 1941.

Eva expresses her disappointment when she arrives at the station in England in 1939. An English organiser, who speaks no German, tells her that her 'English Mother' has been delayed. Eva misunderstands and begins to cry.

Lil tells Faith to put the things away.

Lil greets Eva. She tells Eva that she will have to learn English and takes off her label. Lil smokes a cigarette and lets Eva have a puff.

Faith shows Lil that she has found the Ratcatcher book and asks if it and the photos and letter in the box belonged to the 'little Jewish girl' who stayed with Lil during the war. Faith wonders why her mother has all the girl's belongings. Faith jokes, 'Did you kill her and try to hide the evidence?' Lil becomes upset and Faith realises that her mother is Eva and that she had been lied to about her mother's past. Lil says that Eva/Evelyn's parents are now dead.

Eva shows Lil a letter she has written trying to get permits for her parents to come to England. In Germany, Eva's father had been a bank manager. Lil and Eva discuss the jobs as servants that Eva's parents could hope to get in England.

Lil explains to Faith that Evelyn changed her name and her birth date on her papers when she was 16 because she wanted to 'make a fresh start'.

Lil is angry at Eva when she discovers she has been going door to door at large houses trying to find a job for her parents so they can come to England.

Evelyn comes up to the attic. She says she'll tidy up and tells Faith and Lil to go downstairs. Faith confronts Evelyn with the Ratcatcher book and asks for the truth. Evelyn refuses to discuss it, saying it has nothing to do with her. Faith points out Evelyn's odd behaviour: her constant cleaning, her fear of trains or officials. Faith says, 'I have never been a good enough daughter' and that Evelyn is 'a terrible mother'.

Eva and Evelyn describe the Ratcatcher, with Eva speaking her fears and Evelyn stating, 'He won't take you anywhere ever again.'

# Act Two

## Scene One

In the attic, a dishevelled Evelyn sits.

Helga and Eva are as they were at the beginning of the play, discussing the jewels and that Eva must be a good girl in England.

Faith asks her mother to let her in. Evelyn tells her to go away.

A postman imitates Hitler and gives Eva a parcel from Germany. In the parcel, Helga has enclosed the Ratcatcher book and a Haggadah for Passover. Helga's letter thanks her for helping to arrange jobs for them and encourages Eva to practise Jewish customs.

Lil demands that Evelyn let her in. Evelyn eventually does and the two women smoke together. Lil says that Faith didn't mean what she said and that she is still probably upset about her father leaving.

Continued on next page ▶▶

Lil (Jenny Lee) and Eva (Leila Schaus) share a tender moment in the Queen's Theatre Hornchurch production.

**TIP:**

You might want to consider the playwright's original intentions in writing the play. For example, what might Diane Samuels be saying about the past, families and memory?

**TASK 3.1**

**A** Working in a small group, create a two-minute version of the play, making sure that you cover what you all agree are the most significant events in the plot.

**B** Given your understanding of the play's plot, answer the following questions:

**1** Why does Helga arrange for Eva to go to England?

**2** Why has Evelyn kept her past a secret from Faith?

**3** Why doesn't Eva go to New York with Helga?

**4** What effect does Faith discovering her mother's past have on her own life and choices?

Lil and Eva are at a train station where Eva and other children are being evacuated. Eva imagines that she sees the Ratcatcher and jumps off the train. Lil agrees that she doesn't have to go away.

Lil and Evelyn begin going through her old papers, deciding what to destroy. Evelyn accuses Lil of taking 'too much of me' and making her betray her mother. She calls Lil a 'child-stealer'. Evelyn and Lil begin to destroy each item in the box.

A station guard asks Eva who she is waiting for. She shows him a photograph of her parents. The guard becomes suspicious of Eva. When Lil returns, he says she should take better care of her. Lil says she doesn't think Eva's parents are coming. The guards says that if they do come they'll be interned. Eva says she doesn't want her mother's jewellery any more.

Evelyn stops Lil from tearing the Ratcatcher book. They decide to put this behind them and Lil says Evelyn must make it up with Faith.

A 15-year-old Eva and Lil are watching a newsreel about the liberation of Belsen. Lil is upset by it, but Eva still wants to watch the main feature.

Faith asks Lil and Evelyn to let her into the attic.

Lil is adjusting a hem of Eva's dress. Eva says she is thinking of selling her jewellery. Lil says it's bad luck to sell a 'keepsake'.

Faith enters the attic and sees all the torn papers. She is distressed that they weren't passed on to her. Evelyn tells of the little she remembers of her parents. Evelyn says that her parents were in Auschwitz and that her father died in 1943.

An older 'transformed' Helga meets the 17-year-old Eva in a hotel. They comment on how much each has changed. Eva says she has changed her name to Evelyn as it is more English and explains that she has been adopted by the Millers as, after not hearing from her mother for years, she thought she was dead. Helga wants Eva to start a new life with her in New York. Eva asks if she has to go away with her.

## Scene Two

In the tidied attic, Evelyn and Faith sort through boxes. Faith asks if Lil knew that Helga survived the war. Evelyn says that if she did she would have insisted she go with Helga. Evelyn never saw Helga again after she left England and Helga died in 1969. Evelyn says how proud she was to get her first British passport and that she doesn't feel Jewish. She gives Faith the Haggadah and the Ratcatcher books, as well as the mouth organ.

Helga wants Eva to leave with her on a boat, but Eva suggests that she might join her later. Helga accuses Eva of 'losing' herself. Helga and Eva hurl accusations at each other. Helga says, 'My suffering is monumental. Yours is personal.'

Evelyn begins to cry and asks that Faith stays her 'little girl forever'. Faith is determined to find her relations and says that she and her mother could do it together, but Evelyn says she would rather die. Faith asks if she could take her toys and Evelyn reluctantly gives them to her. Faith exits.

The play ends with a shadow of the Ratcatcher covering the stage.

# Genre

*Kindertransport* is a **historical drama** that explores a historic event and period. *Kindertransport* was the transportation of children from Germany to England at the beginning of the Second World War. Although the playwright, Diane Samuels, makes clear that the characters are fictional, they are inspired by and based on her research, including interviews with *Kinder* (children).

In addition to the historical aspects, the play also has elements of **domestic drama**, which focuses on the everyday lives of the characters and frequently explores **psychological** or social issues. The theme of families, particularly mothers and daughters, is at the forefront of the play, as is the psychology of the character of Eva/Evelyn and how her past has influenced her present behaviour.

**KEY TERMS:**

**Historical drama:** A play set in an earlier period of time than when it was written and explores events of that historical period.

**Domestic drama:** A play focused on the ordinary lives of middle- or working-class characters, frequently set in a home environment.

**Psychological:** Referring to a mental or emotional state and the reasons behind it.

## TASK 3.2

**A** Look at the following elements of historical drama and find an example of each in *Kindertransport*. (The first one has been completed for you.)

- It deals with an actual historic event.
  Eva is shown travelling from Germany to England as part of the Kindertransport, which took place in 1938–39.

- Specific dates are referenced.

- Political events from the period are discussed or shown.

- There are accurate references to items such as clothing, books or transportation appropriate for the historic period.

**B** Now look at some elements of domestic drama and find an example of each:

- The play is largely set in a domestic environment, such as a home.

- There is a realistic depiction of items within the environment.

- Relationships, particularly those of members of a family, are shown.

- The psychology of the characters, including the reasons for their behaviour and emotions, is explored.

A German mother and daughter on their way home from a shopping trip, 1937.

## TASK 3.3

A Read the end of Act One, Scene One, from when Eva is interviewed by the Officer to the end of the scene (pages 19–21). Consider what you learn about the historical period from this extract and answer the following questions:

- Why is Eva on the train on her own?
- Why is she wearing a label?
- Why does the Officer draw a Star of David on her label?
- Why is Eva frightened of the Officer?

B In a small group, experiment with how this scene could be performed to emphasise the sense of fear, urgency and danger. Consider:

- Movements and interactions between the Eva and the Officer
- The pace of the scene: when it might speed up or slow down
- Reactions of the characters, such as facial expressions or gestures
- How they might use vocal skills such as volume, phrasing and emphasis
- How Eva's expression and movements might change to show her relief and joy when she crosses the border.

C Still focusing on this scene, consider how design could be used to emphasise the historical context. Consider:

- The use of sound, including music and sound effects, to recreate the train and the 1930s period
- How costumes might be authentic to the period
- How lighting could establish location and change of mood
- How the setting will show that they are on a train.

D Write a paragraph, or create a series of images for a storyboard, to explain how this scene could be performed and staged. Look especially to highlight the importance of these features in establishing the relationship between the characters and the mood of the scene.

---

## KEY TERMS:

**Chronological:** Presenting events in the order in which they occur.

**Non-linear:** A sequence that is not arranged in a straightforward or chronological way.

**Expressionistic:** Using exaggeration or stylised elements to show emotions and ideas, rather than a realistic depiction.

## TASK 3.4

From your knowledge and understanding of the play, identify examples of the following structural or stylistic features:

- Conflict
- The depiction of an earlier time
- The present and past on stage at the same time
- Dialogue or stage directions that are realistic
- Dialogue or stage directions that are non-naturalistic
- **Resolution.**

# Structure

The play is divided into two acts, with two scenes in each act. The action switches between different periods of time, with the 'historic' period running from 1939 to 1947, and scenes set in 'recent times' taking place in a single day. The 'recent times' are **chronological**, whereas there is some **non-linear** use of time in the past sequences. Act Two, Scene One, for example, returns to the earliest period seen previously in Act One, Scene One, with Helga continuing to prepare Eva for her journey. There are also sections of the play when the past and present are shown at the same time, including a sequence when Lil plays both her younger and older self, speaking at times to Faith and then to Eva. Act One ends with the past Eva and the 'recent times' Evelyn both reacting to the Ratcatcher.

# Style

The play is usually performed naturalistically, with the actors creating believable, three-dimensional characters. The Ratcatcher sequences, however, as well as the fluid handling of time, could be performed in a stylised fashion. Some productions aim for an **expressionistic** style that emphasises the characters' mental state. Some set designs for productions are largely realistic, while others create a more fluid, abstract or stylised quality.

## KEY TERM:

**Resolution:** The solution or bringing together of loose elements of a plot; an ending or conclusion.

## TASK 3.5

Read the statements below about *Kindertransport*. Then work with a partner to put them in order, with the one you agree with most as 1, and the one you agree with least as 5.

- [ ] It is concerned with showing how past events influence the present.
- [ ] It is about the secrets and lies that divide a family.
- [ ] It discusses how parents must let their children go.
- [ ] It is about the evils of Nazi Germany.
- [ ] It shows a daughter discovering her true identity.

**TIP:**

There is no 'right' answer to what *Kindertransport* is about, but, as you study the play, you should consider what aspects of it you find the most compelling and how your interpretation of the play could emphasise those.

# Context

The playwright, Diane Samuels, grew up in Liverpool and attended Cambridge University. She has worked as a Drama teacher and an Education Officer. Some of her plays, such as *Kindertransport* and *Three Sisters on Hope Street* (co-written with Tracy-Ann Oberman) reflect her Jewish background.

In the late 1980s, when Samuels was a young mother, she became interested in the theme of the separation of children from their parents. This, combined with her knowledge of the *Kindertransport*, when German Jewish parents sent their children to live in England to protect them from the Nazis, inspired her to write the first scenes of the play in 1991. The first production of the play was in 1993 by the Soho Theatre Company. It is a popular play that has frequently been revived.

## Historical context

Many of the dates and locations of the historic scenes in the play are given precisely, such as Faith discovering the inscription on the Ratcatcher book of 'Hamburg. 1939' and Eva's arrival in England on 7 January 1939. Evelyn says her father died in 1943. She sees her mother after the Second World War in 1947.

In 1933, Hitler became Chancellor of Germany and initiated actions against the Jews. By 1935, Jews were deprived of many of their civil rights. Kristallnacht ('Crystal Night' or 'Night of the Broken Glass') in 1938 saw many Jews murdered and Jewish homes, hospitals, schools and businesses ransacked and destroyed. In the late 1930s, Jews began to emigrate, although many could not get permission to enter another country. Those who remained faced persecution and many were sent to concentration camps.

Hitler speaks to the Reichstag on 'the Jewish question', January 1939.

Three Jewish children on Kindertransport from Germany and Austria wait to be collected from Liverpool Street Station, London, July 1939.

The British government agreed to allow unaccompanied German Jewish children to come to Britain, with the understanding that they would return to their families after the crisis. Ten thousand children were transported as part of this scheme. *Kindertransport* shows the difficult decision Helga has made to send Eva away and also how she and her husband could not get permits to live in England without a job.

Unable to leave Germany, Eva's father died in the Auschwitz concentration camp. Most of the *Kindertransport* children did not see their parents again. Eva's mother, Helga, survived and, like many Jewish survivors, decided to start a new life in the US. Many of the *Kinder* either remained in Britain, becoming citizens, or emigrated to other countries, such as Israel or the USA.

Many of the *Kinder* went on to have significant careers, but some spoke of the conflicting emotions they had about that time and the choices that were made. Samuels writes of seeing a documentary about a 55-year-old woman who spoke of the 'rage' she felt towards her dead parents for what she perceived as an 'abandonment'.

The dates of the 'recent times' sections are not specified. Evelyn is in her 50s, so, if she was born in 1930, these scenes would take place in the 1980s.

## Cultural context

The most significant prop in the play is the children's book *Der Rattenfänger von Hameln*, known in English as 'The Pied Piper of Hamelin', a traditional fairy tale of which the most famous version is the one by the Brothers Grimm. In the tale, the Ratcatcher agrees to clear the town of Hamelin of its infestation of rats. However, after he leads the rats away by playing his pipe, the mayor of the town refuses to pay him. In revenge, the Ratcatcher lures the children from the village, never to be seen again. The use of this fairy tale underscores the theme of parents being separated from their children.

Films were a popular form of entertainment in the 1930s and 1940s. The main feature film would often be preceded by shorter films, such as newsreels, which, in the days before television, was one way people learned the news. In Act Two, Scene One, Lil and Eva go to see a film, but Lil becomes upset at the newsreel film of the liberation of Belsen concentration camp. When British forces arrived at Belsen, what they saw was horrifying and brought home to many the atrocities of the Holocaust. Lil wants to leave the cinema, but Eva wants to stay, perhaps not making the connection between what she is seeing and the Germany she has left behind.

The Second World War has been a popular topic for many plays. *The Diary of Anne Frank* by a young Jewish girl hiding from the Nazis, has been dramatised and performed frequently. Bertolt Brecht's *The Resistible Rise of Arturo Ui* (1941) uses the **allegory** of a Chicago mobster to trace Hitler's rise to power. *Bent*, the 1979 play by Martin Sherman, explores the persecution of gay citizens in Nazi Germany, including scenes set in a concentration camp. *Kindertransport*, like many acclaimed plays of the 1990s, deals with social and political issues.

**KEY TERM:**

**Allegory:** A story that uses its characters and events to explore real-life people and events, often making a moral point or political criticism.

# Social context

Before the rise of Hitler, it is suggested that the Schlesinger family led comfortable lives. Eva's father was a bank manager and her mother is described as being 'well turned-out' (page 3) in the fashions of the late 1930s. They also have some precious gold jewellery. The family observes Jewish customs, such as Seder, a ceremonial meal for Passover. The Haggadah, one of the two books Eva is given for the journey, is a text recited at Seder. Jewish dietary law forbids eating pork, which is why Eva doesn't want to eat Lil's sandwiches. The Millers don't follow this custom and, with food rationing at the time, view ham as a treat.

Lil Miller lives in Manchester. She says that she wanted to 'keep' Eva in a way that no one ever kept her (page 71), suggesting hardship in her past. 'Uncle Jack' – presumably Mr Miller – is mentioned (page 57), but is not presented as central to their lives. Lil's dialect is less formal than that of Evelyn or Helga and she, at first, shocks Eva with her smoking.

At this time, many British people were not happy about refugees arriving from Germany. Examples of their attitudes can be found in the scene with the Postman, who says that 'All Germans smell' (page 50) and the Guard who says Eva 'should be in Germany' with her parents (page 65).

Helga and her husband might have worn similar outfits to this well-dressed couple in early-1940s Prague.

## EXTENSION

Research Germany in the 1930s and England from the 1930s to 1980s to gain a better understanding of the context. There are many videos and photographs available online, as well as interviews with those who had participated in the *Kindertransport*. Some possible areas of research include:

- Social context: families, housing, roles of women, employment, transportation
- Cultural context: fashion, music, films, interviews with the playwright
- Historical context: the Second World War, Kindertransport, post-war Britain.

Make a note of anything that helps your understanding of the play and how it could be staged or designed.

## TIP:

In your exam, alternative wording might be used instead of 'context', such as 'reflect the time in which the play was written' or 'show when and where the play is set'.

### TASK 3.6

Look at the following list of key moments from the play and write a few sentences about each to explain what it tells you about the social or historical context of the play. (The first one has been completed for you.)

**1** Helga hides some of her jewels in the heels of Eva's shoes.
*The Kindertransport children were not allowed to bring anything but clothing with them. Valuables would be confiscated. In order to give Eva something valuable that might help her later, she must hide it. One of the pieces of jewellery is a Star of David to remind Eva of her Jewish faith.*

**2** Eva's favourite story is *Der Rattenfänger*.

**3** Evelyn has kept her background secret from her husband and Faith.

**4** Evelyn changed her birth date to the day when Lil first picked her up at the train station.

When depicting the context of the play, there are a number of factors to consider, such as:

- How much money a character might have
- Fashions and clothing available at the time (Germany and Britain in the 1930s and 1940s and Britain in the 1980s)
- The influence of the culture of the time, such as literature, art and films
- The backgrounds and occupations of the characters
- The ages of the characters
- Props characters might use, such as the items in the attic
- The types of house and furnishings that characters might have.

**TIP:**

There is no set way to costume the characters, but think about how you could differentiate between them.

---

**TASK 3.7**

**A** Look at the list of costume, make-up and hair ideas below and sort them into whether they would be more appropriate for Helga, Lil or Evelyn:

1930s wool suit

Loose-fitting floral dress

Tailored woollen trousers

Silk blouse

Cardigan

Pearl necklace

Cashmere jumper

Red lipstick

Small, leather, box handbag

Low-heeled, slip-on shoes

Dark hair, styled into a bun

Pale pink lipstick

Short, curled, grey hair

Dark eyebrows

**B** Now sketch a costume for Helga, Lil or Evelyn. Include accessories, make-up and hair ideas that help to convey the character and context.

---

**TIP:**

If you are asked to demonstrate how set design could show when the play is set, you should think about how set and props could show 1930s Hamburg as well as 1980s Manchester.

## Using set design to represent a period in time

A designer needs to convey the period in which the play was written through set design. They might explore, for example, how Evelyn's attic could be authentic to a home of the late 20th century, including:

- Materials the home would be made from (brick, wood, concrete). What would the flooring be? Would there be wooden beams? Would there be any natural light, say from a skylight or dormer window, or would it only have artificial lighting?
- Style and colours, for example is it a renovated Victorian building or a modern red-brick home?
- Items in the attic, such as boxes, old furniture, trunks, toys from Faith's childhood.

**TASK 3.8**

Write two paragraphs in answer to the following question: 'Describe how you could show the social or historical context of the play by your design choices for the set of the play.'

# Interpretations of key characters

You must demonstrate that you understand the main characters in the play, including different ways that they could be interpreted.

**WHAT THE SPECIFICATION SAYS...**

Learners must know and understand:
- How meaning is communicated through:
  - An actor's vocal and physical interpretation of character.

## Helga

A prosperous German Jewish woman. Her husband is a bank manager and they live in an elegant home in Hamburg. When Hitler comes to power, Helga sends her daughter Eva away to save her life. Her husband dies in a concentration camp. After the war, she comes to England to collect Eva on her way to America. She is devastated when Eva refuses to join her.

## Eva

Helga's daughter, shown from the ages of 9 to 17. In early scenes, she is a naïve girl, used to having things done for her. She is frightened to leave and speaks very little English. As she settles with the Millers, her English rapidly improves. She is disappointed when her parents don't join her, but, when she and her mother are eventually reunited, she no longer feels connected to her.

## Lil

Eva/Evelyn's foster mother. In the 1980s scenes, she is in her 80s. She is warm and generous and tries to do her best for Eva, including fighting for her education and trying to get permits for Eva's parents to come to England. Lil doesn't know that Helga survived the war.

## Evelyn

The adult Eva, a mother in her 50s. She and her husband have recently separated and her daughter Faith is planning to move out. Evelyn has kept her past a secret, rejected her Jewish faith and feels conflicted about her relationships with both Helga and Lil.

## Faith

Evelyn's daughter, in her 20s. She is planning to move out, but this prospect of change has been difficult. Faith is shocked when she discovers her mother's past and is determined to learn more.

## English Organiser

The official who greets the children, speaks no German and inadvertently makes the children cry. This rather hapless character provides some comic relief.

## Postman

An Englishman who expresses anti-German sentiments and claims that all Germans smell.

## Border Official

A Nazi officer who searches the children leaving Germany. He is a frightening official figure.

## Station Guard

The guard whom Eva meets when she is looking for her parents. He seems kindly, but becomes suspicious when he learns she is not English. He worries that she or her parents might be spies.

## Ratcatcher

A mythical figure from Eva's favourite book. He symbolises children's fears and the forces that separate parents and children.

**TASK 3.9**

Choose one important line from the play for each character. Write a few sentences to explain its importance in understanding the character and how it could be delivered by the actor. What physical and vocal skills would be most effective?

KEY TERM:

**Repressing:** Hiding, pushing down, controlling or preventing something, such as a thought or emotion.

# Use of vocal skills

Typically in *Kindertransport*, Helga and Eva speak with German accents, while Faith, Evelyn and Lil have English accents. Most productions cast actors who can assume the necessary different accents, but one recent production cast German actors for Helga and Eva and English actors for the other roles. The accents the actors use might suggest particular geographical areas, such as a Manchester accent for Lil.

The characters' vocal idiosyncracies might change during the course of the play, for example Eva's German accent would be less pronounced when she is 17 and has been living in England for several years. The characters' voices will also be influenced by the situations they are in and the emotions they are either expressing or **repressing**.

Vocal skills that actors might consider include:

Accent and dialect    Pace    Volume    Pitch

Pauses and timing    Intonation    Phrasing    Emotional range

## TASK 3.10

With a partner, experiment with vocal skills to interpret the following lines. Note down the choices you make, including reasons.

Faith: Maybe it's not such a good idea to move. (page 6)

Lil: You two have the quietest arguments. (page 13)

Ratcatcher: I will search you out whoever wherever you are. (page 16)

Helga: Snake. Slithering out of yourself like it was an unwanted skin. Worm. (page 85)

Eva: We've got to stop! He'll take us over the edge. Got to get away from him. (page 57)

Evelyn: Stay my little girl forever. (page 86)

## TASK 3.11

For each key character below, give three examples of different vocal skills that the actor playing the role could use. Justify each of your choices by explaining why it is appropriate. (Examples have been given for Eva.)

- **Evelyn**
- **Faith**
- **Helga**
- **Lil**.

| Character | Vocal skill | When vocal skill could be displayed | Justification |
|---|---|---|---|
| Eva | **Volume:** Speaking softly at first, then increasingly loudly. | Act One, Scene One, on the train. | Eva speaks in a quiet, non-confrontational tone with the Officer, trying hard not to make him angry. However, once they cross the border she raises her voice, shouting, 'Stuff your stupid toffees' showing how free she suddenly feels. |
| | **Pause/pace:** Hesitating and speaking slowly. | Act One, Scene Two, with Organiser. | Eva speaks very little English and has to listen hard to try to pick out a few words. She is 'uncertain', so has to consider if she should speak and how to pronounce her words. |
| | **Accent/ intonation.** | Act Two, Scene One | Eva's German accent has almost entirely gone. She has adopted a precise English accent, which contrasts with her mother's German accent. Her tone with her mother is cool and formal. |

# Use of physical skills

Physical skills might be used to reflect the high emotion of much of the play as well as play out the intricate relationships between the characters. The actor playing Eva will need to think about how her physical skills will show her ageing from 9 to 17 and how that might influence her posture, gestures and facial expressions. The actor playing the Ratcatcher might use stylised movements to convey his mysterious and frightening powers.

Physical skills actors might consider include:

**Posture**  **Movement**  **Pace**  **Gestures**
**Facial expressions**  **Proxemics**  **Eye contact**

In this scene in Chickenshed's production, Lil (Evie Edgell) and Evelyn (Michelle Collins) make similar gestures with their cigarettes, but their different expressions and lack of eye contact, as well as proxemics, suggest an emotional distance between them.

## TASK 3.12

**A** In a small group, read Act One, Scene One (pages 15–17), when Helga is reading the Ratcatcher story to Eva. Discuss in your group:

- How realistic or stylised you want this section to be
- How you will show the characters of Eva, Helga and the Ratcatcher through their movements
- What effect you want this section to have on the audience.

**B** Experiment with the following:

- Helga and Eva make eye contact with each other, but avoid doing so with the Ratcatcher
- Helga and Eva get caught up in the story and start acting it out
- The Ratcatcher uses his posture and gestures to create frightening effects
- Eva and Helga react physically to the Ratcatcher, particularly his final line in this scene.

As you explore different physical skills in this scene, note which, in your opinion are most effective and when these physical skills might be used. For example, on what lines might the characters move, use a prop, make a gesture or change facial expressions.

**LOOK HERE**

See pages 200–202 for more rehearsal techniques for exploring characterisation and practising performance skills.

**KEY TERM:**

Mannerism: A slight movement or habit that a person does repeatedly, such as a hand gesture or a facial expression, perhaps without knowing they are doing it.

## TASK 3.13

In your group, read the end of Act One, Scene Two (pages 45–46), when Eva and Evelyn are talking about the Ratcatcher. Experiment with physical skills for this section, considering the following:

- As Eva and Evelyn are the same person, will they share some **mannerisms** and gestures?
- Will they make eye contract? Will they look out at the audience? Will they look at the Ratcatcher?
- As this is the end of the act, could the actors use their physical skills to bring the act to an effective and exciting final image?

## TASK 3.14

Now compare Eva and Evelyn's movements in the first act and the second act. Remember to pick out key examples from each act to support your points. Talk and make notes about:

- Posture
- Movement
- Pace and pause
- Gestures
- Facial expressions
- Proxemics
- Eye contact.

## TASK 3.15

For each key character listed below, give at least three examples of how they could use their physical skills in the play. Justify each of your choices. (An example has been given for Helga.)

- Lil
- Faith
- Ratcatcher.

| Character | Physical skill | When physical skill could be displayed | Details and justification |
|---|---|---|---|
| Helga | **Posture**: She sits with a straight back and delicately crosses her ankles. | At the beginning of the play. | Helga is the very proper wife of a bank manager and tries hard to maintain high standards. Even though she is frightened for Eva, she tries to appear confident in the way she holds herself. |
| | **Facial expressions**: Change from a frowning disapproval to wide-eyed, animated enthusiasm. | The scene in which she reads to Eva. | Helga doesn't want to read the story as it is frightening and not really suitable to read before a separation, but, once reading, Helga brings the story to life for Eva, in part showing why it is Eva's favourite story. |
| | **Eye contact** and **gestures**, to show how disappointed she is in Eva. | Act Two, Scene One. | Helga had hoped for a happy reunion with Eva, but instead finds her distant. She stares at Eva, trying to understand her coldness. She shrugs and points at herself trying to make Eva understand her position when she says, 'These are the pieces of my life.' |

# Stage directions

In addition to the play's dialogue, a way for the playwright to convey what a character is doing, thinking and feeling is through stage directions. For example:

Page 6: Evelyn concentrates on polishing and replacing glasses.

Page 20: Eva grips the toffee tightly and tidies up the clothes into the case.

Page 62: Evelyn tears up the letter into small pieces. She and Lil proceed to destroy each item in the box.

## TASK 3.16

A In a small group, perform each of the stage directions above.

B Discuss and write down what you believe each character is thinking and feeling. For example, what might Evelyn be thinking while she is polishing the glasses and listening to Faith?

C Talk about what the audience learns about the character from the stage directions. From the stage direction on page 62, for example, what do we learn about the relationship between Evelyn and Lil?

In this Nottingham Playhouse production, what might Evelyn (Cate Hamer) be thinking in this enigmatic, private moment in the attic? What does Hamer's expression, posture and body language (for example how she holds the doll) reveal to the audience?

## TASK 3.17

**A** Read this response about stage directions from pages 83 to the end of the play. Highlight three occasions that describe how stage directions help the audience to understand the play.

The audience sees two estranged relationships between mothers and daughters at a moment of parting, reinforced by the stage directions. The sound of 'Boat's hooter' emphasises that Eva and Helga don't have long together, giving the scene urgency. When Helga 'embraces' her daughter, Eva stands 'stock-still', giving no affection or consolation to her mother. In the modern scene, it is Faith, who tries to 'get close' to Evelyn, but Evelyn refuses to 'face' her. It could be interpreted that the trauma of her childhood has made Evelyn unable to express affection: this is underscored by these stage directions. The Ratcatcher's shadow covering the stage shows the audience how the parting of children from their parents casts a shadow over all the play's events.

**B** Focus on the scene with Eva and the Postman (pages 48–50). Note what the audience learns about characters and themes from the stage directions. What effect would this scene have?

**TIP:**

Remember that communication is at the heart of drama. Always consider what the performance and staging choices you make are communicating to the audience. Do they create...

- Sympathy?
- Fear?
- Excitement?
- Suspense?
- Pity?
- Comedy?
- Greater understanding?

# Use of space

As part of their characterisation, actors might use the stage space in many different ways, including:

**Levels** / **Proxemics** / **Positioning on stage**

**Entrances and exits** / **Use of the 'fourth wall'**

In addition, the type of staging configuration and the set design could influence the actors' use of space.

Below is a candidate-style response about how a performer playing the Ratcatcher could use a traverse stage space, and the advantages and disadvantages of this space.

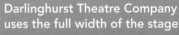

Darlinghurst Theatre Company uses the full width of the stage

The Ratcatcher is a frightening figure, important in the imagination of Eva/Evelyn. **[1]** On a traverse stage, the audience will be near the Ratcatcher, so he could suddenly turn to a section of the audience and reach out as if to touch them in the scene when his story is being read. This would show how frightening he is to Eva as the audience would feel the same childlike fear. **[2]** As the traverse is a long, thin stage, the Ratcatcher could run and prowl across it, creating excitement and a sense of unpredictability. **[3]** A disadvantage of a traverse stage is that it would be difficult for the shadows in the stage directions to be seen by the whole audience. They could be projected on the extreme ends of the stage, but that might not be as effective as shadowy images of which all the audience has the same view. **[4]**

As there is an audience on both sides of the stage, it would be difficult for the actor to hide and suddenly appear. The actor's entrance and exit would have to be carefully blocked in order to be eerie or alarming. **[5]** This could possibly be remedied through the use of trapdoors. **[6]** Although a traverse stage would pose some challenges, it could give an interesting effect of the audience sitting in judgement on the characters and focus them closely on the actors. **[7]**

**[1]** Opens with some understanding of the role of the Ratcatcher.

**[2]** Explains an advantage of traverse staging.

**[3]** Identifies a second advantage of traverse staging, although could identify when in the script this would effective.

**[4]** Identifies a disadvantage of traverse staging, referring to stage direction.

**[5]** Identifies a second disadvantage and uses correct terminology ('blocked').

**[6]** Suggests a technical solution (trapdoor) to problem.

**[7]** Suggests a positive effect created by the use of traverse staging and potential impact on the audience.

**TIP:**

If an exam question asks for advantages and disadvantages, you need to discuss at least two of each. Similarly, if a question asks for examples, you must offer more than one.

**TASK 3.18**

**A** Work in a small group to think about how the following scenes could be produced in different staging configurations:

- The play's opening (pages 3–5)
- The train journey (pages 17–20)
- Lil and Evelyn tearing up the papers (pages 61–62)
- The play's ending (pages 85–87).

**B** Choose one of the scenes and write down, with sketches if helpful, at least two advantages and two disadvantages of performing it in each staging configuration described on pages 8–11.

## WHAT THE SPECIFICATION SAYS...

Learners must know and understand:

How meaning is communicated through:

- The use of performance space and spatial relationships on stage
- The relationship between performers and audience
- The design of: set, props, costume, lighting and sound
- An actor's vocal and physical interpretation of character
- The use of performance conventions
- How performance styles affect the direction, acting and design of a performance.

# Directorial choices

A director of *Kindertransport* needs to consider:

- How to guide the actors' physical and vocal choices
- How to use design to reinforce the play's meaning and impact
- How key moments of the play might be staged
- The style of the play and potential use of performance conventions
- The effect the play should have on the audience.

**TASK 3.19**

**A** Working in a small group, read the section at the beginning of Act One, Scene Two (pages 22–29).

Discuss the impact you want this scene to have for the audience. Is this scene with the Organiser frightening, sad or comic – or a combination?

**B** How will you make clear for the audience the different shifts in time in this section? Experiment with using:

- Changes in pace and volume to increase interest
- Performance conventions, such as still image or mime, or design, such as particular lighting or sound effects, to emphasise the sections that are happening in the past
- Different positions in the stage space, for example will the scenes set in the present and past happen on different sections of the stage or will they overlap?
- Sound or lighting design to heighten a mood or underscore an important moment
- Physical and vocal skills to help explain the situations in which they find themselves.

**C** Now write a paragraph in response to the following question: 'As a director, how would you stage the early section of Act One, Scene Two to create a specific impact on the audience?'

Sarah Savage as the young Eva in Aberystwyth Arts Centre's 2008 production.

## TASK 3.20

Below are excerpts from two candidate-style responses about staging the end of Act One, Scene One. Decide how well you believe the writers have explained and justified their ideas. Look for and highlight the following:

- Clear ideas about what they want to achieve
- Specific examples from the play
- Correct use of theatrical terminology
- Understanding of how a certain impact on the audience can be achieved.

For my concept of the play, I want to create an immersive production. The seats in the auditorium will be like old-fashioned train seats, replicated by the seats on the end on stage where Eva is seated, and there will be signs and banners in German, from the 1930s. For this section, I use will recorded sound effects of a train pulling off and speeding up, and a fogger placed in the wings will create an effect of fog and steam around Eva's ankles as she speaks. On the line 'Is this actually England?', the signs and banners will be turned over to reveal English slogans of the period, as if answering Eva's question. This will help the audience to feel Eva's excitement that she has escaped. I will direct the actor playing Eva to stand downstage centre and deliver her lines directly to the audience.

After the tension of the scene with the Guard, there is a joyous release in Eva's monologue. In my concept, I want to establish the context and mood of this scene and bring it to a dramatic conclusion by using stylised effects. I would stage my version in the round, with a stage that has a revolve. That way, the movement of the revolve could show Eva's journey from Germany, to Holland and, eventually England. During her monologue, the revolve will turn slowly, so all the audience can see Eva's excited facial expressions. Eva would mime eating food and seeing new sights. Her reactions will show how young and immature she is, as she almost makes herself sick.

However, the mood will change when the Ratcatcher music is heard. I would have this played live by the Ratcatcher himself. This will give a sense to the audience that not all is well. The final image of this scene would be Helga seated centre stage, with Faith and Eva huddled, kneeling next to her, and the Ratcatcher behind her, as the revolve slowly turns.

**TIP:**

There is no one right way of interpreting this or any other scene. The choices you make, however, must be rooted in your understanding of the play and how theatre works.

# Design choices

Costume, set, lighting and sound design all contribute to the impact of *Kindertransport*. They are vital in presenting the play's setting, meaning and director's interpretation. For example, the way Helga and Lil dress might suggest that they are very different people and that it will be an adjustment for Eva to move from one to another. Eva at 17 years old will dress very differently from Eva at nine.

Setting and props are important for establishing the context of the play and the contrasts between different characters, such as Lil's use of cigarettes or Eva's mouth organ. Sound can be used to establish location and create atmosphere or tension. Lighting can focus attention on certain characters and suggest a certain mood or location.

**WHAT THE SPECIFICATION SAYS...**

Learners must know and understand:
- How meaning is communicated through:
  - The design of: set, props, costume, lighting and sound.

# Costume design

When writing about costume, it is important to consider what the costume tells the audience about the character's role and personality. It is useful to consider:

**Period and context** **Colour** **Fabric** **Silhouette**

**Fit** **Condition** **Headwear and footwear** **Make-up and hair**

Below is an excerpt from a candidate-style response about Eva's outfit in Act One, Scene One, demonstrating one possible approach to her costume.

**[1]** Shows understanding of character and situation.

**[2]** Describes colour and fabric, with precise details (collar, buttons, belt).

**[3]** Describes fit and silhouette.

**[4]** Describes accessories.

**[5]** Justifies choices with reference to character's situation and context.

**[6]** Considers accessories, hairstyle and make-up and justifies choices.

**[7]** Describes accessories.

**[8]** Considers the effect of the costume.

At the beginning of the play, Eva is nine years old and preparing for a trip to England. As she is inside, she won't yet have her coat or hat on. **[1]** She wears a dark blue and green floral-print cotton dress with short sleeves, a dark, solid-coloured **Peter Pan collar**, buttons down the front and a slim belt at the waist. **[2]** The silhouette will be fitted at the waist with a skirt that slightly flares out. The hemline will be just below knee-length. **[3]** She will wear dark tights and flat black T-bar shoes. **[4]** All these choices are appropriate for a middle-class child in the 1930s undertaking a journey. **[5]** Her dark hair will be in two neat plaits and her face will appear free of make-up as appropriate for her young age. **[6]** As her mother readies her to go out, she will put on a navy blue woollen coat and a matching felt hat. Around her neck she will have her large label with her number on it. She will carry a small brown suitcase. **[7]** She will look neat and well-presented, but the effect of the label and suitcase will also make her appear vulnerable. **[8]**

### KEY TERM:

**Peter Pan collar:** A flat collar with two rounded ends at the front.

### TIP:

These are just some ideas for costumes for Eva and the Ratcatcher. There are many other choices that could be made.

## TASK 3.21

On the right is a sketch of one possible interpretation of a costume for the Ratcatcher.

After studying it, draw your own similar sketches for costume designs for the following characters:

- Lil
- Helga
- Faith.

Grey turtleneck jumper

Small wooden flute

Fitted, dark-grey trousers

Black, mid-calf boots, pointed toes

# Set design

The set designer of *Kindertransport* could help to convey the play's meaning through some of the following:

- Emphasising naturalistic aspects of the play by providing realistic props and set furnishings
- Emphasising non-naturalistic aspects of the play by symbolically suggesting themes such as memory, Germany, politics or family
- Establishing a particular relationship between the audience and the performers, by use of proxemics or levels
- Establishing the period of the play and the passage of time through the use of particular props or set furnishings.

## TASK 3.22

**A** On the right is a design sketch of the attic.

- Add two more details that you think would improve the design.
- Answer the question: 'How does this set help to convey the ideas and themes of *Kindertransport*?'

**B** Then sketch a contrasting set for the play in a theatre in the round, thrust or traverse configuration. What do you want to emphasise in your design and how can it be used at key moments in the play? Remember to consider:

- Colours and textures
- The scale of the set
- Props/stage furnishings
- Positioning of stage furnishings, set items, entrances and exits on stage
- Levels
- Materials.

Room for projections to suit the scene.

Where Helga and Eva will start the play.

Where Faith's toys are kept.

Train scene.

## TASK 3.23

Imagine that you want to create a set for the play that is highly stylised or expressionistic, and which conveys the mood of the play or the mental state of the characters rather than focusing on a realistic depiction of the attic.

Consider what you would like to emphasise and how you could use design to create your set. For example, you might want to use red to symbolise passion or black to represent death. You might want to have a crack down the centre of your 'attic' to show that the family is fractured. You might want to use screens or drapery to show movements between past and present.

Once you have made your decisions, draw and annotate your design.

# Lighting design

The lighting in *Kindertransport* has many functions, including:

- Establishing the time of day and location
- Focusing the audience's attention on certain characters and events
- Highlighting and increasing the intensity of certain moments
- Creating an atmosphere or mood
- Suggesting a transition from one time or location to another.

## TASK 3.24

A Read this candidate-style response about a lighting design for the first Ratcatcher scene (pages 15–18). Highlight the technical terminology.

For this scene, I want to establish how frightening the Ratcatcher is and to foreshadow the frightening separation between Helga and Eva. I will use small clip-on LED lights placed in the Ratcatcher book so that a bright eerie blue light shines up into Helga and Eva's faces, giving a supernatural feeling to their reading of the book and showing the audience that this section will not be entirely naturalistic. The stage will largely be dark, but lowlights placed downstage will cast large shadows of the Ratcatcher on the upstage wall once he appears. These shadows will grow larger on the line 'the shadow growing legs'. When the Ratcatcher says, 'I will take the heart of your happiness away,' there will be a pinpoint spotlight picking out just his face, making this moment particularly frightening. A swirling gobo will appear at the scene, during which the Ratcatcher will sweep out of the scene and the lights will cross fade up to create a sharp rectangle of light to create the railway carriage.

B With a partner, create a lighting design for the play's ending, from page 85 onwards. Consider:

- Changes in the lighting, such as from the past of Helga and Eva to the present of Faith and Evelyn
- How the lighting will contribute to the mood/atmosphere
- How you will achieve technically the lighting effects you want
- What effect you want your final lighting to have on the audience.

# Sound design

Sound design can be used to establish location or a transition, and is also useful in creating an atmosphere or reflecting the psychological state of a character. Sound design can also add to the tension, comedy or mood of a scene, often having a significant impact on the audience's experience of the play. When writing about sound design, you might consider:

- Volume: How amplified will the sound be? Will it grow louder or quieter?
- Will sound effects and music be pre-recorded or performed live?
- Type of sound: Will the sound be naturalistic or abstract?
- Special effects: Will you use distorting effects such as reverb?
- How the sound or music begins and ends: Should it gradually become louder or will there be a burst of sound? Will it end abruptly or fade out?

## TASK 3.25

Look at the following ideas and note at least one occasion in *Kindertransport* when each sound effect might be appropriate:

A boat's horn    Train noises    A mouth organ being played

The sound of crowds    Music    A whistle blowing

A newsreel voiceover

## TASK 3.26

It is possible that, as a sound designer, you will want to create a symbolic or abstract sound design for the play. Some ideas that a designer could consider are:

- Dramatic classical music while Lil and Evelyn tear up the papers in the attic
- A soundtrack of Hitler's speeches
- Eerie, high violin notes when something frightening happens
- A **motif** or recurring piece of music to accompany certain characters, such as the Ratcatcher or Helga.

Note any possibilities for these abstract sound choices and consider how you might create them and what effect you would like them to have.

## CHECK YOUR LEARNING *Kindertransport*

**Do you know…?**

✓ When *Kindertransport* was written.

✓ In which decades it is set.

✓ Where it takes place, including the different locations.

✓ The genre of the play.

✓ How its contexts might affect choices of costumes, sets and props.

✓ How the relationships between the characters, and the changes to these relationships, could be shown.

✓ Advantages and disadvantages of producing the play in different staging configurations.

✓ How key scenes might be staged.

✓ The performance style (or styles) of the play.

✓ How the performers could use their physical and vocal skills to convey characters' motivations, thoughts and feelings and to impart meaning to the action.

✓ The role of the director and how they influence the way an audience responds to and understands the play.

✓ Key moments a director could use to highlight their concept of the play.

✓ Different design choices to be made, why they are important and how they can be effective.

✓ What impact the play should have on the audience and what messages they should be left with.

### LOOK HERE

For more ideas about lighting and sound production and technical terminology see pages 185, 186 and 224–229.

### EXTENSION

One of the important choices a sound designer might make is the Ratcatcher's music. Using the internet, research different types of music and locate some possible music choices. Decide the following:

- Do you want it to be recorded or performed live?
- Should it to be a single piece of pipe music or for several instruments?
- What volume do you want it to be? Will this change?
- What effect should it have on the audience?

### KEY TERM:

**Motif:** A repeated musical theme or tune, often associated with a character or location.

# MISSING DAN NOLAN
## by Mark Wheeller

The OCR specification identifies editions of the texts that are used to set questions in the 'Drama: Performance and response' (Component 04) examination paper. It is not required that centres use these editions for teaching this component.

Page numbers given here refer to the dbda version of *Missing Dan Nolan*, ISBN-13: 978-1-902843-16-2, one of the editions used by OCR for question setting.

*Missing Dan Nolan* is based on the real case of a teenage boy who went missing after a night's fishing. It is based on the playwright's interviews with the boy's family and friends and the police.

# Plot synopsis
## Section 1

The play begins with four teenage boys – Thom, Joe, George and Dan – setting up outside for a night's fishing. The boys drink from a vodka bottle, except for George, who refuses. The boys begin to 'mess around'. George leaves and Joe is sick. Thom helps Joe, and Dan is left on stage alone.

The scene changes to the Nolan house with Clare, Dan's younger sister, shouting at Dan to turn down his music.

Pauline and Greg, Dan's parents, discuss what might have happened to Dan that night and wonder why, if he fell into the water, his body didn't turn up quickly. Pauline says that 21 months after Dan disappeared a body was discovered in Swanage, many miles from where Dan went missing, and identified as Dan. They suspect 'foul play'.

## Section 2

New Year's Day 2002, the day that Dan went missing. Dan asks his parents if he can go out fishing. Greg warns him that it will be a very cold night. Dan says he will be back 2.30 'at the latest'. Greg agrees he can go and Pauline says that Dan is 'trustworthy'.

Greg tells Dan that someone had asked if he was entering another fishing competition, but Dan doesn't know who he means. Dan says they will try another competition soon.

Pauline recalls that she told the boys to 'stick together' and that those were the last words she said to Dan. Pauline and Clare remember the last time they saw Dan as he prepared to go fishing.

Clare explains that Dan was had planned to go fishing two days earlier, but had been grounded for accidentally breaking the TV when play fighting with his brother Liam.

Pauline describes falling asleep while watching a film.

## Section 3

A slide show of Dan's life, showing him as a baby; fishing at five years old; with his four siblings; a newspaper article about Dan going missing; a letter offering him a place on a Royal Navy course; and a school photograph.

Pauline and Greg discuss how they might never know exactly what happened as no one was with him. They say how loved he was and how they will always miss him.

## Section 4

School. Dan's friend Sarah describes him teasing the girls on the day of the school photographs. Later Dan lends her a textbook. She remembers Dan and his friend Max saying 'Have a good Christmas' to her and she wishes she could have said goodbye 'properly'.

## Section 5

Pauline describes telling Greg that Dan still wasn't home by 2.45. Pauline decides to check on the boys. She returns, saying that their belongings are on the pontoon, but the boys aren't there. Pauline wonders if the boys have fallen in the river. She and Greg go to see Andy, Thom's father. Thom is there. He says that he got back around midnight. He explains that he thought Dan was following behind them.

Pauline calls the police. She and Greg describe the questions they were asked and how the emergency services were investigating by 4.30.

A police liaison officer tells them that they should accept that Dan probably fell into the river, despite there being no proof. They ask the police to check all the CCTV cameras and to make posters. Greg and Pauline say how they are disappointed by the lack of action by the police. The local community did try to help.

Sarah describes the reactions at school to Dan's disappearance and says she won't ever forget him.

## Section 6

Pauline says they have managed to piece together a version of what happened.

The four boys take out a bottle of vodka that they had hidden in a bush. Dan has already drunk some of it. They hide it in Dan's backpack. George doesn't drink, but the others are drinking and 'larking about'. George notices the Gaffer, or nightwatchman, who he thinks is 'creepy'. George goes off with his father. Joe is sick. Dan and Thom go to get some chocolate, but the shop is closed. Dan talks to some boys at the bus stop and Thom returns to Joe.

DS Stewart reports that Dan was observed walking drunkenly down the High Street. Thom decides to take Joe home while Dan goes back to pack up his things. Thom feels that it was a difficult decision, but Joe was 'a lot worse off than Dan'.

Andy speaks of the bad decisions the boys made due to the alcohol. Dan and Thom left Joe alone and then Thom and Joe left Dan alone. He says it was 'one experiment with tragic consequences'.

The characters discuss the mystery of Dan's disappearance and wonder what happened to him because 'people don't just vanish into thin air'.

## End

### Deleted scene

After the end of the play, Wheeler includes a 'deleted' scene, which is not usually seen in performance. In it, Dan's little brother, Conor, imagines a magical way that Dan could return to them.

> **TIP:**
>
> Consider the playwright's original intentions in writing the play. For example, what might Mark Wheeller be saying about missing people, families and friendship?

> **TASK 3.1**
>
> **A** Working in a small group, create a two-minute version of the play, making sure that you cover what you all agree are the most significant events in the plot.
>
> **B** Given your understanding of the play's plot, answer the following questions:
>
> **1** What didn't Dan's parents know about his plans for his night's fishing?
>
> **2** How did Dan's parents feel about the police response to his disappearance?
>
> **3** What difficult decision did Thom have to make and why did he make that particular choice?
>
> **4** What mysteries do Dan's parents feel still remain about Dan's death?

> **TIP:**
>
> You might want to refer to Conor's story in your writing about *Missing Dan Nolan*, but it is not essential to include it.

# Genre

*Missing Dan Nolan* is **documentary theatre** or verbatim theatre. Documentary theatre is based on real events, and verbatim theatre is a type of documentary theatre which uses the actual words of people from interviews or other sources. The playwright, Mark Wheeller, interviewed Dan's parents, sister and others involved with the case and used their words to create the play.

Another documentary aspect of the play is shown in Section 3, where a slide show is used to display evidence of Dan's life through images and descriptions. At the front of the playscript, Wheeller emphasises the respect that must be paid to those who have shared their stories: a special concern for documentary or verbatim theatre.

Other examples of verbatim theatre include *The Riots* by Gillian Slovo, about the 2011 riots in some English cities, *London Road* by Alecky Blythe, in which words about the Ipswich murders were set to music, and Wheeller's own *Too Much Punch for Judy*, a much-performed piece about a drink/drive accident.

# Physical theatre

When performing *Missing Dan Nolan*, most productions use aspects of **physical theatre** and the stage directions support this idea, including the use of 'slow motion' and 'brief choreographed horseplay'. The fluid use of location and time suggests that mime and other physical techniques will assist in telling the story.

---

**TASK 3.2**

In a small group, read pages 14–16, from Pauline's line, 'I wake up every day…' to the end of Section 1. Then answer the following questions:

1 Mark Wheeller has said in the OCR teaching guide that Pauline 'carries most of the story'. From this section of the play, what evidence is there that Pauline is leading the narrative?

2 Wheeller says that a few of Greg's lines 'originate from Pauline', but it made sense that they could be said by both parents. In your opinion, what is the effect of the lines said together? What impression does it give you of the parents?

3 Does knowing that Pauline and Greg are real people who are discussing the loss of a much-loved son affect your feelings about this scene and how it should be performed?

4 Does this scene throw up any questions about Dan and his disappearance that you hope will be resolved by the end of the play? If so, what are they?

---

# Style

The play can be performed in a stylised fashion, using only minimal props and costumes. The first production had only four performers – two male and two female – with multi-rolling and some **gender-blind** casting. Other productions have had larger casts, with more ensemble movement.

A student at Aberystwyth University in an intense physical performance.

**KEY TERMS:**

**Documentary theatre:** Theatre based on real people and events and using documentary material, such as interviews, letters, reports and newspaper articles, often without changing the actual words, in order to create a play.

**Physical theatre:** Theatre in which physical movement, such as mime, choreography and other stylised movement, is important and prominent.

**Gender-blind:** Non-traditional casting where parts usually played by men might be played by a woman, or vice versa.

# Structure

The play is divided into six sections. It is **non-linear**, with time moving fluently in Section 1 from the boys fishing to a playful argument Dan has with his sister to his parents reflecting on when his body was found. Throughout the play, however, suspense is created by withholding the known events of the night until Section 6 and building to a recreation of that night. Section 6 ends with Greg and Pauline still seeking answers to some of their questions posed in Section 1 and trying to find something 'constructive from what is every parent's worst nightmare' (page 46).

## TASK 3.3

From your knowledge and understanding of the play, identify examples of the following structural or stylistic features:

- Physical theatre
- A flashback to an earlier time
- Dialogue or stage directions that are realistic
- Dialogue or stage directions that are non-naturalistic
- A climax, when you feel the play is at its most tense.
- The **resolution** of the play.

## TASK 3.4

Mark Wheeller suggests that the director of the play should be 'imaginative' in order to keep the 'visual interest of the audience' high, without detracting from the words of the speakers. Keeping that in mind, work in a group to read the first two pages of Section 2 (21–22). Then create two different ways of staging and performing the scene in order to create interest for the audience. Some techniques you could attempt are:

- Slow motion
- Sound effects
- Physical comedy (falls, exaggerated reactions, and so on)
- Mime
- Changing pace
- Synchronised movement.

## TASK 3.5

With a partner, read the statements below about *Missing Dan Nolan*. Then put them in order, with the one you agree with most as 1, and the one you agree with least as 5.

- [ ] It is about a family's search for the truth.
- [ ] It highlights the dangers of alcohol.
- [ ] It shows how tragedy can happen suddenly and for no apparent reason.
- [ ] It demonstrates the importance of friends looking after one another.
- [ ] It reveals the reality behind the statistics about 'missing' people and those left behind.

**KEY TERMS:**

**Non-linear:** A sequence that is not arranged in a straightforward or chronological way.

**Resolution:** The solution or bringing together of loose elements of a plot; an ending or conclusion.

**TIP:**

There is no 'right' answer to what *Missing Dan Nolan* is about, but, as you study the play, consider what aspects you find most compelling and how an interpretation of the play could emphasise those.

# Context

The playwright, Mark Wheeller, lives in Southampton, not far from where Dan Nolan went missing. He attended a school near Bristol and later became a teacher, playwright and director. His play *Too Much Punch for Judy* (1987) has been performed internationally over 6000 times. Other popular plays he has written include *Hard to Swallow* (1991), about anorexia, and *I Love You, Mum – I Promise I Won't Die* (2017), about a tragic death due to recreational drug use. These plays deal with real cases and raise important issues. Wheeller has a great interest in music, both as used within his documentary plays and in his original musicals. His play *Can You Hear Me Major Tom?* (2017) features interviews with fans of David Bowie to investigate his influence on their lives and their reactions to his death.

## Historical context

On New Year's Day 2002, Dan Nolan, a 14-year-old boy from the village of Hamble in Hampshire, went missing after going night-fishing with friends. Hamble is near Southampton, on the River Hamble. Although many assumed that Dan might have, after an evening drinking, slipped and drowned in the freezing water, there was no sign of his body for many months. Although the case did not initially attract national attention, the Hamble community took part in searches, posters were distributed and a reward was offered for Dan's safe return. In May 2003, a human foot was discovered on a beach near Swanage and it was determined to be Dan's. Although the family accepts that this means that Dan is dead, they feel that the circumstances of his death remain a mystery.

In his introduction to the play, Wheeller writes about seeing a stall with posters proclaiming 'Dan Nolan MISSING' outside a local Tesco. The empathy he felt for the parents led him to write the play, both to raise issues that the case brought up and to help the Nolans gain more attention for Dan's missing status. Wheeller points out that the National Missing Persons Helpline receives 100,000 calls a year. Although most cases are resolved, as many as 30 per cent remain a mystery. Only a handful of these cases receive national attention or retain media interest beyond the initial disappearance. Among the most famous unsolved missing cases are Madeleine McCann, who disappeared, aged 3, while on holiday in Portugal, Ben Needham, a toddler who disappeared on Kos in 1991, and Suzy Lamplugh, a 25-year-old estate agent who went missing in 1986.

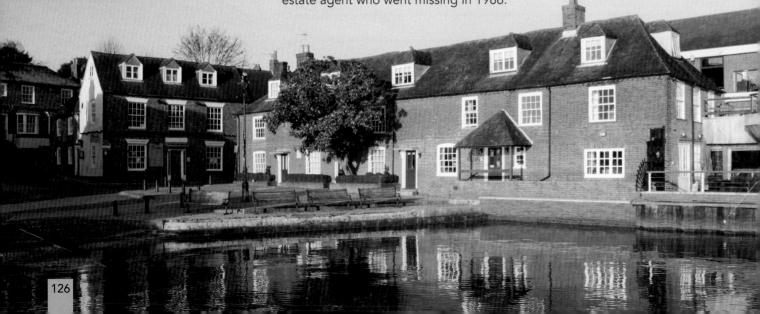

Hamble quayside.

# Cultural context

Wheeller's interest in music is shown throughout the play with his choices of songs to underscore, support and develop the action of the play. He suggests opening the play with Sinead O'Connor's haunting version of the Christmas carol 'Silent Night' and then switching to a song with a 'Skate Punk feel'. The change from slow, sombre, seasonal music to raucous, punk-inspired rock establishes both the post-Christmas setting and the partying mood of the boys. Dan is shown head-banging to the loud music. In contrast, he teases Clare for listening to Westlife, a mainstream boy band. This is an effective way of using music to provide quick insight into the characters.

Mark Wheeller is a champion of youth theatre, and *Missing Dan Nolan* was written to be performed by Oaklands Youth Theatre. For many years, he has written plays with students and youth theatre groups in mind, often developing the work with the performers. Youth theatre is popular throughout the UK, where there are many regional festivals and competitions. His plays feature ensemble work and often have the flexibility to be played by different sized groups.

# Social context

Hamble is a close-knit community where Dan had lived his whole life. He had known his friends George, Joe and Thom from an early age. The familiarity of the community is emphasised in the script when on the night Dan goes missing he is seen by so many people who know him. His parents know his friends well and are able to quickly walk over to Thom's house as he 'only lived two doors away'.

The Nolans, consisting of the two parents and five children, are presented as a happy and loving family. It is stressed that Dan is a 'normal' boy, attending high school and taking part in local activities. His sister lists his interests, often appropriate to their location, as: 'swimming, sailing, fishing canoeing. Sea Scouts…' (page 24). His dream was to be an officer in the Royal Navy.

Travis Barker from Blink 182, a skate-punk band that Dan might have enjoyed.

A Hamble street.

Royal Navy Sea Cadets take part in a Remembrance Day parade.

## EXTENSION

- Research the music mentioned in the play and think about how it could be used to establish aspects of the play's context.
- Research the geography of Hamble and how it could influence a design of the production.
- Find out about the National Missing Persons Helpline and its work.
- Investigate the work of the Oaklands Youth Theatre and other youth theatre groups to see if any of their performance choices could influence your concept of the play.

Make a note of anything that helps your understanding of the play and how it could be staged or designed.

## TASK 3.6

Look at the following list of key moments from the play and write a few sentences about each to explain what it tells you about the social or historical context of the play. (The first one has been completed for you.)

1 Dan and his friends go night-fishing on New Year's Day.
   *In Hamble, it was not considered unusual for teenage boys to go out fishing at night. The parents had some concerns, especially about the weather, but the pontoon was nearby and the boys had been doing this activity for the past year, so they allowed them to go.*

2 Dan and his parents have known his friends for many years.

3 It was a week before the police put up any missing posters and it took 13 months for Dan's disappearance to become a full criminal investigation.

4 Pauline and Greg want to make a difference.

**TIP:**

In your exam questions, alternative wording might be used instead of 'context', such as 'reflect the time in which the play was written' or 'show when and where the play is set'.

When depicting the context of the play there are a number of factors to consider, such as:

- Fashions of the time of the time and location (such as the Henri Lloyd sailing jacket Dan was wearing)
- The influence of the culture of the time, such as music, art, television, films and sport
- The backgrounds and occupations of the characters
- The ages of the characters
- Props that characters might use
- Types of housing and furnishings that families might have.

## Costumes and props in context

In ensemble youth theatre productions, there is often a basic costume that the performers wear, such as black T-shirts or bright shirts combined with black trousers or jeans. In the Oaklands Youth Theatre Production, the cast wore T-shirts with the missing poster of Dan printed on them. Other productions might aim for more conventional costumes, suitable to the age and/or occupations of the characters. Some productions use a combination of non-naturalistic and naturalistic costumes. Below are some additional contextual costume items or props that might be appropriate:

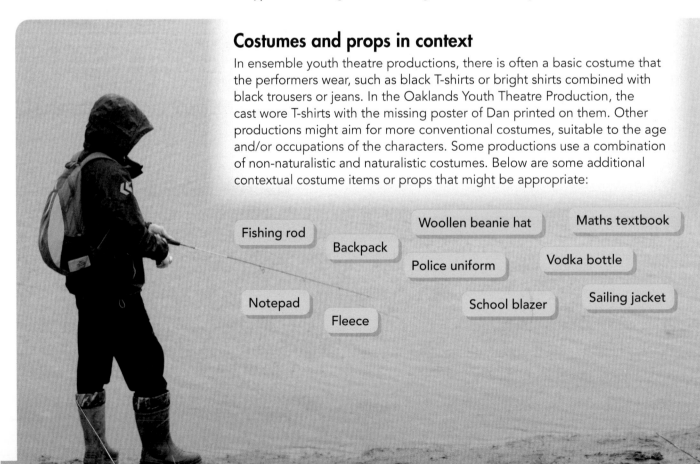

Fishing rod

Backpack

Woollen beanie hat

Maths textbook

Police uniform

Vodka bottle

Notepad

School blazer

Sailing jacket

Fleece

## TASK 3.7

**A** Work with a partner to decide how each prop or costume item listed on the previous page could be used in the play. Make a note of what it tells you, and can inform an audience, about the context of the play.

**B** Draw a costume sketch for Dan. Remember to include any accessories and hair ideas that would help to convey the character and his context.

**TIP:**

There is no one set way the characters should be costumed, but it is worth thinking about how you could differentiate between them.

## Set design in context

In considering the context of the play and how it could be conveyed in a set, a designer might explore how the village of Hamble could be shown. Some other points to think about are:

- What key items could be used to give an impression of the Nolan house, such as chairs, cushions and the television?
- How could outdoor settings be recreated, including where the boys are fishing?
- How could the school be presented, such as the lockers and the school photography session?

**TIP:**

The play was written very shortly after the time it is set, so the contexts are the same.

## TASK 3.8

Write two paragraphs in answer to the following question: 'Describe how you could show the social or historical context of the play by your design choices for the set of the play.'

WHAT THE SPECIFICATION SAYS...

Learners must know and understand:

- How meaning is communicated through:
  - An actor's vocal and physical interpretation of character.

# Interpretations of key characters

You must demonstrate that you understand the main characters in the play, including different ways in which they could be interpreted.

## The Nolans

### Pauline

Dan's mother. A concerned mother of five. She tells the boys to stick together. She is alarmed when she discovers that Dan isn't home and goes out to find him. Pauline is worried that he has been abducted and that the police aren't doing everything they could to help.

### Greg

Dan's father, Pauline's husband. He allows Dan to go night-fishing, but worries about the weather. At first, he isn't as concerned as Pauline that Dan hasn't come back on time, but he becomes alarmed when he discovers he isn't with his friends and takes the lead in questioning Thom.

### Dan

A popular, lively 14 year old who mysteriously goes missing on New Year's Day. He is the oldest of five children and wants to join the navy as an officer. He has a mischievous side and is the one who has brought the vodka on the fishing trip.

### Clare

Dan's sister, 13 years old (18 months younger than Dan). She speaks affectionately of Dan to whom she was just beginning to feel close.

### Liam

Dan's brother. Has a cushion fight with Dan and they smash the television. Has to pick up dog poo with Dan as a punishment.

### Patrick and Conor

Dan's brothers who are mentioned. Neither speak in the play, although Conor's 'story' appears in the deleted scene.

# The friends

## George

Fourteen years old. Possibly a little more serious than his friends. He doesn't drink with the other boys, and his father is said to be 'strict'. His father picks him up at a relatively early time, leaving the three others. George feels guilty that he didn't stay with the other boys or insist that Dan come home with him.

## Thom

Fifteen years old. Appears to be less drunk than Joe. Thom and Dan leave Joe sleeping on a bench in order to try to buy some chocolate. Later, Thom decides to take Joe home, leaving Dan behind. He speaks of the difficulty he has accepting Dan's disappearance.

## Joe

Fourteen years old. He gets very drunk and is taken home by Thom.

## Andy

Thom's father. He believes that the vodka is to blame for the tragedy. He also feels that 'part of our Thom disappeared' when Dan did.

# School

## Sarah

A friend of Dan's, who is fond of him. She wishes they could have 'said goodbye properly'. She says that he made her laugh and that she will never forget him.

## Max

Dan's locker partner, who, with Dan, teases the girls at the school photography session and is pushed over on the final day of term. He and Dan wish Sarah a good Christmas.

## Lorna

Sarah's friend who complains about her school photograph.

# Police

## Police Liaison Officer

As remembered by Pauline, the PLO quickly assumes that Dan slipped into the river, and is slow to take any action.

## DS Stewart

The detective in charge of the investigation. In Section 6, he recounts the known facts of the case.

## TASK 3.9

Select the six characters who you think are the most important in the play. Then select one line for each chosen character. Write one sentence explaining its importance in understanding the character and another one or two on how it could be delivered by the actor. What physical and vocal skills would be most effective?

## KEY TERMS:

**Register:** How formal or informal language is, or language used for a particular purpose or in a certain setting, such as the language of medicine or law. Informal language tends to use less precise pronunciation and might include more slang.

**Repressing:** Hiding, pushing down, controlling or preventing something, such as a thought or emotion.

**Choral speaking:** Several characters delivering lines in unison, as in a choir.

# Use of vocal skills

*Missing Dan Nolan* offers a number of vocal choices for the performers. Actors will need to decide if they are going to adopt a Hampshire accent for the characters, or make another regional choice, or a less geographically specific accent. If multi-rolling, a performer might need to decide how their voice changes when transforming from a teenage character to an adult character. The characters in official roles, such as the Detective Sergeant, might use a certain tone and **register** in order to convey their authority.

The characters' voices will also be influenced by the situations they are in and the emotions they express or **repress**. Mark Wheeller also suggests moments when voices could be used in a non-naturalistic way, such as Dan and his brother speaking in 'slow-motion voices' when they smash the television, Greg ranting in a 'gobbledygook style language' (page 21), or **choral speaking**.

Vocal skills that an actors might consider include:

**Accent and dialect** / **Pace** / **Volume** / **Pitch**

**Pauses and timing** / **Intonation** / **Phrasing** / **Emotional range**

## TASK 3.10

With a partner, experiment with vocal skills to interpret the following lines. Note down the choices you make, including reasons.

Dan: Don't worry! (page 18)

Pauline and Greg: 'Stick together…' (page 20)

Clare: Plans that none of us, at that time, were aware of… (page 22)

Joe: Fine… whatever. What's the time? (page 41)

DS Stewart: Witnesses talked about Daniel Nolan swaying around discussing the quantity of alcohol he'd drunk. (page 44)

## TASK 3.11

For each key character below, give three examples of different vocal skills that the actor playing the role could use. Justify each of your choices by explaining why it is appropriate. (Examples have been given for Dan.)

- **Pauline**
- **Greg**
- **Sarah**
- **Clare**.

| Character | Vocal skill | When vocal skill could be displayed | Details and justification |
|---|---|---|---|
| Dan | **Volume**: Shouting. | Dan's first line (page 13). | He shouts this over his loud music. This is a somewhat comic introduction to Dan, as he is having to shout because he can't hear Clare and because he's playing his music so loud. This makes for a bold introduction to his teenage character. |
| | **Tone** and **pitch**: Teasing/higher. | Section 4 (page 27). | Dan is mocking the girls and imitating their voices by putting on a high, over-the-top 'feminine' voice. He raises his pitch and exaggerates 'my hair'. This shows the light, humourous side to his character. |
| | **Phrasing/ diction**: Hesitation, slurring words. | Section 6 (page 40). | That Dan is beginning to be drunk could be hinted by slurring his words and stumbling or hesitating on his words when he is talking to George. He might blurt out, 'You weirdo!' in a drunken way. |

# Use of physical skills

Physical skills are particularly important in *Missing Dan Nolan* due to its 'physical theatre' style. In addition, physical skills could be used to reflect the different techniques being used to tell the story: re-enactments, supporting monologues and choreographed movement to music. Performers could explore how physical skills might indicate aspects of their characters: a detective sergeant's posture, for example, is likely to be different from that of a 'typical' teenager. A teenager might move differently when messing around with his mates rather from when at home in front of parents.

Physical skills that actors might consider include:

**Posture** **Movement** **Pace** **Gestures**
**Facial expressions** **Proxemics** **Eye contact**

**LOOK HERE**

See pages 200–202 for rehearsal techniques for exploring characterisation and practising performance skills.

## TASK 3.12

**A** In a small group, read the first page of Section 1 (page 13). Discuss:

- How realistic or stylised you feel this section should be
- How physical skills could help to introduce Dan to the audience
- What effect this section should have on the audience.

**B** Then experiment with the following:

- Each of the boys assumes a still image after they enter. Dan enters last and creates an image that shows he is the key figure in the play.
- The boys enter at a normal pace and then move into slow motion when the vodka bottle is revealed, to give it special emphasis.
- The group moves from slow motion to double time when they begin to 'mess around'.
- A change in movement that makes it clear that Dan is now in the family home when he and Clare are speaking and the mood is different.

As you experiment with different physical skills, note which, in your opinion, are most effective and when these physical skills might be used. For example, on what lines might the characters move, use a prop, make a gesture or change facial expression?

**C** Now read the end of Section 1 (pages 14–16), which might seem very different from the previous page. Experiment with your physical skills for this section, considering the following:

- How can Greg and Pauline move to show that they work together as a couple?
- What are the proxemics, in relation to each other and to the audience?
- Are their movements or **mannerisms** similar to or different from each other?
- Will they make eye contact with the audience or each other?
- How might they move at the end of the scene to signal that they are moving on to a new section of the drama?

**D** Finally, compare Dan's and Pauline's movements in the first two Sections of the play. Notice:

- Posture and levels
- Movement and ways of walking
- Pace and pauses
- Gestures
- Facial expressions
- Proxemics
- Eye contact.

**KEY TERM:**

**Mannerism:** A movement or habit that a person does repeatedly, such as a hand gesture or a facial expression, perhaps without knowing they are doing it.

## TASK 3.13

For each character listed below, give at least three examples of how they could use their physical skills in the play. Justify each of your choices. (Examples have been given for Sarah.)

- **Dan**
- **Pauline**
- **Thom**.

| Character | Physical skill | When physical skill could be displayed | Details and justification |
|---|---|---|---|
| Sarah | **Posture**: To show a change from when she is speaking directly to the audience to when she is larking about with her friends. | Section 4. | Sarah is a friend of Dan's whose role is to show what he was like at school. She stands upright, looking directly at the audience for her first line, but then her posture will be more casual when she interacts with her friends. Her weight is more off-centre and she raises her shoulders, laughing. |
| | **Gesture**. | Saying goodbye to Dan and Max. | Sarah is reluctant to say goodbye to Dan, perhaps wishing for a moment alone with him or for the goodbye to have more significance. Her gesture will be a slow wave of the hand. |
| | **Facial expression** and **proxemics**. | The end of Section 4. | When Dan returns, her eyes open wide in surprise and she smiles, as this is what she had hoped for. The two characters stand very close to each other, with Dan perhaps brushing her cheek with his hand, which she reacts to by closing her eyes. This shows an idealised version of a connection between them. |

# Stage directions

In addition to the play's dialogue, a way for the playwright to convey what a character is doing, thinking and feeling is through stage directions. For example:

Page 40: Dan runs round George and pretends to draw a huge knife on him... then suddenly stops in his tracks.

Page 44: Thom shows through his movement the dilemma he is in. He veers towards Joe but remains looking at Dan. Greg moves into his path. Thom still looking towards Dan bumps into Greg prompting him to stop speaking. Thom backs off a little.

Page 45: Pauline and Greg move to the Chocolate truffle cake and put a candle in it. Greg lights the candle.

## TASK 3.14

**A** In a small group, perform each of the stage directions given on the previous page.

**B** Discuss and write down what you believe each character is thinking and feeling. For example, how might George feel when Dan pretends to draw a knife on him?

**C** Talk about what the audience learns about the character from the stage directions. For example, what do they tell the audience about Thom's dilemma and Greg's attitude to the choice he made?

## TASK 3.15

**A** Read the extract below from a candidate-style response about the stage directions at the beginning of the play. Highlight three details that show how the stage directions help the audience to better understand the characters and their relationships.

The opening stage directions create interest in the story to follow. It is an abbreviated version of the boy's night out that will be fully explained in the final section of the play. The stage directions indicate that it is 'lit as though by moonlight', establishing the night-time setting, and the 'slow motion' taking out of the bottle shows how fateful that decision was. The friendly teenage relationship between the boys is established when they 'mess around' and join in each others' 'japes'. When Joe is 'sick', the mood could change. It is important that 'Dan remains on his own' as this is central to the mystery of his disappearance and the message his parents want to make about young people sticking together. The musical choice suggests an otherworldly quality at the beginning, which changes to recognisable music that could cause the boys to be relatable to a teenage audience.

**B** Focusing on stage directions in Section 2 (pages 21–22), make notes about what the audience learns about characters and the play's themes from these stage directions.

- Can you identify any stage directions that could create comedy?
- Any which suggest a change in mood?
- What effect would this scene, including its stage directions, have on an audience?

**TIP:**

Remember that communication is at the heart of drama. Always consider what the performance and staging choices you make are communicating to the audience. Do they create…

- Sympathy?
- Fear?
- Excitement?
- Suspense?
- Pity?
- Comedy?
- Greater understanding?

# Use of space

As part of their characterisation, actors might use the stage space in many different ways, including:

| Levels | Proxemics | Positioning on stage |
| Entrances and exits | Use of the 'fourth wall' |

In addition, the type of staging configuration and the set design could influence the actors' use of space.

Below is a candidate-style response about performing Section 3 on a thrust stage, and the benefits and drawbacks of that staging configuration.

[1] Opens with some understanding of the play and characters.

[2] Explains an advantage of thrust staging.

[3] Identifies a second advantage of thrust staging, though could identify when in the script this would be effective.

[4] Identifies a disadvantage of thrust staging.

[5] Identifies a second disadvantage and uses correct terminology ('blocking').

[6] Suggests a positive effect created by the use of traverse staging and the impact on the audience.

In Section 3, Dan's family provide a short biography of his life, with the help of a slide show. It is an important scene for portraying Dan as a well-rounded character and providing a greater understanding of how his family are feeling. [1] An advantage of a thrust stage for this scene, is that, even though there is an audience around three sides of the thrust portion of the stage, the upstage section could be used for projections. I would have Pauline and Greg stood at either side of the screen, sharing the images with the audience, with Clare sat cross-legged to one side. [2] Another advantage of the thrust space is that the area closer to the audience gives a sense of interaction and intimacy. Therefore when Clare exits and the conversation becomes less 'public' and more 'private', Pauline could move downstage towards the audience, but lost in her own concerns. As she moves around this downstage area, the audience could see her facial expression and Greg's concern as he follows her. [3]

A disadvantage of a thrust stage is that sightlines can be tricky, especially on the far sides. The screen could not be simply placed centre stage as a large portion of the audience wouldn't see it. [4] Another disadvantage is that audience members sees the show from different angles so blocking a pleasing stage picture for the final moment could be more demanding. [5]

Overall, a thrust stage could provide a useful staging configuration for the technical demands of the scene and the intimacy of the acting at the end of the scene, making it visually interesting and engaging for the audience. [6]

## TASK 3.16

A Working in a small group, experiment with staging the following scenes in different staging configurations:
- The play's opening (pages 13–14)
- Discovery that Dan isn't home (pages 29–32)
- The boys fishing (pages 38–40)
- The scene with DS Stewart (pages 42–44).

B Then, note at least two advantages and two disadvantages of performing each scene in the staging configurations described on pages 8–11.

### TIP:

If an exam question asks for advantages and disadvantages, you need to discuss at least two of each. Similarly, if a question asks for examples, you must offer more than one.

### WHAT THE SPECIFICATION SAYS...

Learners must know and understand:
- How meaning is communicated through:
  - The use of performance space and spatial relationships on stage
  - The relationship between performers and audience
  - The design of: set, props, costume, lighting and sound
  - An actor's vocal and physical interpretation of character
  - The use of performance conventions
- How performance styles affect direction, acting and design.

# Directorial choices

A director of *Missing Dan Nolan* needs to consider:
- How to guide the actors' physical and vocal choices
- How to use design to reinforce the play's meaning and impact
- How key moments of the play might be staged
- The style of the play and use of performance conventions
- The effect that the play should have on the audience.

## TASK 3.17

**A** Working in a small group, read Section 6, from the point when George leaves (page 41) to Thom saying he feels guilty (page 44.) Discuss the impact you want this scene to have. For example, do want to create suspense or tension about what the boys are going to do? How will you make clear for the audience the different shifts between the re-enactment of events and DS Stewart's report?

**B** Experiment with the following:

- Changing pace and volume to increase interest in the scene
- Using performance conventions or design to establish that some of the action is taking place the night when Dan disappeared and some is a later report by DS Stewart.

- Different ways of using the stage space. For example, will you show the boys moving around different parts of the stage to show their journey around the town or will they stay in the same place? Will DS Stewart be separate from the boys or walk among them?
- Using sound or lighting to heighten a mood or underscore a key moment.
- Having the actors use their physical and vocal skills to show the situations in which they find themselves. For example, will the boys be still when DS Stewart is speaking, or will they be acting out what he says? Will their emotions and motivations change throughout the scene?

**C** Now write a paragraph in response to the question: 'As a director, how would you stage part of Section 6 to create a specific impact on the audience?'

## TASK 3.18

Below are excerpts from two candidate-style responses about staging the beginning of Section 6. Decide how well you feel the writers have explained and justified their ideas. Highlight the following:

- Clear ideas about what they want to achieve
- Specific examples from the play
- Correct use of theatrical terminology
- Understanding of how a certain impact on the audience can be achieved.

My minimalistic version will depend largely on the skill of the actors and physical theatre techniques to convey the story. For the opening of the section, it is important for the audience to understand that the mood is, at first, innocent and playful. They should like and identify with the boys. I will have the boys leap on stage and assume a comic pose when they shout their names. Throughout, I will use still images, as if piecing together what happened like a series of photographs. The boys will have their arms around each other and will say the line 'Four boys... out for a night...' in chorus. Instead of having a vodka bottle prop, the actor will mime holding up a bottle, and a pinspot light will flash onto his hand. All the boys will, in slow motion, crane their necks to look at this bottle, which will be so important. This will create anticipation, but be followed by the 'choreographed horseplay'.

I will stage my production in the round and have the audience sitting around the playing area on cushions, so that they feel close to the action, as if spending time with their friends. Pauline will start this section centre stage, and the boys will enter through different sections of the audience, laughing and joking as they push past. This interaction will make the audience feel involved and increase the sense of loss when Dan disappears. For the choreographed horseplay, the boys will move in slow motion, performing elaborate comic lifts and climbing on top of each other. When they begin the narration, each will break out of the tight group and address a particular part of the audience, except for Dan, who will have replaced Pauline centre stage and mime fishing. The other three boys will be on the outside edge of the stage, with their backs to Dan, symbolic of their having left him.

**TIP:**

There is no one right way of interpreting this or any other scene. The choices you make, however, must be rooted in your understanding of the play and how theatre works.

WHAT THE SPECIFICATION SAYS...

Learners must know and understand:

- How meaning is communicated through:
  - The design of: set, props, costume, lighting and sound.

# Design choices

Costume, set, lighting and sound design all contribute to the impact of *Missing Dan Nolan*. They are vital in presenting the play's setting, meaning and interpretation. For example, if all the characters are dressed identically, you might be making the point that this is an ensemble company where everyone is equally responsible for telling the story. If you then add costume items, you might be pointing out a character's job or social role. If only Dan is in full costume, that signifies his importance in the play, as well as the importance of what he was wearing that night.

The setting might be complex and multi-levelled or minimal. You might use technology or have a deliberately simple and straightforward way of conveying the story. Sound can be used to establish location and create atmosphere or tension. Lighting can focus attention on certain characters and suggest a certain mood or location.

## Costume design

When writing about costumes, it is important to consider what the costume tells the audience about the character's role and personality. It is useful to consider:

**Period and context**  **Colour**  **Fabric**  **Silhouette**
**Fit**  **Condition**  **Headwear and footwear**  **Make-up and hair**

Below is an excerpt from a candidate-style response demonstrating one possible approach to Sarah's costume.

[1] Shows understanding of the character and their importance in the play.

[2] Describes costume, including colour and fabric.

[3] Describes how costume could be adapted for different characters.

[4] Describes and justifies details.

[5] Describes and justifies fabric, trim (buttons) and fit.

[6] Considers accessories and hairstyle and justifies choices.

[8] Considers make-up and the overall effect of the costume.

In my production of the play, the same performer will play Sarah, Clare and Thom, so it is important that the costume can be adapted easily for each character.

Although Sarah does not have a large role, she is important for showing another side of Dan and the impact he had on his school friends. [1] To emphasise that she is a school friend, I would dress Sarah in a school uniform of grey trousers, with a grey wool long-sleeve jumper, white cotton shirt and a navy wool school blazer. [2] The blazer could be removed or replaced when the performer is playing Clare or Thom. [3] I will design a red, blue and gold boat on rolling waves for the badge on the blazer, which will subtly reinforce the play's images of water and boats. [4] The blazer will be made of a good-quality wool, have gold buttons and be well-fitted, suggesting the school's high standards. [5] Sarah has lace-up black school shoes. She will wear her hair up in a high, neat ponytail, which could easily be tucked into a cap when she is playing Thom. [6] As Sarah, she will wear light make-up, a subtle pink lipstick and a natural foundation.

The impression of Sarah should be of a studious, kind girl who tries to do the right thing at all times. [7]

## TASK 3.19

Here is a sketch of one possible interpretation of a costume for Pauline.

Draw your own costume designs for the following characters:

- **DS Stewart**
- **Greg**
- **Joe**
- **Dan.**

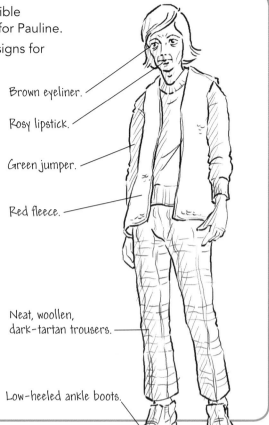

Brown eyeliner.

Rosy lipstick.

Green jumper.

Red fleece.

Neat, woollen, dark-tartan trousers.

Low-heeled ankle boots.

**TIP:**

These are just some ideas for costumes for Sarah and Pauline. Other designers have made other choices, such as having an identical ensemble outfit for all the characters.

# Set design

The set designer of *Missing Dan Nolan* could help to convey the play's meaning through establishing and/or emphasising:

- Naturalistic aspects of the play in realistic props and set dressings
- Non-naturalistic aspects of the play by symbolically suggesting water, families or loss
- A particular relationship between the audience and the performers, by the use of proxemics or levels
- The period of the play and the passage of time through certain props or set furnishings.

## TASK 3.20

Draw a set for a theatre in the round, thrust or end on configuration. What do you want to emphasise in your design and how can it be used at key moments in the play? Consider:

- Colours, textures and materials
- The scale of the set
- Levels and positions
- Props and stage furnishings.

## TASK 3.21

Imagine that you want to create a set that is highly stylised or expressionistic to convey themes of missing people or loss, or the mood of the play.

Consider what to emphasise and how you could create your set. For example, you could have the whole set in black and white, perhaps with bands of red, in the style of a 'missing' poster or to symbolise the change from light to dark in the Nolans' life. A crack down the centre of the set could suggest the before and after of the family's life. Or you could surround the set with water to show the location of the play and the danger of the water. You could project maps charting the travels of the boys on the night.

Once you have decided, draw and annotate your design.

# Lighting design

The lighting in *Missing Dan Nolan* has many functions, including:

- Establishing the time of day and location
- Focusing the audience's attention on certain characters or events
- Highlighting and increasing the intensity of certain moments
- Creating an atmosphere or mood
- Suggesting a transition from one time or location to another.

## TASK 3.22

**A** Read the candidate-style response below, which describes a lighting design for the end of the play, from page 44 to the end. Highlight the technical terminology used.

For this section, there are three moments in particular that I want to highlight with my lighting design: Thom being torn between going with Joe or Dan; Pauline and Greg's imagining what could have happened to Dan; and the sad ending when Dan disappears. For the moment when Thom makes his decision, I will have three large pools on the stage floor created by profile spots. Each of the boys will be stood in one of the pools of light, while the rest of the stage is in near darkness. When Thom tries to move towards Joe, Greg will move from the darkness into Thom's spotlight. When Thom makes his decision, he will move into Joe's spotlight and Dan's will gradually fade to darkness. Greg's spotlight will become smaller and focus on his anguished face.

Later, when Pauline and Greg are imagining what might have happened to Dan, there will be a brief use of strobe lights to show the quickly mimed 'murder' of Dan. This will suggest the horror of what they suspect might have happened. Greg will light the practical candle on the cake and this will cast a slight upward light onto their faces.

At the play's end, foggers attached to the lighting rig and low angle lights will create the effect of a silver mist on water. Dan will walk into this mist as the lights gradually fade to black out. The audience should feel the loss of Dan and how his family will always miss him.

**B** With a partner, create a lighting design for the play's beginning (pages 13–16). Consider:

- Changes in the lighting, such as alterations to suggest moves from outside to inside
- How the lighting will contribute to the mood or atmosphere
- How you will achieve technically the lighting effects that you want
- What effect you want your final lighting to have on the audience.

# Sound design

Sound can establish location or a transition, create atmosphere or reflect the **psychological** state of a character. Sound design can also add to the tension, comedy or mood of a scene, often having a significant impact on the audience's experience. When writing about sound design, consider:

- Volume: How amplified will the sound be? Will it grow louder or quieter?
- Will sound effects and music be pre-recorded or performed live?
- Type of sound: Will it be naturalistic or abstract?
- Special effects: Will you use distorting effects such as reverb?
- How the sound or music begins and ends: Will it end abruptly or fade out?

## TASK 3.24

Throughout the play, Wheeller gives song choices, but says they are 'suggestions only'. As you read the play, listen to the songs he mentions.

Identify at least three songs for which you could suggest alternatives. Explain and justify your choices.

## TASK 3.25

A designer might want to create a symbolic or abstract sound design for the play. Some ideas to consider are:

- A low cello piece to suggest sad moments
- A **motif** or recurring piece of music to accompany certain characters such as Dan, Clare or Sarah
- A drum beat to highlight each key event described by DS Stewart or each time a sip of alcohol is taken
- A loudly ticking clock, to suggest the passing of time
- Recurring sounds of water lapping against a shore.

Note where in the script there are possibilities for these abstract sound choices and explain what effect you would like to create with them.

## CHECK YOUR LEARNING *Missing Dan Nolan*

### Do you know...?

✓ When *Missing Dan Nolan* was written.

✓ When and where it is set, including specific locations.

✓ How its contexts might affect choices of costume, sound, set and props.

✓ How the relationships between the characters could be shown.

✓ Advantages and disadvantages of producing the play in different staging configurations.

✓ How key scenes might be staged.

✓ How the performers could use their physical and vocal skills to convey characters' motivations, thoughts and feelings and to impart meaning.

✓ Key moments a director could use to highlight their concept of the play.

✓ Different design choices that could be made.

✓ What impact the play should have and the messages it should present.

 **LOOK HERE**

For more ideas about sound and lighting production and technical vocabulary see pages 185, 186 and 224–229.

## TASK 3.23

Look at the following ideas and note at least one occasion in the play when each sound might be appropriate:

- Loud music
- A television programme
- Classical music
- Water lapping
- Voices from a pub
- A car horn
- Breaking glass.

## KEY TERMS:

**Psychological:** Referring to a mental or emotional state and the reasons behind it.

**Motif:** A repeated musical theme or tune, often associated with a character or location.

## EXTENSION

At the beginning of the script (page 13), Mark Wheeller suggests that stage right there is a 'small selection of musical instruments, used during the play'. Find at least three moments when you think live music would contribute to the play. Write a composition or brief instructions for what would be played, when and how (softly, loudly, quickly and so on). Indicate what musical instruments could be used and the effect you hope to create.

# MISTERMAN
## by Enda Walsh

The OCR specification identifies editions of the texts that are used to set questions in the 'Drama: Performance and response' (Component 04) examination paper. It is not required that centres use these editions for teaching this component.

Page numbers given in this chapter refer to the Nick Hern Books version of *Misterman*, ISBN-13: 978-1-84842-263-6, one of the editions used by OCR for question setting.

# Plot synopsis

*Misterman* tells the story of a crucial day in the life of Thomas Magill, a troubled, isolated, 33-year-old man living in a small Irish town, Inishfree.

The play opens with Thomas in a huge warehouse or industrial building preparing his breakfast, which is disturbed by a Doris Day song coming from one of his tape players. Thomas attempts to stop the music by hitting the tape player with a hammer. When it continues to play, he tapes teddy bears over his ears to block the sound. Once the tape recorder stops, he takes off the 'teddy-bear mufflers' and begins working with two reel-to-reel tape machines.

On the tape players there are voices of local people, such as Simple Eamon Moran, Dwain Flynn and Mrs O'Donnell. Mrs O'Donnell's voice says Thomas has blood on his face and he should go home.

Thomas straps on his portable tape recorder, 'like a holster' and closes his eyes. In the blackout that follows, he begins speaking of mystical religious events. The lights fade up to reveal a number of playing areas.

Thomas plays a recording of his Mammy's voice. He holds a conversation with the recording, discussing breakfast as he eats it. The voice asks for a 'sugary surprise' from Centra. He mimes stepping outside and plays outside sound effects. He enacts a conversation between Mrs O'Leary and himself. Mrs O'Leary complains about her son, Timmy. Thomas offers to have a word with Timmy. He makes a note: 'Timmy O'Leary. Cleanliness.'

Thomas adopts the voice of Dwain Flynn who teases Thomas about making notes and complains about Denis Boyle, who threw him out for bad language. 'Dwain' smacks Thomas and calls him a 'headcase'. Thomas notes: 'Dwain Flynn. Profanity.' On the tape player, Roger the dog begins barking.

Thomas then creates a conversation with Mr McAnerny who calls him 'Mister Weatherman' and 'Misterman'. He asks Thomas if he will be going to the community dance that evening. Thomas says he's going to the cemetery and McAnerny remembers Thomas's father, who ran a grocery story. Thomas imagines being an angel in heaven. Thomas notes: 'Charlie McAnerny. Immodesty.' McAnerny's recorded voice tells him, 'This behaviour has to stop.' The dog is barking and Thomas screams at it to go away.

An intense Thomas Keegan as Thomas in Solas Nua's production.

Thomas reveals a large piece of plywood with crosses made from drinks cans. He enters the 'cemetery' and begins speaking to his father's grave, sharing gossip with 'Daddy'.

Thomas enacts a conversation with Simple Eamon Moran, with whom he imagines having a cup of tea. They speak about how they could form a team to save the town – 'Crusaders is what we'd be!' The friendly atmosphere changes when Thomas sees a calendar with a photograph of a naked woman on Eamon's garage wall. Thomas runs away. The barking Roger chases him. Thomas punches and kicks the dog, killing it.

Thomas imagines Mrs Cleary's Café. He wants cheesecake, but Mrs Cleary apparently only wants to flirt and dance with him. Thomas notes: 'Mrs Cleary. Indecent.' Mrs Heffernan reports that the dog is lying dead in the road.

Thomas is mesmerised by Edel, a beautiful young girl. He feels she is an angel who will change Inishfree, which is being 'altered by her hope'.

Thomas voices Mrs O'Donnell, who says that Eamon has told people that Thomas killed Roger. She warns Thomas that her husband will take his revenge. On the tape, Mrs O'Donnell asks if it is true that he killed the dog and Thomas says he doesn't know. Thomas smashes one of the reel-to-reel tape machines.

Thomas returns home and massages a table which he uses as a substitute for his mother. He has a row with Mammy because she refuses to keep out the cold with extra layers of clothing and Thomas can't cope with the cost of heating her room. He asks for respect from Mammy and Trixie, their cat, whose kittens he has drowned. Dogs bark outside, which agitates Thomas.

He turns on the street noises on the reel-to-reel and walks in the town again. He meets Timmy O'Leary, whom he scolds for mistreating his mother. He imagines Edel is leading him and talking to him.

Thomas describes a magical walk with Edel, his angel. He speaks of a beautiful orchard and a grassy bank where they sit. He asks if he can hold her hand. It begins to rain and Thomas stands up 'furious and hurt'. He hears someone laughing at him. He tells the story of Noah.

He returns home, and the taped voice of a furious Mr O'Donnell is heard. O'Donnell beats Thomas for killing his dog. Thomas changes into his father's suit. He plays a recording of his Mammy and him discussing his going to the community dance.

Thomas mimes going outside again and plays the outside noises. He sees the townspeople. He can't hear them, but he knows they are mocking him. He walks into the dance hall: 'I walk... I walk into Hell.'

Speaking into a microphone, Thomas tells all the villagers what he thinks of them for mocking him and the way they treated his family. He then plays a recording of his murder of Edel, a 14-year-old English girl. On the recording, she refuses to hold his hand and says she has gone out with him for a dare. Furious, he beats her to death with his tape recorder. He imagines talking to a 'good angel' and kisses the angel's hand (the microphone). He says, 'Nobody's listening' and drops the microphone where it smashes on the ground.

**TIP:**

You might want to consider the playwright's original intentions in writing the play. For example, what might Enda Wash be saying about mental illness and isolation?

## TASK 3.1

A Working in a small group, create a two-minute version of the play, making sure that you cover what you all agree are the most significant events in the plot.

B Given your understanding of the play's plot, answer the following questions:

1 What type of notes does Thomas make?

2 What is Thomas's relationship with his mother like?

3 How do his religious beliefs affect his actions?

4 What are some examples of violence from Thomas?

## KEY TERMS:

**Monologue:** An extended speech by one character.

**Social drama:** A genre of plays that deal with the interactions between different social groups, an exploration of a social group, or the place of an individual within a society.

**Psychological:** Referring to a mental or emotional state and the reasons behind it.

# Genre

*Misterman* is a **monologue** or a one-person show. It is, however, also populated by the many other characters in the town, whose voices the audience hears either through the tape recordings or in Thomas's imitation of them. The play has aspects of **social drama**, as it explores the effects of social isolation and religious obsession in rural Ireland. Enda Walsh depicts the details of this society, in which Thomas is to some extent tolerated, but is also mocked and kept apart. The play could also be considered a **psychological** study of a disturbed character.

### TASK 3.2

Below are some advantages and disadvantages of a one-person play. Consider them and then write a paragraph to explain why you think Walsh wrote *Misterman* to be performed by one person.

Some advantages:

- A powerful role for a performer is offered, with a chance to show a range of skills.
- There is a clear focus on one character and one story.
- It provides an opportunity to explore how stories can be told.
- It creates an intimacy between the audience and performer.

Some disadvantages:

- Only one point of view or perspective is represented.
- There is a risk of the play becoming monotonous.
- An audience might be told rather than shown the action.
- It is difficult to show scenes that involve more characters.
- The drama can become like a lecture or a spoken short story rather than a play.

Cilliian Murphy's Thomas is an ominous figure, who casts an eerie shadow, amid the sawdust and debris of this dark set.

### TASK 3.3

Examine some of the social aspects of the play given below. Then write a sentence or two explaining what we learn from them about the Magills and the other inhabitants of Inishfree. (The first one has been suggested for you.)

- Thomas visits his father's grave.
  *Thomas's father ran a grocery shop. After his death, the Magill family seems to have lost status and Thomas has to take over as head of the household.*
- Thomas attends the community dance.
- Mr O'Donnell beats Thomas.
- Edel is English.
- Thomas uses religious ideas and imagery in this speeches.

### TASK 3.4

There are a number of examples of Thomas's unhappiness and instability, as well as possible causes for it. Look at the following points and select three to discuss what they suggest about Thomas's psychology:

- He has drowned all of Trixie's kittens and killed a dog.
- His father has died.
- His mother is dependent on him.
- He wants to record and note everything.
- He is traumatised by Edel's rejection of him.
- He is 'heavily bruised and scarred'.

## TASK 3.5

**A** Read Thomas's speech at his father's graveside (pages 23–24). Then, working with a partner, take it in turns to hot seat Thomas, with questions put by a social worker, who asks Thomas about his feelings towards his father and his life.

**B** Then read the scene again, this time experimenting with using:

- Your voice, including volume and tone, to create a sense of closeness with his dead father
- A range of vocal and physical skills, such as inflection, pitch, gesture and posture, to show what Thomas feels about Mickie-Joe-Goblin-McAllister and the people waiting for the clinic.
- Facial expression and voice to show how Thomas feels about his father.
- Changes in his voice and expression when he sings.

**C** Make notes about what you learn from this scene about Thomas's psychology and beliefs and how they could be conveyed, in this scene and at other points in the play.

## TASK 3.6

**A** Focusing on the same scene as above, consider how design choices could emphasise what Thomas is feeling and what his town is like. Think about how the following ideas might work:

- Sound effects appropriate for a rural Irish cemetery
- Sound effects that give an impression of Thomas's feelings and thoughts
- Lighting to create a suitable atmosphere in the cemetery
- A set design that shows how Thomas might create something to represent the cemetery from the objects he has available to him.

**B** Now write a paragraph, or create a series of images for a storyboard, to explain how the scene could be performed and staged. Look especially to highlight the importance of these features in establishing the character and the mood of the scene.

# Structure

The play is written as a single act to be performed without interval. The timeline of the play switches from Thomas in his space to his recreation of the significant day. With his use of the tape recorders, Thomas is attempting to create his day from breakfast to the community dance.

Although much of the play is **chronological**, there are some **non-linear** sections, particularly when one of the tapes plays a conversation about an event which has not happened yet.

**KEY TERMS:**

**Chronological:** Presenting events in the order in which they occur.

**Non-linear:** A sequence that is not arranged in a straightforward or chronological way.

# Style

The play could be performed naturalistically, with the actor playing Thomas displaying all the realistic psychological symptoms of someone traumatised and lost in an imagined world. Or, a production could aim for an **expressionistic** style that presents the various characters that Thomas recreates in a stylised way. He might, for example, use physical techniques such as slow motion, mime or choreography. An expressionistic set could represent Thomas's mental state rather than attempt to recreate an actual place.

## KEY TERMS:

**Expressionistic:** Using exaggeration or stylised elements to show emotions and ideas, rather than a realistic depiction.

**Resolution:** The solution or bringing together of loose elements of a plot; an ending or conclusion.

## TIP:

There is no 'right' answer to what *Misterman* is about, and you might have very different ideas from those above, but, as you study the play, think about what aspects of it you find the most compelling and how an interpretation of the play could emphasise those.

## TASK 3.7

**A** From your knowledge and understanding of the play, identify examples of the following structural or stylistic features:

- Conflict
- Thomas's version of events contradicted by a voice on tape
- Dialogue or stage directions that are realistic
- Dialogue or stage directions that are non-naturalistic
- Dialogue or stage directions that reveal the emotional state of the characters
- A **resolution**.

**B** Read the statements below about *Misterman*. Work with a partner to put them in order, with the one you agree with most as 1, and the one you agree with least as 5.

- [ ] The play is about the lack of understanding and treatment for mental illness.
- [ ] The story is about the loneliness and isolation of Thomas.
- [ ] The play offers insight into what can cause someone to kill.
- [ ] It is about rural Ireland and its effects on the characters.
- [ ] It is a play about storytelling and how worlds can be created by one performer.

# Context

The Irish playwright, Enda Walsh, was born in North Dublin in 1967. He acted in youth theatre and professionally, including playing Thomas in an early version of *Misterman*. As a playwright, his major breakthrough occurred in 1996 when *Disco Pigs*, a play about the intense relationship between two teenagers, won the Best Fringe Production at the Dublin Theatre Festival. Walsh began writing *Misterman* in 1997, inspired by a murder that occurred in 1994 in East Clare. Many years later, Cillian Murphy, one of the two actors in *Disco Pigs*, read the script and wanted to perform it. This version was performed by Murphy, directed by Walsh, at the Black Box Theatre, Galway in 2011 and went on to New York and the National Theatre in London. Walsh continues to write for the stage, screen and radio, with other successful plays including *Chatroom* (2005), *The Walworth Face* (2006) and *Ballyturk* (2014). He wrote the screenplay for the award-winning film, *Hunger* (2008).

# Historical context

In a 2012 interview for the *Guardian* about *Misterman*, Walsh said, 'Basically, I wanted to do a rural Ireland that looked like somebody had taken a hammer to it.' One inspiration for the play was the case of Brendan O'Donnell who, after spending months in East Clare exhibiting troubling and threatening behaviour, murdered the artist Imelda Riney, her young son and a priest. The murders and subsequent trial made headlines. Although many of the details of *Misterman* vary from the O'Donnell case, Walsh has focused on an isolated, troubled man in rural Ireland, whose erratic behaviour goes untreated until it escalates to a horrific crime. Walsh has said that he wanted to counter the idealised version of Ireland that was seen in television programmes, such as *Ballykissangel*. He says that, in rural Ireland, 'There seem to be a lot of potential Thomas Magills… the guy that everyone knows who's wandering around the town, muttering to himself.'

Irish Gaelic is spoken as the first language in some areas of Ireland and in others as a second language. It has a rich history and it is a source of pride for many to keep the language alive. When Thomas drinks tea with Eamon, Thomas says, 'Slainte mhath!', which means 'Good health!' When Eamon replies with a longer and humorous Gaelic toast in return, however, it is clear that Thomas doesn't understand it. This might reflect a weakness in his education or lack of commitment to learning Gaelic.

John Hurt in Samuel Beckett's *Krapp's Last Tape*.

Maureen O'Hara and John Wayne in John Ford's *The Quiet Man*.

# Cultural context

Ireland has a rich literary heritage. One of its most influential writers was Samuel Beckett (1906–1989), who is most famous for his plays, *Waiting for Godot* and *Endgame*. His one-act play, *Krapp's Last Tape* (1958), about a 69-year-old man in a room on his own playing audio tapes of key moments in his life, bears some resemblance to *Misterman*. In each, an isolated character is editing and trying to make sense of his life through his use of reel-to-reel tapes, though the mood of the two plays is very different. While *Krapp's Last Tape* is slow and melancholy, *Misterman* is intense, fast-moving and always threatening to spiral out of control. Enda Walsh's later play, *Ballyturk*, also explores some similar themes to *Misterman*. In it, two men who are apparently imprisoned in a dwelling spend their time reflecting on and re-enacting rituals from an Irish town. Both plays emphasise a sense of place, despair and isolation.

Thomas lives in Inishfree, which recalls similar names in other literature and media. The Irish poet, W.B. Yeats wrote about an idyllic but isolated island in Lough Gill, in 'Lake Isle of Innisfree'. A different Inisfree is the fictional Irish village in the 1952 film *The Quiet Man*, about an Irish-American man travelling to his birthplace. The film was famous for its depiction of the beautiful Irish countryside. It also inspired a 1950s song, 'Isle of Innisfree', in which a man dreams of returning to Ireland. These portrayals of a romantic, idealised Ireland are very different from the one in *Misterman*, which is riddled with gossip, bullying and violence.

# Social context

The primary religion in Ireland is Catholic, with over three-quarters of the population identifying as Catholic in the 2016 census. The importance of religion is apparent throughout *Misterman* and Thomas views himself as a type of preacher or prophet. Thomas's beliefs, however, often have a childlike quality to them, for example by relying on popular Old Testament tales, such as that of Noah, or a simplistic belief in angels. He also feels that he has a role in discovering and punishing the sins of others. Thomas's age, 33, is the same age that Jesus was at his death, which might be significant. One way that a respect for religion is shown by the play's characters is when they say 'Jaynee' as an alternative to taking Jesus's name in vain.

After the death of his father, Thomas is his mother's carer. It could be that Thomas's family has been neglected by social services and therefore is not receiving the support they need. This was an issue raised in the case of the murderer Brendan O'Donnell, who was unable to get psychiatric help. Thomas is also unemployed and concerned about money.

There are many indications of Thomas's life being strongly tied to, and affected by, his parents. The song that disturbs him at the play's beginning is by the wholesome, popular singer of the 1950s, Doris Day, a favourite of his Mammy's, and its cheerful tune is at odds with Thomas's situation. The lyrics 'everybody loves me' are ironic given Thomas's outsider status in his community. The technology he uses is also of an earlier era. Instead of cassette tapes or digital recordings, Thomas has old-fashioned reel-to-reel players, possibly salvaged from different sources. Throughout his dialogue with his Mammy, there appears to be an unhealthy dependency between the two.

## EXTENSION

Research Ireland in the late 20th and early 21st centuries. Possible areas to explore include:

- Social context: Religion, social care, employment
- Cultural context: Plays and films, music, fashion
- Historical context: Politics, rural Ireland.

Make a note of anything that helps your understanding of the play and how it could be staged or designed.

## TASK 3.8

Look at the following list of key moments from the play and write about what each one tells you about the social or historical context of the play. (The first one has been completed as an example.)

1 Thomas is bothered by a Doris Day song. *Although in a strange warehouse rather than his family home, Thomas cannot escape reminders of his mother. The song is from an earlier era and* **incongruous** *in Thomas's situation. The mood of the song does not fit with his concerns. His efforts to stop the sound hint at his future violence.*

2 Thomas uses old-fashioned reel-to-reel tape to play recordings of conversations he has had in Inishfree.

3 Thomas is worried about the cost of heating his mother's room.

4 Thomas tells Eamon that a 'prophet of God needs a following' (page 27).

**KEY TERM:**

**Incongruous:** Out of place; appearing wrong in a certain location or situation.

Learners must know and understand:
- How meaning is communicated through:
  - An actor's vocal and physical interpretation of character.

# Interpretations of key characters

You must demonstrate that you understand the main characters in the play, including different ways that they could be interpreted. Although this is a one-person play, with only Thomas appearing on stage, you need to be able to demonstrate how the unseen characters, portrayed in the recordings and Thomas's imitations, could be conveyed to the audience.

## The Magills

### Thomas

The play's 33-year-old protagonist. His father has died and he is an only child. He lived with his mother but is now in a disused depot or warehouse. He recreates a recent important day through his tape recordings and his own enactments. In his imagination, he is a powerful preacher with a mission to help Inishfree, but his version of events is often contradicted by the recordings and his own tendency to violence. He becomes obsessed with a young English girl called Edel, whom he believes to be an angel.

### Mammy

A widow and Thomas's mother. She has a pet cat, Trixie. She thinks of Thomas as the 'best boy in Ireland' and relies on him. She never goes out, feels the cold and requests little sweet treats. Thomas has large sections of her dialogue on tape and conducts conversations with the tape.

## The neighbours

### Simple Eamon Moran

Heard both in Thomas's recreation and on tape. A garage owner who speaks fondly of Thomas's parents and refers to Thomas as 'Tommy'. He shows kindness to Thomas, making him a cup of tea and jokingly comparing the two of them to Starsky and Hutch, two television detectives. Thomas turns on Eamon, however, when he sees the nude calendar on his wall.

### Dwain Flynn

Heard on tape and in Thomas's imitations. Dwain is a bullying, foul-mouthed man who has been barred from the pub. Dwain shouts at Thomas for recording him and hits him. Thomas notes: 'Dwain Flynn. Profanity.'

### Mrs O'Donnell

A neighbour to Thomas and wife of Marty O'Donnell. She is first heard on tape telling Thomas that he has blood on his face and that he should go home. Although her words seem sympathetic, when Thomas imitates her later, he makes her sound harsh and 'nasty'.

### Mr O'Donnell

Marty, Mrs O'Donnell's husband and owner of Roger, the dog. On tape, he is heard screaming angrily at Thomas. Thomas enacts being beaten up by him.

### Mr McAnerny

An older man who knew Thomas's father. He is heard both on tape and in Thomas's imitation, when he assumes a voice that is 'gloriously pompous'. He tries to give Thomas advice, which he says is 'for your own good' and 'that this behaviour has to stop'. Thomas notes: 'Charlie McAnerny. Immodesty.'

### Mrs O'Leary

Thomas acts out meeting her when she tells Thomas of her problems with her lazy son, Timmy. In Thomas's imagination, Mrs O'Leary loves Thomas and would like to kidnap him for her own son.

## Timmy O'Leary

Mrs O'Leary's 32-year-old son. Thomas has noted: 'Timmy O'Leary. Cleanliness.' Thomas talks to Timmy when he is walking with Edel. Thomas imagines that he has given Timmy an effective lecture about how he treats his mother, but Timmy seems more interested in Edel and is wondering if she is in a relationship with Thomas.

## Mrs Cleary

Café owner. In Thomas's re-enactment she is inappropriately flirty and overpowering. But this contrasts with her matter-of-fact comments on the tape: 'Your cheesecake, Thomas.' Thomas's note is 'Mrs Cleary. Indecent.'

## Mrs Heffernan

Heard on the tape talking about the dead dog. She presumes it has been hit by a car.

## Billy

A neighbour who greets Thomas with 'Howya, Thomas' each time Thomas leaves the house.

# The visitor

## Edel

A 14-year-old English girl, described by Thomas as an angel in a blue dress. She is a symbol of hope to him and he imagines they will bring about a beautiful 'new world'. Her voice is finally revealed at the end of the play. She says she only came with him for a dare. He beats her to death, with her screams heard on the recording.

Thomas Campbell in an energised portrait of Thomas Magill at the Old Fitzroy Theatre, Sydney.

### TASK 3.9

There is often a contrast between how a character is presented in Thomas's imitations and the impression gained from their own words on tape. As you read the play, note the times when what is heard on tape seems in contradiction with the character as presented by Thomas.

### TASK 3.10

Choose one line from the play that you think is important for each character. Explain its importance in understanding the character and how it could be delivered by the actor (on tape, or by Thomas). What vocal skills would be most effective?

# Use of vocal skills

Typically in *Misterman*, the characters will speak with rural Irish accents, except for Edel, who has an English accent. The accents might suggest particular geographical areas of Ireland and could be researched for authenticity. In the dialogue, Walsh suggests some informal pronunciations such as Billy's 'Howya' or Thomas omitting the 'g' from some words, such as 'chattin'' and 'laughin''.

In addition to his own voice, the actor playing Thomas also assumes the voices of other characters. There is evidence that his imitations are not entirely accurate, but convey his attitude towards the characters, exaggerating or even inventing how they speak and what they say.

The actor playing Thomas must also use his vocal skills to convey his emotional journey.

Vocal skills that actors might consider include:

**Accent and dialect**  **Pace**  **Volume**  **Pitch**

**Pauses and timing**  **Intonation**  **Phrasing**  **Emotional range**

**EXTENSION**

Consider how Edel's voice might surprise the audience. What elements of her accent, pitch and tone might be unexpected? What effect might her English accent and youthfulness have on the audience?

## TASK 3.11

With a partner, experiment with vocal skills to interpret the following lines. Note down the choices you make, including reasons.

Thomas: Everything is not good, Daddy. (page 11)

Mammy: You might give me a rub with the Vicks when you get back from your travels? (page 13)

Mr McAnerny: This behaviour has to stop. (*Slight pause.*) Now, if you ever need to… (page 22)

Simple Eamon Moran: Sure where's the harm in a calendar?! (page 29)

Thomas: All the chat about Thomas Magill and his mocky-a angel? Well, it's me who's laughin' now, ya hear me! (page 49)

Edel: I told the girls I'd be back by five to get ready for the dance… (page 51)

## TASK 3.12

For Mammy and Eamon Moran, give three examples of different vocal skills that the actors could use. Justify each choice by explaining why it is appropriate. Examples have been given for Thomas.)

| Character | Vocal skill | When vocal skill could be displayed | Justification |
|---|---|---|---|
| Thomas | **Accent** and **tone**. | When Thomas begins his 'It all began with Nothing' speech. | He speaks in his rural Irish accent, but as formally as he can. The tone is solemn and mystic as if intoning a passage from the Bible. |
| | **Pitch**: Lower and higher. | Enacting his conversation with Mrs O'Leary. | He alternates between his own naturally lower pitch and a higher, more feminine voice for Mrs O'Leary. |
| | **Volume** and **emotional range**. | When Thomas explodes at his mother 'You stupid woman!' | He shouts this line loudly. Whereas previously he would speak in moderate tones to his mother, he loses control – finally escalating to a very loud volume on 'JUST DO IT!' |

# Use of physical skills

Physical skills might be used to reflect the high emotion of much of the play as well as the intricate relationships between the characters. The actor playing Thomas will need to think about how he can show when he is being himself and when he is impersonating another character. He will also need to demonstrate how he changes physically throughout the piece, for example when he is emotionally distressed, violent or reacting to being beaten. Physical skills to consider include:

**Posture** / **Movement** / **Pace**

**Gestures** / **Facial expressions**

**Proxemics** / **Eye contact**

## Differentiating between characters

### TASK 3.13

**A** Working with a partner, read the conversation Thomas enacts between himself and Mrs O'Leary on pages 14–17. Discuss:

- Thomas's usual posture, way of walking and gestures
- How he will alter these in order to inhabit Mrs O'Leary
- How he will switch between the two characters.

You could experiment with:

- Establishing a set posture, gesture and facial expression for Mrs O'Leary and Thomas to manifest their characters
- Different uses of eye contact (For example, does Thomas look the imaginary Mrs O'Leary in the eye or look straight forward or down at the ground? Is one character taller than the other so that to make eye contact they have to look up or down?)
- Movements and use of facial expression to suggest when the characters are approaching each other or parting
- Gestures to suggest how they are reacting to what each other says.

**B** Discuss which techniques appeared most effective. Do you want the audience to be amused, tense, frightened or concerned?

### TASK 3.14

**A** In some scenes, instead of imitating another character, Thomas is reacting to a tape of their voice, such as the scenes with Mammy. In a pair or small group, read pages 38–41, when Thomas begins massaging his mother. Discuss:

- The different physical actions that Thomas undertakes, including massaging 'his mother', reacting to what she says, reacting to the dogs
- How the actor could use their physical skills to indicate Thomas's emotional state
- What effect you want this section to have on the audience.

**B** Experiment with the following:

- Thomas makes eye contact with where he imagines his mother is and mimes massaging her realistically, as if she is actually there.
- Thomas goes through the motions in a more abstract way, without creating his mother as a realistic character, instead lost in his thoughts.
- A gradual change to his gestures, posture and facial expression, showing him becoming slowly angry with his mother.
- A sudden and violent change in gestures, posture and facial expressions to show a burst of fury with his mother.

### TASK 3.15

**A** As you experiment with different ways of using physical skills in these scenes, note which seem to be most effective and when these physical skills might be used best. For example, on what lines might Thomas move in a certain way, use a prop, make a particular gesture or change facial expression?

**B** Now compare Thomas's use of the following physical skills in the same two sections of the play. Give precise examples to explain your ideas.

- Posture, including sitting or standing (How would this change, for example, as Thomas shifts between himself and Mrs O'Leary? Perhaps as Thomas he would be upright, facing straight, evenly balanced; then, as Mrs O'Leary, turn his head, put his chin down, weight into one hip with a slightly bent knee.)
- Movement and ways of walking
- Pace of movement and actions
- Gestures (Are they slight and subtle or bold and exaggerated?)
- Facial expressions.

## TASK 3.16

For the two key moments given below, give at least three examples of how Thomas could use his physical skills, justifying your choices. (An example of the grave scene has been provided.)

- Thomas as Eamon (pages 25–29)
- Thomas with Mrs Cleary (pages 30–32).

| Scene | Physical skill: details | Justification |
|---|---|---|
| At the graveside (pages 22–24) | Facial **expression**: Eyes alert, mouth tightly shut, serious, concentrated before he begins talking to his father. | The visits to his father's grave are an important part of Thomas's rituals and, at the beginning of this section, his expression shows that he is intent on getting everything right in terms of the sound effects and props. |
| | **Movement**: Respectful approach and kneels down next to grave. | Thomas moves with a stiff-legged formality as he nears the grave. He is respectful of his father and perhaps a little frightened. He kneels slowly next to the grave and leans over to place the flowers carefully. |
| | **Gesture** on 'I really miss ya, Daddy.' | Thomas moves away from his lively gossip to a more tender section. He tenderly touches the 'grave' when he says 'Daddy'. He sits cross-legged and confides his more intimate thoughts. When he says, 'Being an only child is tough', he rests his head in his hands, showing a touch of self-pity. |

# Stage directions

In addition to the play's dialogue, a way for the playwright to convey what a character is doing, thinking and feeling is through stage directions. For example:

Page 8: [Thomas] walks quickly to the back of the space, bends down and picks up something. He walks back towards the tape recorder holding a hammer. He smashes it down on the tape recorder.

Page 16: [Thomas] does a gesture to say goodbye to her but it's not right… He does the line again… He gestures to her in a new way. That's correct… He takes out a small notebook and writes.

Page 25: Thomas turns off the cemetery reel-to-reel, grabs a chair and quickly sets up Eamon's garage space. He turns on a reel-to-reel inside there. Sound of music.

## TASK 3.17

**A** In a small group, perform each of the stage directions above.

**B** Discuss and write down what you believe Thomas is thinking and feeling. For example, what might Thomas be thinking when he replays his goodbye to Mrs O'Leary? How does he feel when he smashes the tape recorder with a hammer?

**C** Talk about what the audience learns about Thomas from the stage directions. For example, are there any signs of his tendency to violence and clues to the importance of this particular day?

# Pauses

At several points, Enda Walsh notes pauses in the stage directions. Pauses can mean many different things, or be significant for a range of reasons, including a hesitation because of indecision, lack of understanding or extended thought, a reaction, a change in mood or simply a calm silence.

## TASK 3.18

Look at the following pauses indicated by the stage directions and explain what you think they mean in terms of the characters and action of the play:

> Page 22: Mr McAnerny: Do you hear me, Thomas? (*A slight pause.*)

> Page 25: A slightly uncomfortable pause as Thomas waits for an invitation from Eamon.

> Page 51: Thomas: Can I hold your hand? (*A slight pause.*)

## TASK 3.19

**A** Read the extract below from a candidate-style response about the stage directions on pages 49–50, when Thomas addresses the community dance. Highlight three details that show how the stage directions help the audience to better understand the character of Thomas.

In this scene, the audience sees a different side to Thomas. The stage direction 'Suddenly he has the confidence' shows that, while Thomas might have entered 'all hunched', he changes at this point. This is the moment the play has been building up to. The urgency of what he now does is reinforced by the stage direction 'runs' and 'fires on' the reel-to-reel. Although Thomas has been the hero of his own story, it is clear from what the audience learned earlier from the tapes and re-enactments that he is a lonely and mocked figure. In this scene, he suddenly becomes dominant when he 'stands on a chair' and his previously ignored voice is amplified by a 'microphone'. The most unusual stage direction, and the one that indicates his mental instability and **religious mania**, is when he 'puts on a pair of shabby angel wings'. This connects with the final stage directions of the play when he believes he is kissing an angel. The stage directions for this section show Thomas's lack of grasp on reality and what has led up to the horrific murder of Edel.

**B** Focusing on the stage directions at the beginning of the play (pages 7–10), make notes on what the audience learns about characters and the play's themes. What effect do you think this scene, including its stage directions, would have on an audience?

### LOOK HERE

See pages 200–202 for more rehearsal techniques for exploring characterisation and practising performance skills.

### KEY TERM:

**Religious mania:** An abnormal mental state with symptoms of high energy, extremes of emotion and impaired judgement, which involves an obsessive interest in religion and personal faith.

### TIP:

Remember that communication is at the heart of drama. Always consider what the performance and staging choices you make are communicating to the audience. Do they create…

- Sympathy?
- Fear?
- Excitement?
- Suspense?
- Pity?
- Comedy?
- Greater understanding?

# Use of space

As part of their characterisation, actors might use the stage space in many different ways, including:

Levels / Proxemics / Positioning on stage

Entrances and exits / Use of the 'fourth wall'

This set for the Orange Tree Theatre in Richmond was designed by Max Dorey with a theatre in the round configuration. It cleverly includes part of the auditorium structure to house Thomas's tape recorders. Thomas (Ryan Donaldson) has no furniture except low pallets – and he also uses the trapdoor – so his physical skills, especially in terms of changing levels, are very dynamic, even within a relatively small stage space.

In addition, the type of staging configuration and the set design could influence an actor's use of space.

Below is a candidate-style response about how Thomas could use a black box stage space arranged with raked seats to create a small theatre in the round.

[1] Opens with some understanding of the role of Thomas.

[2] Explains how the performer could use the space.

[3] Identifies an advantage of a black box theatre.

[4] Identifies a second advantage of a black box stage and explores its use in a specific scene.

[5] Explains how the performer could use the space.

[6] Explains a disadvantage of the space with specific reference to a stage direction.

[7] Gives another disadvantage of the space.

[8] Discusses a positive effect of the space on the audience.

Thomas is an intense character and in this space he has organised everything he needs to tell his story, from his father's suit to the reel-to-reel tape players. [1] Although the audience is very close to Thomas and surrounding him, I want him to perform the role as if no one else is there. He will never break the fourth wall and he will be lost in his own world. [2] An advantage of a small black box space is that the audience might feel as if they are in the warehouse with Thomas. [3] In the scene when the storm breaks out, when Thomas is talking to Edel, he could be positioned centre stage when a pipe overhead 'breaks' to create the effect of the rain. The audience's closeness will make this moment very powerful – some might even be splashed, making it more exciting. [4] The actor playing Thomas could turn around in a fury, giving all the audience the chance to see his expression. [5]

A disadvantage of this space, however, is that it is relatively small, and Walsh has said that, at the end, he wants Thomas to look 'small' in this 'huge space'. [6] It will also be harder to create effects with staircases, and so on for levels or large set pieces which could give some exciting staging possibilities. [7] An intimate black box theatre space would, however, focus the audience on the performance and give them a sense of the claustrophobia of the town of Inishfree. [8]

## TASK 3.20

**A** Work in a small group to discuss – and describe using sketches, for example – how these scenes could be produced in different staging configurations:

- The opening of the play (pages 7–9)
- The cemetery (pages 23–25)
- Mammy and Thomas (pages 36–40)
- The community dance (pages 49–53).

**B** Then write down at least two advantages and two disadvantages of performing them in the staging configurations described on pages 8–11.

**TIP:**

If an exam question asks for advantages and disadvantages, you need to discuss at least two of each. Similarly, if a question asks for examples, you must offer more than one.

# Directorial choices

A director of *Misterman* needs to consider:

- How to guide the actor's physical and vocal choices
- How to use design to reinforce the play's meaning and impact
- How key moments of the play might be staged
- The style of the play and potential use of performance conventions
- The effect the play should have on the audience.

## TASK 3.21

**A** Working in a small group, read the scene with Eamon leading to Thomas killing the dog (pages 22–30).

Discuss the impact you want this scene to have for the audience. Do you want it to be tense, for example? Frightening? Surprising? Alarming? Sad? A combination of these? How will you make clear for the audience the different shifts in mood in this section?

**B** Experiment with:

- Changing pace and volume to increase interest in the scene
- Using performance conventions and/or design elements to emphasise Thomas's thoughts and his relationship with Eamon
- Different ways of using the stage space, for example will Thomas change position when he is enacting Eamon, or will the characters move around at key moments? How will you show that Thomas has left the garage?
- Creating sound or lighting that would heighten a mood or underscore a key moment.

**C** Now write a paragraph in response to the following question: 'As a director, how would you stage the scene between Eamon and Thomas in order to create a specific impact on the audience?'

### WHAT THE SPECIFICATION SAYS...

Learners must know and understand:

How meaning is communicated through:

- The use of performance space and spatial relationships on stage
  - The relationship between performers and audience
  - The design of: set, props, costume, lighting and sound
  - An actor's vocal and physical interpretation of character
  - The use of performance conventions
- How performance styles affect the direction, acting and design of a performance.

## TASK 3.22

Below are extracts from two candidate-style responses about staging the scene with Mrs Cleary (pages 30–33). How well do you believe the writers explain and justify their ideas? Look for and highlight:

- Clear ideas about what they want to achieve
- Specific examples from the play
- Correct use of theatrical terminology
- Understanding of how a certain impact on the audience can be achieved.

In my production, I want to highlight the differences between what is going on in Thomas's head and reality. The audience will understand that what he thinks is happening is not the truth. In order to convey this, when Thomas imitates Mrs Cleary, I will have samba music begin and a disco ball lighting effect, showing that this couldn't possibly be real. Thomas will speak in a low but feminine voice, at a very quick pace, punctuated with a low chuckle. When she says, 'Grab a hold of Mrs Cleary', she will complete a number of samba dance steps, eventually leaning backwards over the table. Thomas will then roll back into his seat and say in a **deadpan** way 'I've just come in for a cheesecake.' This will be a comic moment, but will also show that Thomas views himself as being the only reasonable person in Inishfree, surrounded by cartoon-like characters. When Mrs Cleary's voice is heard on the tape, however, it will be clear that she is an ordinary café owner and that it is Thomas who has behaved irrationally by killing the dog.

My concept of the play is that it takes place in Thomas's head and I want the audience to experience how extreme and chaotic it is. For this scene, in addition to the dialogue, there will be several sound effects, showing that Thomas has to compete with many conflicting thoughts. I will have him break the fourth wall and speak directly to the audience when he says 'Cheese? And cake?' This should surprise the audience and make them laugh. At all times, I want the audience to feel unsettled by Thomas, not knowing whether to feel sorry for him, laugh at him or be frightened of him. After the comedy of Thomas gyrating as Mrs Cleary, there will be a sudden shift in mood when Mrs Heffernan's voice is heard talking about Roger's death, as the audience will know that Thomas is responsible. The scene goes from the silliness of dancing and cheesecake to the violent death of a beloved pet.

## KEY TERM:

Deadpan: Without showing expression; blank.

## TIP:

There is no one right way of interpreting this or any other scene. The choices you make, however, must be rooted in your understanding of the play and how theatre works.

## WHAT THE SPECIFICATION SAYS...

Learners must know and understand:

- How meaning is communicated through:
  - The design of: set, props, costume, lighting and sound.

# Design choices

Costume, set, lighting and sound design all contribute to the impact of *Misterman*. They are vital in presenting the play's setting, meaning and director's interpretation. The way Thomas is costumed, for example, will give hints to his status in the community and how he is perceived by others. When he makes costume changes, such as putting on the blue suit or adding the angel wings, these moments will show a new stage in his character's journey.

Setting and props are important for establishing the context of the play and Thomas's life. Sound can help to establish location and create atmosphere. Lighting can focus attention on certain features and suggest a mood or location.

# Costume design

When writing about costume, it is important to consider what the costume tells the audience about the character's role and personality. It is useful to consider:

**Period and context** / **Colour** / **Fabric** / **Silhouette**

**Fit** / **Condition** / **Headwear and footwear** / **Make-up and hair**

Although there is only one character on stage in *Misterman*, you might want to consider if Thomas alters any aspects of his appearance when imitating other characters and how his costume might change during the play.

Below is a candidate-style response about the outfit at the end of the play.

The Thomas the audience sees at this point looks very different from the Thomas at the beginning of the play. Before he was a simple outsider, but now his appearance is distinctly odd. **[1]** He is wearing his father's light blue suit, which is too large for him and also of a somewhat old-fashioned style, with slightly flared trousers. Although the suit is important to Thomas, it is not particularly high quality and is made out of shiny polyester. **[2]** With it, he wears a ruffled, white dress shirt, like something his father might have worn to a wedding. It will be loose on Thomas and gape at the neck. **[3]** To complete the incongruous effect, Thomas will be wearing the trainers he has worn throughout the piece. **[4]** The wings he puts on are described as 'shabby'. I imagine that they are something Thomas might have stolen from a local nativity play. They will be made out of cardboard, with greyish feathers glued on and they will fit on Thomas with white elastic which he will loop over his shoulders and under his arms. **[5]** With his face made-up to show bruises from the beating he has received from O'Donnell, the effect should be unnerving. **[6]**

**[1]** Understanding of character.

**[2]** Describes colour, fabric and silhouette/fit, including why they would be appropriate for the context.

**[3]** Describes style, using correct terminology, and colour and fit.

**[4]** Describes footwear.

**[5]** Makes imaginative choice, references text, describes practical details.

**[6]** Describes make-up and the effect of it.

## TASK 3.23

Here is a sketch of one possible interpretation of a costume for Thomas at the beginning of the play.

Draw your own sketches of Thomas's costume, make-up and accessories at these points in the play:

- As Mrs Cleary (page 31)
- After the beating by O'Donnell (page 46)
- At the very end of the play (page 53).

**TIP:**

These are just some ideas for costumes for Thomas. Other designers will make different choices.

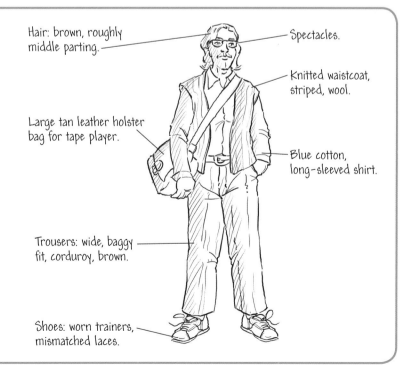

Hair: brown, roughly middle parting.

Spectacles.

Knitted waistcoat, striped, wool.

Large tan leather holster bag for tape player.

Blue cotton, long-sleeved shirt.

Trousers: wide, baggy fit, corduroy, brown.

Shoes: worn trainers, mismatched laces.

# Set design

The set designer of *Misterman* could help to convey the play's meaning through some of the following:

- Emphasising naturalistic aspects of the play by providing realistic props and set furnishings
- Emphasising non-naturalistic aspects of the play by symbolically suggesting themes such as memory, the unseen forces in Thomas's life and Thomas's mental state
- Establishing a particular relationship between the audience and the performers by use of proxemics or levels
- Establishing the period of the play and the passage of time through the use of particular props or set furnishings.

The set designer should consider how realistic or stylised the set should be. One choice they will have to make is whether the depot is a real place or a representation of Thomas's mental state. Is it a place that Thomas has discovered and where he has hidden objects that he now uses to relive his day or is it all a product of his imagination?

## TASK 3.24

**A** Here is a sketch of a set design for *Misterman* in an end on staging configuration.

- Add two more details that you think would improve the design.
- Answer the question: 'How does this set help to convey the ideas and themes of *Misterman*?'

**B** Then draw a contrasting set for the ending of the play, produced in a theatre in the round.

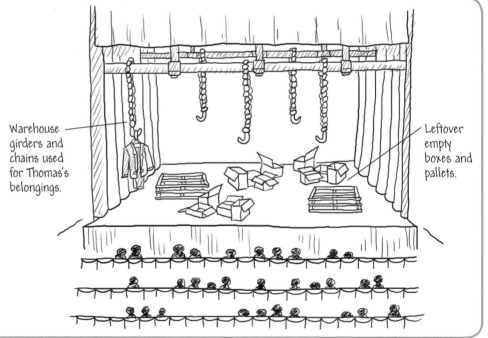

Warehouse girders and chains used for Thomas's belongings.

Leftover empty boxes and pallets.

## TASK 3.25

Draw and annotate a set design to recreate the scene of Thomas in the park with Edel (pages 43–45). Remember that the scene needs to be quickly established and understood by the audience. Consider:

- Colours and textures
- The scale of the set
- Positioning of the set dressings on stage
- Levels
- Materials
- Props and stage furnishings.

# Lighting design

The lighting in *Misterman* has many functions, including:

- Establishing the time of day and location
- Reflecting Thomas's mental state
- Focusing the audience's attention on certain characters and events
- Highlighting and increasing the intensity of certain moments
- Creating an atmosphere or mood
- Suggesting a transition from one time, location or impersonated character to another.

## TASK 3.26

Enda Walsh provides some interesting lighting directions in the play. On page 10, when Thomas closes his eyes, there is a blackout. When the lights come up afterwards, there are small 'playing areas' 'dotted' around the space. With a partner, discuss what effect you think Walsh wants to achieve with lighting directions such as these.

## TASK 3.27

**A** Read this description of a lighting design for the scene with Edel in the park (pages 43–45). Highlight technical terminology.

*In Thomas's imagination, the beginning of this scene is both religious and romantic, and I want to create a mystical mood through my use of lighting. Most of the stage will be in darkness, but a profile lantern with a gobo will project a moonlight effect upstage. Thomas and 'Edel' will be lit with fresnels with green filters, to reinforce the park location and the green carpet upon which they are sitting. When the mood is broken by Edel's refusal to hold Thomas's hand, I will have the rain backlit, making it more beautiful and strange. There will be flashes of a strobe light when the thunder occurs, which reinforces the change in mood and the fracturing of Thomas's hopes. The green light will change to a red gel to reflect the following violence.*

**B** On page 29, Walsh suggests that there is a 'dramatic lighting change as the music and Thomas stop'. With a partner, discuss what effect you would hope to achieve with this dramatic lighting change and what technical equipment you would use to create it.

**C** Now work together to create a lighting design for the play's ending, from Thomas leaving the house on page 48. Consider:

- Changes to the type, direction, colour and so on of the lighting
- How the lighting will contribute to the atmosphere
- How you will achieve technically the lighting effects you want.

**LOOK HERE**

For advice on technical aspects of lighting design and how to create a lighting cue sheet, see pages 224–226.

# Sound design

Sound design can be used to establish location or a transition, and is also useful in creating an atmosphere or reflecting the psychological state of a character, which could be particularly relevant for this play. Sound design can also add to the romance, comedy or tension of a scene, often having a significant impact on the audience's experience of the play.

Walsh's suggestions about the sound in *Misterman* are unusually complex and varied. He uses sound to create other characters, provide a background soundscape and to amplify Thomas's speaking. When writing about sound design you might consider:

- Volume: How amplified will the sound be? Will it grow louder or quieter? (Consider, for example how the Doris Day song affects Thomas? Would you 'muffle' the sound when Thomas tapes the teddies over his ears?)
- Recorded or live: Will sound effects and music be pre-recorded or performed live?
- Type of sound: Will the sound be naturalistic or abstract?
- Special effects: Will you use distorting effects such as reverb?
- How the sound or music begins and ends: Should it gradually become louder or will there be a sudden burst of sound? Will it end abruptly or fade out?
- Are microphones used and, if so, what type?

## TASK 3.28

Look at the following ideas and note at least one occasion in *Misterman* when each sound effect might be appropriate:

- Thomas speaks into a microphone
- An unseen character's voice
- A dog barking

- A car horn
- Music
- A gate opening
- Church organ music.

## TASK 3.29

A recurring sound in the play is a dog, or dogs, barking. As a sound designer, one of your choices is how realistic or abstract you want the barking to be and how the audience should experience it. Read the candidate-style response below about sound design based on the stage directions on pages 39–40. Note examples of technical language. Then write your own paragraph about the sound effects for page 30.

The play is reaching its climax and I want to the audience to realise that the dogs are no longer actual dogs, but a symbol of what is tormenting Thomas. In order to achieve this effect, I will record and distort the sound of dogs barking for the sound of 'Dogs outside have started to bark.' The sound will snap on abruptly and be shockingly loud, with a hint of reverb giving them a mysterious, echoing effect. For the direction, 'the dogs go crazy', I will have the sound coming from a number of speakers around the auditorium so the audience can experience the sound all around them and increase the volume even more. Under it, I will have classical music playing, making it sound distressing and odd. When Thomas opens the door, the sound will snap off and be replaced by gentle low volume outdoor sound effects of birdsong.

## TASK 3.30

Working with a partner, look closely at the opening of *Misterman*, up to page 11, and create a sound design for it. Think of ways that you could use sound to:

- Generate interest
- Create tension
- Suggest Thomas's mental state
- Draw attention to the play's themes
- Create a realistic sound effect
- Create an abstract sound effect.

### LOOK HERE

For advice on technical aspects of sound design and how to create sound cues, see pages 227–229.

## CHECK YOUR LEARNING *Misterman*

**Do you know…?**

- ✓ When *Misterman* was written.
- ✓ When it is set.
- ✓ Where it takes place, including the specific location/s within the wider setting.
- ✓ The genre of the play.
- ✓ How its context might affect choices of costumes, sets and props.
- ✓ How the psychology of the main character and relationships between characters might be shown.
- ✓ Advantages and disadvantages of producing the play in different staging configurations.
- ✓ How key scenes might be staged.
- ✓ The performance style of the play.
- ✓ How the main actor could use their physical and vocal skills to convey motivations, thoughts and feelings and to impart meaning to the action.
- ✓ The role of the director and how they influence the way an audience responds to and understands the play.
- ✓ Key moments a director could use to convey their concept of the play.
- ✓ Different design choices to be made, why they are important and how they can be effective.
- ✓ What impact the play should have on the audience and what messages they should be left with.

# PRACTICE QUESTIONS FOR COMPONENT 04, SECTION A: SET TEXTS

## SECTION A

You are advised to spend about 55 minutes on this section.

*Blood Brothers* – Willy Russell

*Death of a Salesman* – Arthur Miller

*Find Me* – Olwen Wymark

*Gizmo* – Alan Ayckbourn

*Kindertransport* – Diane Samuels

*Missing Dan Nolan* – Mark Wheeller

*Misterman* – Enda Walsh

State the performance text you have studied: _____

1 Select one line from the list below. Explain how it has an impact on this character in the performance text you have studied. [4]

*Blood Brothers*
Mrs Lyons: Where did you get that… locket from Edward? Why do you wear it?

*Death of a Salesman*
Linda: Get out of here, both of you, and don't come back!

*Find Me*
Verity: Oh Verity! Oh Verity! I'm the underdog female in this family.

*Gizmo*
Manny: Because that's naughty that is. And we always agreed good behaviour, didn't we?

*Kindertransport*
Eva: Am I in the abyss?

*Missing Dan Nolan*
Sarah: I'll remember the little things…

*Misterman*
Simple Eamon Moran: Sure where's the harm in a calendar?!

2 Select one lighting design from the photographs below. Justify why this could be suitable for a production of the performance text you have studied. [4]

**3** Select the character from the performance text you have studied.

*Blood Brothers*: Linda

*Death of a Salesman*: Biff

*Find Me*: Edward

*Gizmo*: Cevril

*Kindertransport*: Lil

*Missing Dan Nolan*: Clare

*Misterman*: Mammy

Complete the table below by listing three ways in which an actor could use their vocal skills to portray the character. Justify your choices with examples from the performance text you have studied.        [6]

| Use of vocal skills | Justification |
|---|---|
|  |  |
|  |  |
|  |  |

**4** Explain, using examples from the performance text you have studied, how stage directions can be used to support the actors in communicating their role to the audience.        [6]

**5** Compare the advantages and disadvantages for an actor when presenting the performance text you have studied on a proscenium arch stage.        [6]

**6** Discuss how a director could stage the ending of the performance text you have studied to make the play's resolution effective. You may refer to the direction of the performers and/or design of the scene in your answer.        [8]

**7** Describe one suitable prop or piece of scenery from the performance text you have studied. Justify why your choices are appropriate. In your answer, indicate the scene or scenes from the performance text you have studied in which the prop or set might be used. You may include a sketch of your design with annotations in your answer.        [8]

**8** Explain, using two examples, how the social and/or historical context can be seen in the design or acting skills of the performance text you have studied.        [8]

# SECOND PRACTICE PAPER

## SECTION A

You are advised to spend about 55 minutes on this section.

*Blood Brothers* – Willy Russell     *Gizmo* – Alan Ayckbourn     *Missing Dan Nolan* – Mark Wheeller

*Death of a Salesman* – Arthur Miller     *Kindertransport* – Diane Samuels     *Misterman* – Enda Walsh

*Find Me* – Olwen Wymark

State the performance text you have studied: _____

1  Select one line from the list below. Explain how it has an impact on the characters in the
   performance text you have studied.                                                    [4]

   ***Blood Brothers***
   Mickey: That's why I take them. So I can be invisible.

   ***Death of a Salesman***
   Howard: Willy, you can't go to Boston for us.

   ***Find Me***
   Miss Everitt: She is your child, Mrs Taylor.

   ***Gizmo***
   Hezza: I was terrified. Never seen anything like it…

   ***Kindertransport***
   Officer: Know your number. If you don't know it you might forget who you are.

   ***Missing Dan Nolan***
   Dan: I'll come back as well. Can you help me with my stuff?

   ***Misterman***
   Edel: It was a dare, that's all! A DARE!

2  Choose two moments in the performance text you have studied when the movements of the characters
   indicate a change in mood. Explain your answer.                                       [4]

3 Select the character from the performance text you have studied.

*Blood Brothers*: Mrs Johnstone

*Death of a Salesman*: Willy Loman

*Find Me*: Jean

*Gizmo*: Ben

*Kindertransport*: Evelyn

*Missing Dan Nolan*: Thom

*Misterman*: Thomas

Complete the table by listing three ways in which the actor could use their physical skills to portray the character. Justify your choices with examples from the performance text you have studied.　　　　　　　　　　　　　　　　　　　　　　　　　　　　　　　　　　　　[6]

| Use of physical skills | Justification |
|---|---|
|  |  |
|  |  |
|  |  |

4 Choose a different character from the one listed in Question 3 from the performance text you have studied:

Character: _____

Give three examples of how dialogue can be used to support the actor in communicating this role to the audience.　　　　　　　　　　　　　　　　　　　　　　　　　　　　　　　　　　[6]

5 Draw a sketch showing how an important moment from the play could be performed in the round. Show the set and the positioning of key characters.　　　　　　　　　　　　　　　　[6]

Then list the advantages and disadvantages for an actor when presenting the performance text you have studied in the round.

6 Discuss how an actor could perform two different moments from the play in order to show the audience how the character has changed or developed.　　　　　　　　　　　　　　　[8]

7 Describe one suitable costume for a character from the performance text you have studied. Justify why your choices are appropriate. In your answer, name the character from the performance text you have studied. You may include a design with annotations in your answer.　　　　　　[8]

8 Explain, using two examples, how sound and/or set design could reflect the social and/or historical context of the performance text you have studied.　　　　　　　　　　　　[8]

**SECTION B**

# EVALUATION OF LIVE THEATRE PERFORMANCE

## WHAT THE SPECIFICATION SAYS...

Learners should:

- Analyse and evaluate the work of others through watching live drama and theatre.

Learners must know and understand:

- The meaning of drama and theatre terminology used by theatre makers
- How genre is used in live performance to communicate meaning to an audience
- How to analyse a live theatre performance
- How to evaluate the work of others, drawing considered conclusions.

## HOW YOU WILL BE ASSESSED

AO3: Demonstrate knowledge and understanding of how drama and theatre is developed and performed. (10 marks.)

AO4: Analyse and evaluate their own work and the work of others. (20 marks.)

### TIP:

The play you write about must be different from the performance text you write about in Section A. You might well see a live performance of your Section A text, but you cannot write about it in Section B.

### TIP:

To gain good marks for AO3, you will need to use correct theatre terminology.

## Evaluating the success of a production

For Section B of your exam, you will be asked about an aspect of the live theatre you have seen. The question could be about acting, design, direction or characteristics of the play, such as its genre or style. Whatever you are asked, you will be expected to evaluate how successful the work was and, in doing so, provide examples from the performance to support your comments. There is only one question for Section B and you must answer it. It is important, therefore, that you are secure in writing about many different aspects of the play you have seen.

When you first see a performance, you might find it difficult to analyse and evaluate the different elements. It is easy to be caught up with the play's story, spectacle or acting, without considering which specific details of the production are responsible for its success or failure. As an informed student of Drama, however, this is a skill that you need to develop.

You will learn to read the semiotics of the production. These are all the signs that are being provided by production elements to convey specific meanings. For example, certain costumes or props, by their colour or style, will suggest to the audience certain ideas about the play and its characters. The semiotics or signs of a pantomime, with its bright colours, audience interaction and non-naturalistic sets, are very different from those for a naturalistic thriller, with its realistic set, dark colours and use of the fourth wall.

# Production elements

You need to be aware of the production elements that you could be analysing. Some are listed here:

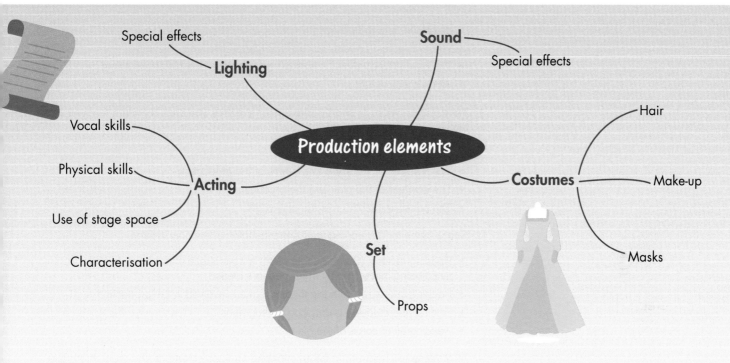

Production elements

- Special effects — Lighting
- Sound — Special effects
- Vocal skills, Physical skills, Use of stage space, Characterisation — Acting
- Costumes — Hair, Make-up, Masks
- Set — Props

## TASK 4.1

Recall a theatre performance you have seen and create a mind map similar to the one above. Identify, if appropriate, at least two examples for each element. Try to think of, for example:

- Two lighting effects, such as the use of a certain colour or a blackout
- Two uses of vocal skills, such as a change in volume or use of an accent.

In order to write well about these different elements, you need to be able to:

- Describe what you have seen
- Use correct theatrical terminology
- Discuss the effects you believe were attempted
- Analyse how these effects were created
- Evaluate how successful they were.

# Preparing to watch a performance

Before you go to see the show, it could be worth learning a little bit about it, including:

- ▶ Its full title and the playwright
- ▶ Where it is being performed and the type of theatre it will be in
- ▶ The genre (type) of play it is, such as a musical or a historical drama
- ▶ When it was written.

Then, either before or shortly after seeing the play, you should ensure that you are familiar with the play, including:

- ▶ The **plot** and **characters**
- ▶ The features of the **style** and **genre** of the production
- ▶ The **context** of the play and the production.
- ▶ The possible intentions of the playwright.

Suggestions for developing your understanding of the play include:

- ▶ Reading reviews (Some people prefer to read these after seeing the play to avoid being influenced by other people's ideas.)
- ▶ Reading interviews with the theatre makers involved in the production
- ▶ Finding and studying production photographs
- ▶ Reading all or some of the play.

All of these will help you to be an informed audience member and more attuned to seeking out details of the production.

# Making notes about the performance

In order to have a set of accurate points about the performance, it is advisable to make detailed notes as soon as possible after seeing the show. You shouldn't write during the show, but you may make initial notes before it begins. If, for example, the stage is visible before the performance begins, you could note the staging configuration and set design. An interval would give an opportunity for quick notes and sketches of what you have observed so far. Then, complete your detailed notes after seeing the show.

**TIP:**

Production photographs are a good way reminder of visual details, such as costumes, the set or the expressions of the actors.

An observational sketch of a prison-scene set for Arthur Miller's *The Crucible* on a thrust stage.

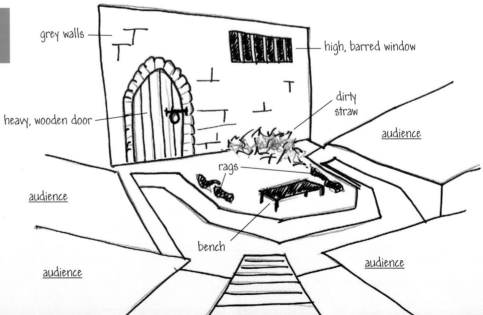

grey walls

high, barred window

dirty straw

heavy, wooden door

audience

rags

audience

bench

audience

audience

You might find the chart below helpful in making your notes about the performance.

| Production element | Details and notes | Sketches |
|---|---|---|
| Acting | Vocal skills:<br>Physical skills:<br>Characterisation:<br>Use of stage:<br>Interaction with other characters or audience: | |
| Costume | Type:<br>Period:<br>Fabric:<br>Colour:<br>Style:<br>Fit and condition:<br>Accessories:<br>Hair, make-up and masks: | |
| Set | Type:<br>Period:<br>Size and scale:<br>Colours:<br>Entrances and exits:<br>Levels, ramps, revolves:<br>Drapes, curtains, flats, backdrops:<br>Technology (projections, multimedia): | |
| Lighting | Types:<br>Colours:<br>Angles and positioning:<br>Special effects:<br>Transitions, blackouts, fades: | |
| Sound | Types:<br>Music:<br>Volume/amplification and direction:<br>Live or recorded:<br>Use of mics and positions of speakers:<br>Sound effects: | |

**TIP:**

Try to select a few key moments in preparation for writing about different production elements. For example, you could look for a character's entrance or the play's climax and note how performance, lighting, costume, set and sound were used at those moments.

# Writing about acting

When watching a performance by an actor, you need to consider:

- What they want to communicate to the audience
- What skills they are using to do this
- How successful they are at this communication.

## Example: *Romeo and Juliet*

In a performance of Shakespeare's *Romeo and Juliet*, for example, the actor playing Romeo might want to communicate that:

- Romeo is young and impulsive
- He instantly falls in love with Juliet
- He is highly emotional, leading him eventually to taking his own life.

Next, you should consider how the actor used his skills to convey this. Did he:

- Move in a light, athletic way and use dramatic gestures?
- Maintain eye contact with Juliet and stay near to her?
- Use gestures and vocal skills to show his despair?

Then, isolate a few key moments to discuss in detail, such as:

- Use of **voice**
- **Movement**
- Stage-fighting
- **Position** on stage.
- Handling of **props**

> **TIP:**
>
> Don't confuse the character with the actor. You are writing about the actor's approach to the character. You might dislike a character, but appreciate the actor's skill in portraying them.

## TASK 4.2

**A** Look at these photographs from different productions of *Romeo and Juliet*. Focus on the actor playing Romeo to discuss each photograph:

- What do you think the actor wants to show the audience about Romeo (for example, his mood, age, desires, personality)?
- What evidence is there of the actors' use of physical skills to convey this characterisation? Can you note anything about their:
  - Facial **expression**
  - **Posture**
  - **Gestures**
  - Use of costumes, set, props or stage space
  - Relationship or **interaction** with other characters?

**B** Which of these interpretations interests you most, and why?

2 Richard Madden, with Lily James, Kenneth Branagh Theatre Company.

1 Sam Troughton, with Mariah Gale, RSC.

4 David Dawson, with Anneika Rose, RSC.

3 Adetomiwa Edun, with Ellie Kendrick, Shakespeare's Globe.

# Choosing key performance moments to write about

When writing about performance, you will need to choose which character or characters you wish to write about and which sections of the play. There is no one right way of doing this but it is important to make choices that will give you the chance to demonstrate your skills. You might look for particularly interesting moments such as when:

- A character is introduced
- A secret is revealed
- A character undergoes a change
- There is a moment of high emotion
- There is a difficult technical demand on the actor, such as a stage fight, multi-rolling, use of disguise or choreography.

## Example: *The Glass Menagerie*

Tennessee Williams' *The Glass Menagerie* follows the desperate efforts of Amanda Wingfield to find a boyfriend for her extremely shy daughter, Laura. Laura's brother, Tom, invites a workmate home and Laura is shocked to discover it is Jim, a boy whom she had a crush on in high school. In Scene Seven, Jim encourages and flatters Laura, only to reveal at the end of the scene that he has a girlfriend. On the next page is one analysis of the acting from parts of that scene.

Rafael Jordan as Jim and Phoebe Fico as Laura in California Shakespeare Theater's production of *The Glass Menagerie*.

| Key moment | | What is being communicated | Acting skills | Evaluation |
|---|---|---|---|---|
| Jim and Laura are left alone together. | Laura | Shocked to discover Jim is their dinner guest. She feels excited, but almost ill with nerves. Her lack of ease in social situations is clear. | **Physical skills**<br>• Posture: Sits slightly hunched, head down.<br>• Gesture: Hand flutters towards her neck as she tries to clear her throat.<br><br>**Vocal skills**<br>• Tone: Breathy.<br>• Pitch: Slightly high.<br>• Pace: Slow, hesitant. | Effectively shows the contrast between the characters and how the moment means so much more to Laura than it does to Jim. |
| | Jim | Confident and friendly. He doesn't remember Laura, but is always happy to meet someone new. | **Physical skills**<br>• Posture: Upright, hands in pockets.<br>• Expression: Smiling.<br>• Eye contact: Looks directly at Laura.<br>• Handling of props: Courteously presents her with a glass of water. | |
| Jim tries to teach Laura to dance. | Jim | Caught up in the moment; enjoying teaching Laura. | **Physical skills**<br>• Movement/choreography: Makes large sweeping gesture in time with music. Dances a few waltz steps on his own, then stretches out arms for Laura to join him.<br>• Expression: Small smile, enjoying himself.<br><br>**Vocal skills**<br>• Volume: Loudly exclaims, 'There you go…'<br>• Tone: Laughs when saying, 'What do you bet I can't?' | Audience feels hopeful for Laura. Her actions demonstrate transformation, but did it go far enough? Could her facial expression show her delight more?<br><br>A greater transformation would have been more dramatic and made more impact. |
| | Laura | Thrilled to be so close to Jim but unsure what to do; frightened she will make a fool of herself. | **Physical skills**<br>• Movement/choreography: Slowly steps towards Jim and allows herself to be swept into his arms.<br>• Eye contact: At first looks down at her feet, but meets his eyes on 'Am I?' | |

| Key moment | | What is being communicated | Acting skills | Evaluation |
|---|---|---|---|---|
| Jim reveals that he won't call again, as he has a girlfriend whom he loves. | Jim | Seeing something in Laura's reaction, he suddenly feels guilty, knowing he might have led her on. | **Vocal skills**<br>• Pace: Slower, more deliberate and, at times, hesitant.<br><br>**Physical skills**<br>• Eye contact: Looks down on 'I hurt your feelings,' feeling ashamed. | Creates a total change in mood. The audience feels sorry for Laura. Her attempt at generosity and bravery are made particularly powerful by the actor's choice to try to hide sorrow with a sweet smile and gentle gesture. |
| | Laura | Her dreams and hopes are dashed. | **Physical skills**<br>• Posture: Resumes hunched posture seen at the beginning of the scene.<br>• Facial expression: Tries to smile and cover her disappointment, but is trembling.<br>• Handling of prop: Gently picks up the broken unicorn and presses it into Jim's hand.<br><br>**Vocal skills**<br>• Volume: Very soft; can barely be heard.<br>• Pace: Slow, hesitant. | |

## TASK 4.3

Use the template of the grid above to discuss key moments from the play you have seen. Make sure that you have chosen a section with enough scope to describe and analyse a variety of acting skills and effects.

# Useful performance vocabulary

Using specialist vocabulary can help you to isolate and describe accurately the different elements of the performance. The following terms should be helpful when writing an analysis of an actor's performance.

## Characterisation

**Motivation:** What a character wants or needs in a scene.

**Style:** The way in which something is performed, such as naturalistically or comically.

**Subtext:** The unspoken meaning, feelings and thoughts 'beneath' the lines.

**Naturalistic:** Lifelike, believable.

**Stylised:** Non-naturalistic, in a particular conceptual style.

## Physical skills

**Movement:** Changing positions or moving across a space.

**Posture:** The way a person stands or holds themselves.

**Gestures:** Movements, such as hand or head movements.

**Facial expressions:** Emotions (or lack of them) shown on a person's face.

**Entrances and exits:** How an actor comes on stage or leaves it.

**Use of stage space:** How an actor moves around the stage, for example using levels or moving through the audience.

**Interaction:** How a character reacts to other characters, including moving closer to or farther from them (proxemics); any physical contact between them and reactions to each other.

**Handling of props:** Use of portable items, such as walking sticks, books, mirrors, glasses and so on.

**Choreography:** Setting movements to create dance or other movement sequences.

**Stage fights:** Blocked movements to create the impression of violence.

**Stage business:** Minor movements or blocking that an actor might do, such as tidying a room, reading a book or closing a window, to establish a situation.

## Vocal skills

**Pitch:** The vocal register used (high or low).

**Pace:** How quickly or slowly something is done.

**Pause:** A hesitation or silence.

**Emphasis:** Stressing or highlighting something.

**Inflection:** Saying a word in a particular way to stress its meaning.

**Accent:** A way of pronouncing words that is associated with a particular country, region or social class.

**Volume:** How loud or quiet something is.

**Delivery:** How lines of dialogue are said in order to convey meaning.

**Emotional range:** The feelings expressed by the way lines are said.

**Phrasing:** How lines of dialogue are shaped, such as by use of hesitation, rhythm, metre and grouping certain words together.

---

### TASK 4.4

Choose an actor's performance you have seen and use at least three terms from those given here to describe their work.

# Including analysis and evaluation in your writing

It will be necessary to describe what you have seen in the show, but you must also analyse the work and evaluate how successful it was. An evaluation does not simply mean saying something was good or bad, but instead, explaining the reasons why you thought it was or was not successful.

**TIP:**

Be careful of 'waffling' and taking too long to get to the point. The timing for the exam is tight, so you must begin answering the question right away.

## TASK 4.5

**A** Read the following excerpts from two candidate-style responses on watching a performance. Mark (or highlight) every:
- Technical terminology, **T**.
- Evaluative comment, **E**
- Detail from the production, **D**

**B** Decide which response most effectively analyses and evaluates the performance seen.

The actor playing Juliet conveyed the tenderness and youth of the character through her vocal skills and use of facial expressions. **[1]** In Act 2, Scene 2, the balcony scene, she appeared young and vulnerable, with no apparent make-up and in a simple nightgown. She spoke with a soft, slightly high-pitched youthful voice. Her gestures on 'What's Montague?' – spoken with an outraged tone and her arms wide open – showed her innocence in the face of the families' disputes. When Romeo spoke to her, she pulled her bedroom curtain across her body in an understandable and slightly humorous reaction to being seen outside in her nightgown. This highlighted her youth and modesty and, in my opinion, added to the eventual tragedy of the piece. Throughout the play, her **rapport** with the actor playing Romeo was outstanding and was conveyed particularly through their close contact and use of eye contact.

There were good and bad things about the performance of Juliet. Her presence was pleasant, meaning that she looked right for the role, and she wore all the costumes well. She also spoke up loudly enough. In the balcony scene, she appeared on a high platform, as I expected. However, the negative part is that I just didn't find her interesting, perhaps it is was the old-fashioned language, but she was boring and hard to understand. **[2]** Also, I didn't understand why she wasn't just honest with her parents.

**[1]** It is good to focus early on acting skills and desired effects like this.

**KEY TERM:**

**Rapport:** A strong understanding or communication between people.

**[2]** Beware of saying something is 'boring' or 'hard to understand'. It could indicate that you have not made enough effort to engage and comprehend. It is better to say what you believe the actors or production were attempting and why they fell short.

**TIP:**

Think TED:

**T:** Technical vocabulary

**E:** Evaluation

**D:** Detail and examples from production.

177

# Writing about costumes and sets

For Section B, you could be asked about costumes and/or sets, specifically or as part of the overall visual impact or contribution to the genre of the piece.

When analysing and evaluating set and costume design, you should consider:

- What they communicate to the audience
- What skills are used to communicate this
- How successful they are at this communication.

If you were writing about *Romeo and Juliet*, for example, you might say:

- How the design helps to establish aspects of the play, such as setting
- What the design indicates about the characters and their backgrounds
- How the design helps to communicate that the play is a Shakespearean tragedy
- The materials used to create the designs
- Colours and textures apparent in the design
- Effects created by the designs, such as making a character more beautiful or frightening, or making a location more exciting or ominous
- How successful the design was in communicating the play to the audience and adding to their experience.

## TASK 4.6

Look at the range of costume and set designs here. Make brief notes for each photograph on what you learn about the play and production from the designs. For example:

- What is the **mood** of the production?
- What **impression** do you get of the characters?
- What **genre** might the play be, and what demands are associated with that genre?

Also note any details you see about:

- **Materials**, such as different clothing fabrics, wood, plastic and metal
- **Colours**
- **Size** and **scale** of set
- **Fit**, **shape** and **condition** of costumes.

### TIP:

When writing about design, don't just say whether you find a costume or set attractive, but consider how it serves the play and adds to the audience's understanding.

Allegro.

Foreign Wars.

Loving v. Virginia.

# Vocabulary for costumes

Using correct terminology when writing about design will help you to express your ideas clearly and in sufficient detail, while demonstrating your understanding of how theatre is made. Here are some helpful terms when you are analysing the costume of a production.

## Costumes, hair, make-up and masks

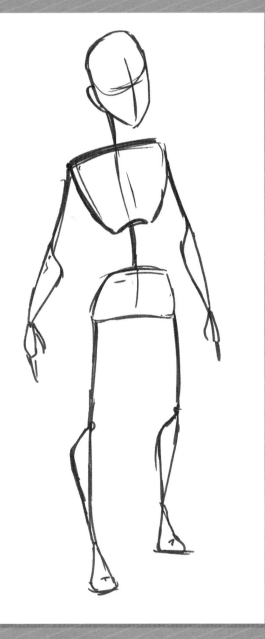

**Headwear:** Hat, cap, scarf, crown, headband, ribbon, clasp and so on.

**Hair:** Colour, length, style.

**Wigs:** Natural, period or theatrical.

**Make-up:** Natural, character, stylised or fantasy.

**Facial hair:** Moustache, sideburns, beards.

**Masks:** Covering part or all of the face.

**Neckline:** High, low, scooped, collar, V-neck and so on.

**Accessories:** Jewellery, ties (bow tie, cravat).

**Fabrics:** Silk, wool, cotton, polyester, chiffon, rubber; with a print or plain.

**Decorations** on fabric: Sequins, rhinestones, lace, and so on.

**Trim:** Buttons, braid, embroidery, faux fur.

**Padding:** Protective padding, character padding (to make a character heavier or to create a pregnancy belly, for example), fashion padding (such as shoulder pads), to give a different silhouette.

**Silhouette/fit:** Tight; loose; oversized, high waisted; drop waist, hourglass and so on.

**Colour palette:** The range of colours used; these might be bright, pastel, natural; toning and complementary or clashing.

**Colour coding:** Using certain colours to suggest something about characters, such as characters in a particular group all wearing the same colour.

**Footwear:** Sandals, boots, brogues, slippers, lace-ups, trainers, loafers, heels and so on.

**Footwear embellishments:** Buckles, laces, stitching, straps, ribbons.

**Condition:** 'Distressed' to look worn or old; pressed, clean, soiled, ripped, mended, faded.

# Vocabulary for sets

Using technical terminology correctly in your analysis will help you to gain marks. It is unlikely that the production you watch will use all of the following, but see if any can be accurately included in your writing about set design.

## Set design

**Box set:** A setting of a complete room, often naturalistic, with three walls and a 'missing' 'fourth wall' facing the audience.

**Cloth:** A piece of scenic canvas or cloth. A **backcloth** or **backdrop** is a cloth that hangs at the rear of scene. It might have a design or scenery painted on it.

**Cyclorama:** A curved plain cloth or screen filling the rear of the stage.

**Drapes:** Curtains or other hanging fabric.

**Dressing:** Decorative props and furnishings added to a stage set, such as paintings, cushions or vases. Also called **set dressings**.

**Flat:** A piece of scenery mounted on a flat frame.

**Fly:** To raise and lower scenery or other items onto the stage using a system of ropes and pulleys. You can refer to 'flying a set in'.

**Furnishings:** Furniture on the set, such as chairs, cushions or tables.

**Gauze** or **scrims:** Curtains that might hang loose or be mounted on a frame, which, if lit a certain way, are transparent.

**Multimedia:** Using film or other media in the production.

**Projection:** Projecting a film or still image onto the stage.

**Props:** Moveable items on the stage, such as hand props that the actors can carry, such as books, cups or phones.

**Revolve:** A large turntable device that can be turned to reveal a different setting.

**Scaffolding:** A large structure, usually constructed of metal, that creates different levels on a set.

**Symbolic:** Using something to represent something else. A symbolic stage design might be a non-naturalistic one that suggests something about the play and its themes, such as using red to suggest violence, or a house with a crack down its middle to suggest a family that is torn apart.

**Trap** or **trapdoor:** A door in the floor of a stage that allows objects or performers to be dropped, lifted or lowered.

**Truck:** A platform on wheels upon which scenery can be mounted and moved.

**Wing space:** An unseen area to the side of the stage, from which actors, props, furnishings or sets can be moved onto stage.

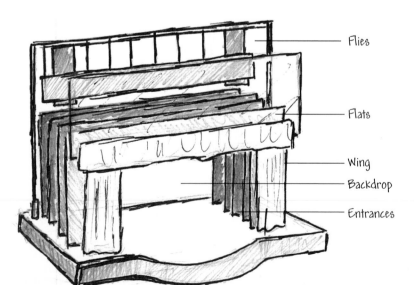

Flies

Flats

Wing

Backdrop

Entrances

> ## TASK 4.7
> Choose a performance you have seen and write a paragraph or two to describe it and analyse the visual impact of its set and costume design. Use at least five of the terms given on this page.

# Writing about style and genre

The genre of the play you see could influence the set and costume designs. A costume designer for a musical, for example, might need to consider whether characters are able to move and dance fluidly in the costumes. A set designer for a thriller might need to create spooky and eerie effects, perhaps by using technology such as trap doors or revolves.

## Costume styles

Three basic styles of costumes are:

**Period/historical**: Intended to replicate or suggest specific periods in time.

**Fantastical/stylised**: Designed to suggest non-naturalistic characters or situations, such as representing animals or objects or futuristic, exaggerated, abstract or symbolic figures.

**Modern/contemporary**: Representing current fashions and naturalistic clothing.

*The Crucible*, Royal Lyceum Theatre, Edinburgh.

*Animal Farm*, Soulpepper.

*Edith Can Shoot Things and Hit Them*, Company One.

Depending on the genre, and the play, however, the designer might use a combination of features. *Equus*, for example, is usually performed with contemporary, naturalistic costumes for most of the characters, but stylised or fantasy costumes for the horses.

A Broadway production of *Equus*, with costumes designed by Amy Ritchings and Costume Armour.

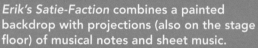

A *Great Wilderness* at the Williamstown Theatre Festival.

# Set styles

Three basic types of set design are:

**Naturalistic**: These sets have realistic details. Some might be highly lifelike, for example, recreating a complete room with three walls and precise set dressings. Some might have naturalistic features, such as doors and furniture, but omit other details. Naturalistic settings can be used for historic settings and contemporary ones.

*Erik's Satie-Faction* combines a painted backdrop with projections (also on the stage floor) of musical notes and sheet music.

**Stylised**: These are non-naturalistic and might highlight certain aspects of a play's themes or ideas. For example, a play about greed might have a backdrop created from replica £50 notes or a set spray-painted gold.

This simple design for *The Scottsboro Boys* by Beowulf Borritt turns chairs on their sides to create a prison cell.

**Minimalistic**: These sets are very bare, with only a few items that, often, could be used to represent many things.

In addition, you might see a play in which there is a single set, or many different sets requiring set changes, or a composite set, in which different locations are represented by a single set.

## TASK 4.8

Consider a production you have seen and decide which of the descriptions above is most appropriate to the costumes and set you saw. Explain whether you think this was a suitable choice for the play, and why (or why not).

## TASK 4.9

Identify the genre of a play you have seen and write a paragraph explaining whether or not you believe the set and costume design supported the play's genre well. If not, which areas could have been improved, and how?

# Choosing key details of costume or set design to write about

## TASK 4.10

Read the example analyses below (about a version of *Hansel and Gretel*), then complete your own version of the table with your observations from a production you have seen.

| | Detailed description | What the costume or set conveys about characters, location, plot, genre or style | How the costume or set is used in the play | Evaluation |
|---|---|---|---|---|
| **The costume of the Hen** | • Fabric: Brown felt.<br>• Silhouette: Oversized, padded, round.<br>• Headwear: Large yellow rubber gloves inflated to make the chicken's comb.<br>• Actor's face is seen protruding from yellow 'beak'.<br>• Footwear: Bright yellow Wellington boots.<br>• Make-up: Nose painted yellow to go with beak. | The style was non-naturalistic and the costumes were fantastical. Some characters were talking animals, which fitted in with the fairy tale aspects. The costumes were also comical, adding to the humour. | When the Hen first appears, the effect of the costume is comical. Her large padding makes it difficult to fit in small spaces. When she 'sits' on her egg, it disappears into the large globe of the costume's body. When she walks, the comb waggles humorously. | The costume was largely effective, especially in highlighting the comedy of the piece. It gave the effect of an overweight, middle-aged woman who found everything quite annoying. However, given the fairy tale quality, I would have liked the costume to be been more colourful, and the 'feathers' could have been designed to create more movement. |
| **Stage and set** | • Configuration: Thrust.<br>• Materials: Light wood (pine?).<br>• Flooring: Rough wooden planks.<br>• Backdrop: Cloth, painted with a forest scene, and a star cloth with fairy lights embedded.<br>• Stage furniture: Long wooden table, two benches, stove, large wicker cage.<br>• Props: Bowls of fruit, vases of flowers.<br>• Levels: Two small ramps SL and SR, leading to platform with wheat on it. | The set establishes the simple country home in a forest where the woodsman lives. Everything looks home-made.<br><br>The painted backdrop is non-naturalistic and adds to the fairy tale quality. | The early scenes show a happy family gathered around a table or enjoying food from their orchard. However, as the play progresses, the comforting props of fruit and flowers disappear, showing that the family is now poorer.<br><br>When the children leave, they slowly climb up the ramp and fall asleep in the wheat field. | The setting succeeds in establishing the woodsman cottage and the simplicity of the family's life. The use of colours, except for the backdrop, lacks variety. The scenes in the wheat field have more visual impact, as the 'wheat' sways when the children fall asleep and the fairy lights gradually come on, changing the mood of the scene. The audience was clearly enchanted by this section. |

# Writing about lighting and sound

When writing about sound and/or lighting design, you should consider:

- What the designer wanted to communicate to the audience
- What skills and technology were used to accomplish this
- What effects were created and how successful they were.

Sound and lighting designers might want to convey:

- The setting, including location, season and time of day
- The period, for example, 19th century or modern day
- The mood, such as comic or ominous
- Key plot points, including changes of location, entrances of characters or changes in circumstances, such as a sudden storm or a gunshot
- Themes, such as childhood, memory or the passing of time
- The genre, such as a thriller or a musical.

## TASK 4.11

Read the excerpts from the two candidate-style responses below and identify what you believe the sound or lighting designers were trying to communicate with these design choices. Highlight examples of technical terminology used.

The lighting design emphasised the power of the King. When he entered through the archway, he was backlit, so the audience's first impression of him was his powerful silhouette. In addition to the profile spots used to light him when he ascended to the throne, a golden pinspot light was focused on his gold crown so that it glinted, highlighting his role as king. The lighting changed when the Messenger arrived, however. There was a cross fade, with the lights on the throne dimming, and a dull, murky grey, filtered light fading up on the Messenger, showing his lowly status. Throughout, the design showed the relative power of some characters, while others emerged from near darkness.

The sound design was used to increase the sense of mystery. When the couple arrived at the house, there was an over-amplified recorded sound of dripping water. The source of the sound was unclear, with the speakers around the auditorium making it sound like it was present throughout the building. When the Sailor entered, there was a short recording of a naval musical motif, which was slow and slightly mournful. This created a sense of foreboding. Silence was also important in the play, because, when it was suddenly broken, there was a sense of shock, similar to when the gunshot was heard in the second act.

# Useful vocabulary for lighting design

## Angles and sources of lighting

**Backlight:** Light projected from an upstage source. It highlights the outline of actors or scenery.

**Barndoors:** Metal flaps used on fresnel lanterns to force the light beam into a particular shape, such as a square. They also control the 'spill' of light, ensuring that the correct area is lit.

**Flood:** A lantern without a lens, which produces an unfocused wash of light.

**Floor lighting:** Lanterns placed on low stands, often used to cast shadows.

**Followspot:** A powerful lantern that can follow an actor around the stage.

**Footlights:** Low lights placed on the downstage edge. These were popular in Victorian theatres and musical halls and are sometimes used today to create period lighting effects.

**Fresnel:** A lantern with a lens that produces a soft-edged beam of light.

**General cover:** Lanterns that are used solely to light the acting areas.

**House lights:** The lights in the auditorium, which are usually up while the audience is being seated and turned off at the start of the performance.

**Pinspot:** A lantern so tightly focused that it lights only a very small area, such as a single object or an actor's face.

**Profile:** A type of lantern with a lens that can project clear outlines.

**Wash:** Light that covers the whole stage.

## Transitions

**Blackout:** Switching off all stage lights. This can be sudden or gradual.

**Cross fade:** A lighting transition involving changing lighting states by bringing up the new state while reducing the old state.

**Fade:** To gradually bring up (fade up) or diminish (fade down) lights.

## Intensity and colour

**Colour filter:** A coloured piece of plastic inserted into a case on the lantern to alter the colour of the light. These are also called **gels**.

**Focus:** How tightly or sharply defined a beam of light is, such as a well-focused circle or square.

## Special effects

**Fogger:** A machine that produces a smoke to create atmospheric fog effects.

**Gobos:** Metal or glass plates, used with profile spotlights, to create special effects, such as leaf patterns or waves, or to create scenic effects such as cityscapes or neon signs.

**Pyrotechnics:** Special effects that create dramatic effects such as fireworks, starbursts or flashes, which might involve real flames or controlled explosions.

**Smoke or haze machine:** A machine that produces clouds or mist.

**Strobe:** A lighting device that gives short bursts of bright light.

# Useful vocabulary for sound design

## Types of sound

**Abstract:** Not realistic; symbolic, such as a loud heartbeat to suggest tension, or a ticking clock to suggest the passing of time.

**Motivated sound:** Sound effects required by the script, such as a gunshot or an alarm.

**Musical theme or motif:** A recurring section of music. It might be associated with a particular character or mood.

**Naturalistic:** Realistic sound effects, such as traffic, birdsong or crowds.

**Volume:** How loud or soft a sound or voice is.

## How sound is produced

**Actor-musicians:** Performers who play musical instruments as part of their acting roles.

**Composer:** Someone who writes music. Some productions have a composer to create original music.

**Live sounds:** Sound created either by the stage management, technicians or actors during the performance. In some productions, where the theatricality of the performance is being highlighted, the sound effects are created in front of the audience.

**Musical instruments:** Drums, guitars, violins and so on, which might be played by a band, orchestra or actors.

**Recorded sounds:** Sound that has been recorded specially for playback during the performance or selected from sound effects archives.

## Equipment and environment

**Acoustics:** The sound quality in a given space, including how the size and shape of the theatre or stage space affects the warmth or clarity of sound.

**Microphones:** Devices for converting and amplifying sound. Radio mics, for example, allow actors and singers to be amplified with no visible means of connection.

**Speakers:** Means of amplifying sound. The placement of speakers will influence how the audience experiences the sound.

## Transitions

**Curtain-call music:** Music played during curtain call. Sometimes the curtain call is choreographed to a particular song.

**Fade:** Gradually turning sound up or down.

**Snap:** Turning sound suddenly off or on.

**Scene changes:** How music or sound is used during transitions or scene changes, often to establish a new location or change in mood.

## Special effects

**Reverb:** An echoing effect; sustaining the sound longer than usual.

**Soundscape:** Using sounds to create an aural environment, such as sea sounds or repeated words.

**Sound effects:** Special sounds created either through the use of recorded effects or creating them live. Typical recorded sounds include birdsong and traffic. Typical live effects include door slamming and offstage voices.

# Choosing key moments of sound or lighting design

Some useful moments to consider when selecting aspects of sound or lighting to design to analyse include:

- **Transitions**, such as beginnings, scene changes, endings
- **Dramatic moments** or **climaxes** of scenes, such as important entrances, stage fights, choreography
- **Unusual** or technically **complex** demands, such as special effects, unconventional use of sound or light, effects that have a strong impact on the audience.

## TASK 4.12

Read the candidate-style notes on lighting and sound design in the table below, then use the same format to make your own notes for the production you have seen.

| Specialism | What the designer hopes to communicate | Skills and technology used to create effects | Evaluation of impact and success of design |
|---|---|---|---|
| **Lighting** | <ul><li>Style: Non-naturalistic.</li><li>Genre: Musical.</li><li>Mood: Cheerful, comic.</li><li>Locations: Many different settings.</li><li>Themes: Circus, Ambition, Success</li></ul> | <ul><li>Followspot: Followed lead character to give him prominence, enlarged to include his wife in their duet.</li><li>Colour: Pink-tinted gel.</li><li>Fresnel: Barndoors created a sharp rectangle to symbolise a cage.</li><li>Gobos: Heart-shape, cage bars.</li><li>Pyrotechnics: Used after first kiss.</li><li>Transitions: Slow fades and two blackouts.</li></ul> | <ul><li>The lighting was deliberately artificial and non-naturalistic, in keeping with the show-business/circus content and theme of the play.</li><li>Variety added to the entertainment, with the audience's focus taken to different areas of the stage, never knowing where to look next.</li><li>At times, the lighting was perhaps too romantic, such as the pink gel and heart-shaped gobo, which gave a Valentine effect to the moment. The use of pyrotechnics, however, was exciting.</li></ul> |
| **Sound** | | <ul><li>Music: Live five-piece band on stage.</li><li>Speakers: Throughout the auditorium, including at the front of the stage.</li><li>Sound effects: Recording of a lion roaring; crowds applauding; whip snapping.</li><li>Microphones: Performers wore body mics; additional area mics were suspended above the stage.</li><li>Volume: Loud, especially for songs.</li></ul> | <ul><li>The band was accomplished, with some musicians playing more than one instrument. The use of offstage sound effects created humour and excitement. The recorded applause had the added effect of encouraging the audience to applaud.</li><li>The music was well-performed, but the sound balance was not always right, with the band sometimes drowning out the words of the singers. The sound effects were more effective and added to the play's theme of ambition by showing that the Lion Trainer would do anything to get the audience's attention.</li></ul> |

# Answering a question about a live production

For Section B, you will be presented with a single question. There could also be additional advice and bullet points to guide your answer. For example:

In a live performance you have seen, analyse the impact the design had on you as an audience member. In your answer, you should consider:

- How one or more of the designers created and communicated meaning
- What skills one or more of the designers used, such as use of materials, colours or stage space
- How effective the designers' choices were.

**You should use appropriate drama and theatre terminology.**

At the start of your answer, write the name, venue, and month and year of the piece you saw. Include examples from the performance in your answer.

**TIP:**

When discussing how effective production choices were, you should consider both what worked well and what could have been improved.

## TASK 4.13

Read the following extract from a candidate-style response to the question above, and then answer the following questions:

1 What design specialisms does the candidate discuss?
2 What meaning does the candidate think was being conveyed?
3 What skills does the candidate identify and what technical vocabulary do they use?
4 Where does the candidate evaluate the work?
5 Does the candidate justify their opinions?

In the musical *Company*, designer Bunny Christie has created a surreal set that shows Bobbie's mental and emotional state. One way of doing this was by using sets and props of an unusual scale, for example, either too small, so Bobbie has to crawl through a tiny door, or too large, like the huge balloon '35' to emphasise her fear of growing older. This unrealistic use of scale suggests how Bobbie is struggling with the reality of her situation.

The costumes are also used to show that Bobbie is an outsider. She is constantly dressed in bright red, making her stand out from her married friends who wear more muted colours. Her sleeveless, knee-length red dress, with its close silhouette and matching red shoes, make Bobbie appear both non-conforming and as if she is constantly on the lookout for a partner.

One of the most inventive uses of design was in the song 'Not Getting Married Today', where the singing vicar constantly appears from unlikely places: the refrigerator, a counter, behind a door, under the wedding cake (which suddenly seems to transform into an elaborate hat the vicar is wearing), making both Bobbie and her friend's fears of marriage comic and frightening.

Throughout, the set changes are handled fluidly, with electronic lifts moving the flats and staging up and down, and sliders moving them off and on, keeping the musical fast-moving. In my opinion, the design works extraordinarily well, in terms of how it shows what Bobbie is feeling. However, with the emphasis on Bobbie, some of the other characters fade into the background. More specific costume or set choices for them might have made them more interesting or relatable.

Rosalie Craig as Bobbie in *Company*.

## TASK 4.14

Now attempt to answer the same question for the live production you have seen. When you have finished, check over your work, answering the same set of questions as in Task 4.13 about your own writing.

# Sample Section B questions

Evaluate the impact the design choices of the live production had on you as an audience member. [30]

Evaluate the impact of the acting choices of the performer or performers in the live production had on you as an audience member. [30]

Evaluate the effect the use of sound, including voice, in the live production had on you as an audience member. [30]

Evaluate how visual aspects of the play supported the genre or style of the live production you saw and the impact it had on you as an audience member. [30]

## TASK 4.15

Make detailed plans for how you would answer each of the example questions above.

**TIP:**

You will only be given one question to answer for Section B.

You are advised to spend about 35 minutes on it.

Remember to include examples from the performance you have seen in your answer.

**TIP:**

You must answer this question referring to a different play from the one you have studied for Section A.

### CHECK YOUR LEARNING Drama: Performance and response: Evaluation of live theatre performance

**Do you know...?**

✓ What the different production elements are.

✓ How to make notes about the different aspects and successes and failures of a performance.

✓ The technical vocabulary for analysing performance.

✓ The technical vocabulary for analysing design.

✓ How to choose key moments from a performance to write about.

✓ How to provide detailed points about different features of the production.

✓ How to evaluate production elements, including finding positive and negative points.

✓ How to justify your opinions by making reference to specific relevant examples from the show.

# 5 COMPONENT 01/02: Devising Drama

## WHAT THE SPECIFICATION SAYS...

Learners should work collaboratively to create, develop, perform and evaluate their own piece of devised drama as either performers or designers.

## ASSESSMENT OBJECTIVES

AO1: Create and develop ideas to communicate meaning for theatrical performance. (Assessed in Portfolio, Sections 1 and 2.)

AO2: Apply theatrical skills to realise artistic intentions in live performance. (Assessed in Performance.)

AO4: Analyse and evaluate their own work and the work of others. (Assessed in whole Portfolio.)

## HOW YOU WILL BE ASSESSED

You will create an original devised piece in which you will participate either as a performer or a designer, and you will be assessed on your supporting portfolio, your performance and your evaluation. This assessment will take place at your learning centre.

# What is devising?

Devising is a way of creating drama without already having a script. Many professional theatre companies use this approach to explore new ideas and to develop work. They can shape the work so that it suits the skills of their performers and creative team. Usually, they will have an audience in mind and will consider how the piece will meet the needs of that audience.

When devising a piece of drama, you should consider:

- What you want to say
- How you will make the drama meaningful and engaging
- Who the audience is.

# Working successfully in a group

At the heart of devising is collaboration and group work. For this specification, your group must contain **between two and six performers** and can have **one designer per design role**: lighting, sound, set or costume. So, throughout the process you will need to work constructively with your group members. This means considering the viewpoints of others and being flexible in your approach and vision.

## TASK 5.1

**A** Working in a small group, imagine that you have been asked to devise a short educational play for 11 year olds about what to expect when they start secondary school. You have 15 minutes to decide on:

- What you think is important for the children to learn
- How you will make it interesting for them
- A title for the piece, and how it will begin.

**B** When you have completed the first part of this task, reflect on your work. Ask yourself:

> Did I contribute ideas?

> Did I think of practical ideas that could help the piece?

> Did I listen to others?

> Did I consider the audience?

> Did I help the group complete the task in the time allowed?

> Was I a good group member?

**C** Considering how you approached the group work, note one thing that you believe you did well, for example coming up with a good title or encouraging other members to contribute. Then, note at least one target for improvement. Should you, for example, listen to others more, or do you need to be more positive?

Some groups find it helpful to create a 'contract' in which they agree how they will work together, as it is best to set off on the process with agreed, positive goals. Some points that might be included are:

- How often the group will meet for rehearsals
- Each member's responsibilities
- That they will treat each other respectfully
- How they will resolve problems.

# Responding to stimuli

Your teacher will present you with a choice of **stimuli** that will provide the initial ideas for your devised piece. Your choice of stimulus will help you to create a story or concept for your drama. The stimuli are provided by OCR and will change every year. They will be from a number of sources, such as:

> Historic event    Instrumental music    News article    Painting

> Person or people    Photograph    Poem    Prose

It is a good idea to consider the dramatic potential of several of the stimuli that are presented before you make a final decision on which to use. When responding to a stimulus, you should explore what themes, dramatic ideas and questions it offers.

> **TIP:**
>
> The three most common group-work complaints are about those who contribute nothing, are unreliable or block the ideas of others. Make sure that you are a positive group member who helps to move the project forward.

> **KEY TERM:**
>
> **Stimuli:** Artefacts, such as photographs, letters, art, stories or poetry, used as a starting point for original creative work.

# Dramatic questions, themes and ideas

## TASK 5.2

Below is an example of a prose stimulus: an excerpt from Charles Dickens' Victorian novel *Great Expectations*. In this extract, the young hero and narrator, Pip, first sees a rich, elderly woman, Miss Havisham, who, as a young woman, was rejected on her wedding day. Although Miss Havisham has grown old, her surroundings are frozen in the despair of that day. Later in the novel, the reader discovers that she spends her life plotting revenge against men.

**A** Read the extract and the sample responses to it, including dramatic questions, themes and ideas. Do any ideas seem particularly interesting and worthy of further exploration?

**B** Add any other points of your own that you would like to explore.

**[1] What inspired Dickens to write about Miss Havisham? What did he want to say about Victorian women, wealth and marriage?**

**Themes**: Victorian women, Victorian writers.

**Idea**: Scenes from Dickens' life in which he meets characters who might have been inspirations for Miss Havisham.

**[2] Does wealth make you happy?**

**Theme**: Wealth versus poverty.

**Idea**: A central character who seems to have everything but is unhappy.

**[3] What do the external fashions and conventions of weddings mean?**

**Theme**: Marriage and rituals.

**Idea**: Someone rejecting the conventions of the white wedding.

Someone agrees to be a contestant on a reality show about weddings, but ends up spoiling the show by refusing to behave as expected.

**[4] How can you portray on stage the most important moment in a person's life?**

**Theme**: Choices.

**Idea**: Show the most dramatic moment in a person's life, for example when they had to make an important choice and whether or not they could move on from it. Trace two narratives depending on the choices made.

**[5] What are the effects of time? What happens if someone tries to cling on to youth?**

**Theme**: Time/ageing.

**Idea**: A time-travel drama in which a character goes back to their youth to right a wrong.

Miss Havisham [1]

She was dressed in rich materials – satins, and lace, and silks – all of white. [2] Her shoes were white. And she had a long white veil dependent from her hair, and she had bridal flowers in her hair, but her hair was white. [3] Some bright jewels sparkled on her neck and on her hands, and some other jewels lay sparkling on the table. Dresses, less splendid than the dress she wore, and half-packed trunks, were scattered about. She had not quite finished dressing, for she had but one shoe on – the other was on the table near her hand - her veil was but half arranged, her watch and chain were not put on, and some lace for her bosom lay with those trinkets, and with her handkerchief, and gloves, and some flowers, and a prayer-book, all confusedly heaped about the looking-glass. [4]

It was not in the first few moments that I saw all these things, though I saw more of them in the first moments than might be supposed. But, I saw that everything within my view which ought to be white, had been white long ago, and had lost its lustre, and was faded and yellow. [5] I saw that the bride within the bridal dress had withered like the dress, and like the flowers, and had no brightness left but the brightness of her sunken eyes. [6] I saw that the dress had been put upon the rounded figure of a young woman, and that the figure upon which it now hung loose, had shrunk to skin and bone. Once, I had been taken to see some ghastly waxwork at the Fair, representing I know not what impossible personage lying in state. Once, I had been taken to one of our old marsh churches to see a skeleton in the ashes of a rich dress, that had been dug out of a vault under the church pavement. Now, waxwork and skeleton seemed to have dark eyes that moved and looked at me. I should have cried out, if I could. [7]

**[6] What happens when a wedding doesn't end in 'happily ever after'?**

**Theme**: Marriage/love.

**Idea**: Two stories about weddings: one person being forced into a marriage they don't want and someone finds love just when they had given up.

**[7] What would someone do to get revenge for the ruin of their life?**

**Theme**: Revenge/hatred.

**Idea**: A story about a rejected person seeking revenge on the world.

TIP:

At this stage, try to generate a number of different responses. Don't be too quick to reject an idea or settle on the first thing that comes to mind.

# Responding to different stimuli

## TASK 5.3

Spend some time exploring the other sample stimuli below and on the following pages. Annotate them with dramatic questions, themes and ideas.

Your stimulus might be a biography or speech by an important person.

### Shirley Chisholm

Shirley Chisholm was the first black woman elected to the United States Congress.

She was born in 1924 in Brooklyn, New York, to parents who had immigrated from the West Indies. Her father was a factory worker, and her mother was a seamstress. She was educated both in Barbados and in New York. She served in Congress from 1969 to 1983. She was the first black person from a major party to run for nomination as presidential candidate.

Chisholm's interest in politics started when she worked in education. As a state legislator, she championed programmes to provide benefits for domestic workers and improve educational opportunities for the disadvantaged.

In Congress, she served on the Education and Labour Committee and she was a founding member of the National Women's Political Caucus.

In her famous speech delivered to the House of Representatives in May 1969, in support of equal rights for women, she said:

**Why is it acceptable for women to be secretaries, librarians and teachers, but totally unacceptable for them to be managers, administrators, doctors, lawyers and Members of Congress?**

The unspoken assumption is that women are different. They do not have executive ability, orderly minds, stability, leadership skills, and they are too emotional…

More than half of the population of the United States is female. But women occupy only 2 per cent of the managerial positions… In Congress, we are down to one Senator and ten Representatives…

It is for this reason that I wish to introduce today a proposal that has been before every Congress for the last 40 years and that sooner or later must become part of the basic law of the land – the equal rights amendment…

What we need are laws to protect working people, to guarantee them fair pay, safe working conditions, protection against sickness and layoffs, and provision for dignified, comfortable retirement. Men and women need these things equally…

Other stimuli include a piece of music, such as *Canon in D* by Johann Pachelbel...

A poem...

### 'The Leader'

I wanna be the leader
I wanna be the leader
Can I be the leader?
Can I? I can?
Promise? Promise?
Yippee I'm the leader
I'm the leader

OK what shall we do?

*Roger McGough*

A painting or other work of visual art, such as *The Persistence of Memory* by Salvador Dali.

# The break-up of The Beatles

The Beatles – John Lennon, Paul McCartney, George Harrison and Ringo Starr – were a hugely successful and extremely influential rock group of the 1960s. From humble beginnings, they became the best-selling band in history and had devoted fans worldwide.

After a series of incidents, including the death of their manager, Brian Epstein, conflicting goals and interests, and new romantic partners, strains began to appear between the band members. In September 1969, John Lennon informed the others that he was leaving the group. After a number of personal and legal disputes, the break-up was formalised in 1974.

For many years, fans hoped they would reunite, but this hope ended in December 1980 when John Lennon was assassinated by a former fan.

**The Beatles enjoy early success, in 1963.**

Your stimulus might be a news report, a photograph or other image like this...

**TIP:**

Your final performance must reflect the stimulus. If your chosen stimulus is something like the *Great Expectations* extract on page 192 and you create a piece about an alien invasion, you might struggle to show a believable creative journey from the stimulus to your final piece.

...or a song, such as 'Clown' by Emeli Sandé.

NOW PLAYING

**Clown**
Emeli Sandé

## WHAT THE SPECIFICATION SAYS...

Learners should be able to:

- Use research to inform creative decisions when devising their drama
- Examine the social, cultural or historical context of the chosen stimulus
- Explain how research has impacted on their artistic intentions.

**LOOK HERE**

See pages 210–213 for details of how to complete your portfolio.

**TIP:**

Your research should be highly developed and detailed. It should link to the stimulus material.

# Research

You need to research your stimulus and record your research in your portfolio.

Your research should not be a series of random dates and facts, however, but should provide an underpinning of ideas and practical considerations for your final piece. For example, using the Miss Havisham extract on page 192, you might want to find out about:

- Victorian and modern wedding fashions
- How Miss Havisham has been depicted in illustrations, on stage and in films
- Why marriage was important to Victorian women
- Any figures from Dickens' life who might have provided inspiration for Miss Havisham
- Modern examples of people who were left at the altar on their wedding day
- Popular music at Victorian and modern weddings
- What happens to Miss Havisham at the end of the novel.

Helena Bonham-Carter as Miss Havisham in Mike Newell's 2012 film version of *Great Expectations*.

Some forms of research for your chosen piece could include:

- Exploring the artists and subjects of relevant paintings, illustrations and photographs
- Listening to music from the period
- Discovering the details of important political or social events
- If appropriate, trying to learn the intentions of the creator of the prose, poem or artwork
- Identifying differences between the present day and the time of the original stimulus, if you are updating a story based on a stimulus from an earlier time
- Viewing examples of fashions or settings from the appropriate time period.

# Generating dramatic ideas from your research

## TASK 5.4

Choose one stimulus from pages 192–195 to research. Start to think how it could inform a dramatic production. Use a table like this to organise your notes and ideas.

| Type of research | What we learned | How this could influence artistic decisions in our work |
|---|---|---|
| Read and researched the full 1969 Shirley Chisholm speech and watched a video discussion of it. | The speech begins with an example of a woman being asked if she could type — the assumption being that she could only aspire to be a secretary. | A scene where our main character is asked if she can type, despite having a higher degree... |
| | | |
| | | |

> **TIP:**
> Avoid just 'cutting and pasting' research into your portfolio. You should select particular material that will influence your production. For example, you might find fashions from the period that you could then annotate with how they have influenced your costume designs.

# Developing ideas
## Moving on from your stimulus

Your first ideas will lead to a fuller exploration of a theme and the creation of a narrative. You might base your devised piece closely on the stimulus or you could closely link certain details of the stimulus to your final piece. You must, however, be able to show how your stimulus and your response to it led to an advanced piece. In Task 5.2, for example, one of the ideas inspired by Miss Havisham was a reality TV programme. This is just an initial idea, so you would need to discuss and explore:

- The target audience for the drama you will devise from it, and how it will appeal to that audience
- What you want to communicate to your audience (For example, are you criticising marriage or the expense associated with it? Do you want to make fun of stereotypical wedding rituals or do you want to make a point about commitment?)
- The main characters and how will they contribute to the narrative
- The style and tone of the work (Are you creating a comedy? A historical drama? A naturalistic piece? A stylised piece?)
- How you will use design
- How you can show the links between the stimulus and the final work.

> **WHAT THE SPECIFICATION SAYS...**
> Learners should know and understand:
> - How to develop an idea to progress from a simple to a more complex stage.
>
> Learners should be able to:
> - Show the progression of their idea from initial thoughts to the realised form.

> **TIP:**
> Be aware of the needs of your performers and your audience. You may explore a challenging or controversial topic, but it must be done artistically and sensitively. If in doubt, avoid content that could be traumatic for those performing or viewing it.

## EXTENSION

Research the work of professional companies that use devising, such as Splendid Productions and The Paper Birds to discover further inspiration for your work.

## WHAT THE SPECIFICATION SAYS...

Learners should know and understand:

- How workshops can move the development of the performance forward
- How to rehearse in preparation for a performance to an audience.

Learners should be able to:

- Plan for effective use of rehearsals.
- Refine and amend work throughout the devising process so that clear dramatic intentions are communicated to the audience.

### TIP:

If you are working as a designer in your group, you are still responsible for contributing to the development of the piece. Additionally, you could take a leadership role in guiding and polishing performances or you could provide materials to assist with rehearsals.

### TIP:

A common problem that groups have is arguing too much about ideas. it is important to find a way of solving disagreements. You might select one group member to be the 'director', or you could take votes on important decisions.

## TASK 5.5

**A** Choose either one of the stimuli on pages 192–195 or the stimulus you are already working on, and, as a group, respond to the bullet points and questions on the previous page. Some of your ideas might change as you work, but it is good to come to a shared vision before you begin rehearsals.

**B** Write a paragraph that sums up what will be in your piece, including the characters, the main events of the story or the plot and what you want the audience to get from seeing it.

# Rehearsing

To create your piece of drama and to complete your portfolio, you need to organise a series of rehearsals. It is your responsibility to guide your own rehearsals. The content of them will depend on the type of piece you are creating and the challenges and obstacles you encounter. It is good practice to have a focus for every rehearsal and, at the end of each rehearsal, to confirm what you want to accomplish in the next one. Goals for a given rehearsal might be to:

- Create an opening scene
- Develop a music and movement section
- Improvise or block a given scene
- Explore the background of the characters and their relationships
- Rehearse the dialogue or monologue for a scene
- Work with props or costumes
- Rework or troubleshoot a section that is not yet working
- Polish a section that is 'nearly there'
- Hold a technical rehearsal, including sound and lighting.

## A rehearsal schedule

You will probably find it helpful to create a rehearsal schedule. Be aware that it might need to be adapted as your piece develops.

A sample schedule is provided on the next page, with some examples. It is for a group who have already agreed the stimulus and their basic approach to the piece and have a rough narrative idea. You may use this as a guide for creating your own rehearsal schedule, but bear in mind that the number of rehearsals and weeks you have to work are likely to be different from those given here. Note too that the demands of a naturalistic piece, for example, will be very different from those of a stylised, movement-led piece.

### TIP:

The recommended time for a devised performance is between 5 and 15 minutes. Be aware of these timings as you rehearse. The absolute minimum performance time is 4 minutes, and if you do not meet this requirement, you risk not being awarded any marks for AO2.

| Rehearsal week and type | Aims and activities | | Next steps Individual work |
|---|---|---|---|
| **1 Character work** | Goal | • Develop characters and their relationships.<br>• Create possible opening scene. | • Research characters and background/context.<br>• Write in-character monologue. |
| | Rehearsal | • Hot seating.<br>• Improvise a backstory scene for each character. | |
| **2 Dialogue** | Goal | • Create outline of piece and agree some key dialogue. | • Make detailed notes or, if ready, begin creating script.<br>• Find music possibilities for next week. |
| | Rehearsal | • Improvise key scenes.<br>• Create conflict scenes where characters have different objectives. | |
| **3 Movement** | Goal | • Create a synchronised movement section to move the narrative on. | • Record music and make notes of movement choices (use video?).<br>• Research different companies' use of stylised movement. |
| | Rehearsal | • Still image.<br>• Choreography. | |
| **4 Structure** | Goal | • Agree structure and style features.<br>• Set beginning and ending and, if relevant, climax. | • Note scene order.<br>• Check that all members are making sufficient contributions and, if not, make necessary adjustments.<br>• Agree costume and set designs and who is responsible for acquiring what. |
| | Rehearsal | • Scene mapping.<br>• Experiment with techniques, such as narration, breaking the fourth wall. | |
| **5 Shape and timing** | Goal | • Check timing.<br>• Respond to feedback. | • Make any last-minute adjustments. |
| | Rehearsal | • Small sharing rehearsal for feedback.<br>• Target-setting. | |
| **6 Dress/technical rehearsals** | Goal | • Check and coordinate all technical aspects of the performance.<br>• Polish any remaining performance issues. | • Complete final outline of piece.<br>• Create lighting and sound cue sheets.<br>• Check timing of piece and adjust accordingly. |
| | Rehearsal | • Stop-and-start technical rehearsal and a speed run for pace.<br>• Full dress rehearsal with small invited audience. | |
| **Performance** | Goal | • Warm-ups: troubleshoot any problem sections. | • Gather audience questionnaires.<br>• Complete final evaluation. |
| | Rehearsal | • Final pre-performance rehearsal.<br>• Full audience. | |

# Rehearsal techniques

There are a great many different rehearsals techniques you could try. A few examples are given here which you might find helpful.

## For content and form

### Improvisation

Performing without a script. This is used in many different ways when devising, for example:

- As a warm-up or when generating ideas, a group might use a series of very short improvisations in reaction to a stimulus, theme or title.
- When beginning to create a character, you might improvise how they would react in different situations.
- When developing a scene, you might know your starting and ending point, but improvise how the characters get from the start to the end.

### Backstory

A period of time before the action of your piece begins through which you gain insight and depth into your characters and your drama. You might want to explore a character's recent past, such as what they were doing five minutes before a scene begins, or heir distant past, such as their childhood. These discoveries might just enrich your work, or you could include some of the backstory in the performance through **cross-cutting** or **flashbacks**.

### Objectives/obstacles/conflict

Conflict is at the heart of drama and this exercise helps you to define what a character wants in a scene and what is preventing them from getting it. At the beginning of a scene, state what each character wants, such as, 'I want to escape' or 'I want a promotion', then agree on the obstacle: 'I want a promotion (objective), but the boss thinks X is better for the job than I am (obstacle),' or 'I want to escape (objective), but my friend is lonely and wants me to stay (obstacle).'

Try performing the scene first without any dialogue, just by pursuing your objectives physically and trying to overcome your obstacles. Then, keeping the same intensity in your approach, add some lines. This is a useful way to avoid aimless scenes. It should, instead, generate dramatic interest and excitement.

## KEY TERMS:

**Cross-cutting:** Changing back and forth between different scenes or episodes. This can occur in a finished piece or be used as a rehearsal technique, with someone calling 'Cut' to switch between scenes.

**Flashback:** A scene from an earlier period of a character's life than that shown in the play's main timeline.

## For characterisation

### Role-on-the-wall

Used early in rehearsals, this can be a helpful way of discovering different aspects of your character.

Place a large outline of a figure on a long sheet of paper on the wall to represent the character and then fill it with facts and information about the character. You could divide the figure, so that you put:

- In or around the head: The character's thoughts and some key lines they say
- Torso: Feelings
- Limbs: Actions
- On the area around the figure: External influences, such as location, age and nationality and what others think about the character.

### Writing in role

Write a letter, diary entry, report or journal as if written by the character, to develop greater insight. A variation is to have each character write a letter or email to another character, perhaps to apologise for something they have done, reveal a secret or explain their actions. This writing might lead to a monologue or even a full scene.

### Hot seating

One person is put, in character, in the 'hot seat' and others ask them a series of questions. Discoveries made about the character can be developed into scenes or provide detail in a performance.

### Thought-tracking

An actor 'freezes' during a scene, and speaks their thoughts aloud. This is a way of developing effective subtext; showing the meaning beneath the lines and actions.

## For movement and positioning

### Still image

This creates a picture that represents a frozen moment or a key image from a drama. It could show one or more characters. It is useful for exploring positioning of characters (and levels and proxemics), as well as facial expression, body language and gesture. It can also be used as way of beginning or ending a scene or marking an important moment.

### Tableau(x)

A dramatic stage picture showing a group of characters and, often, stage furniture, props and costumes. A tableau provides visual clues as to how to interpret a scene, such as what the characters are wearing, where they are and what their relationships are, for example, who is powerful.

When developing your piece, you might create a series of tableaux to show how the characters change during the piece. When rehearsing, for example, you might want to create a tableau that sums up the dramatic action of each scene. Some productions use a tableau to begin or end their performance. Tableaux can be useful for checking the visual interest of your piece.

### EXTENSION

There are many online examples, including videos, of different movement exercises, which, depending on the style of your piece, you might find helpful and inspiring. You could Look at the work of companies such as Complicité, Kneehigh and Frantic Assembly, to see how they create movement for their performances.

Movement involving a puppet in a Complicité production, *Shun-Kin*.

# Structure

Depending on your choices, you might have a play that simply presents a series of events from a single day, or you might switch back and forth between different time periods. Your work could be a naturalistic 'slice of life', or you might use a narrator or other storytelling techniques to fill in the characters' backgrounds or changes in locations. You might follow a single protagonist or have multiple story strands.

There are no right or wrong choices, but it should be a positive decision, not something that you just fall into. Some structural options are described here.

### WHAT THE SPECIFICATION SAYS...

Learners should know and understand:

- How to plan, create and structure drama
- How to edit and adapt the work as a result of new ideas or the development of the drama.

## Choosing a narrative structure

### Linear

A **chronological** plot, in which one event leads on to the next one. A play might present, in order, the events of one day, for example, or one week or one year.

### Non-linear

A play in which events are not presented chronologically. A scene set in the present day, for example, might be followed by a scene that takes place ten years earlier or a hundred years later.

### Bookended

The first and last scenes are connected in some significant way. For example, a narrative could start with an important event, such as an awards ceremony or a train accident, and then, after following a series of events, end at the same place.

### Circular

A plot structure that suggests that the same action will occur again. For example, a play that begins with someone being robbed, and has a plot that follows what happens to them, might end with a new person being robbed, suggesting that the story will be repeated.

### Episodic

A series of loosely connected scenes that might be united by a shared theme or location.

### Parallel or multiple plots

A narrative that follows several protagonists' connected stories.

In *Into the Woods*, the Narrator (Jim King) punctuates the action to offer the audience guidance on the developing plot.

### KEY TERM:

Chronological: Presenting events in the order in which they occur.

**TIP:**

With any of these techniques, check to make sure that your plot is clear and makes sense. Does it communicate what you hoped it would?

**TIP:**

As you rehearse, you may decide to change the order of your narrative, especially if you think it will make the piece clearer or more engaging.

## TASK 5.6

**A** Write down, on small pieces of paper or sticky notes, all the scenes in in your play and place them in chronological order on a large sheet of paper. Then, in your group, consider if that is the best structure for your piece. (It might be.) Try experimenting with the following:

- Start the scene order with the most exciting, climatic moment.
- Create at least one flashback.
- Make a strong connection between the beginning and the ending.
- Set a scene order that gradually builds to a climax.

**B** Discuss the advantages of the different structures and agree which would be the most effective for your piece.

**C** Now test your planned structure with one or more of these activities:

- Have a narrator tell the 'story', while the rest of the group mimes the action.
- Draw a storyboard of the plot.
- Create a two-minute version of your plot.

**WHAT THE SPECIFICATION SAYS...**

Learners should know and understand:

- How to communicate meaning to an audience through engaging drama.

# Communicating ideas through performance

Acting and design both play a vital role in how ideas are communicated in drama. For example, if a man enters to the sound of a fanfare, wearing a golden crown and an embroidered cloak and sits down on a spotlit golden throne surrounded by kneeling subjects, the audience will understand from these semiotics, that he is a powerful king, before he has even said a word. In performance, an actor will communicate to the audience through the use of gestures, facial expression and tone of voice the type of king that is being presented.

How ideas are communicated to an audience is at the centre of all drama. In order to do this well, you must be clear about:

- What your ideas are
- How you will put them across
- Who your audience is.

If your goal is, for example, to inform a teenage audience about an important historic figure, the ways you will convey this might be very different from the methods for creating a dynamic movement piece about the effects of climate change for an adult audience.

Throughout your work, don't lose sight of your intentions. If you want to make a political or social point or to entertain or inform your audience in a particular way, make sure that you remember this during rehearsals and when you write up your devising log.

# Conveying meaning through style and conventions

You can communicate to your audience through the style of your piece and how you use the conventions of drama. You might create a naturalistic piece that addresses a realistic problem or you might work on a stylised, highly theatrical piece. Either way, some conventions to consider include:

- **Narration**: When one or more characters tell some of the story by speaking directly to the audience
- **Ensemble movement**: Stylised group movement, often performed to music
- **Multi-role**: When actors play more than one role.

**TIP:**

Match the style and conventions of your piece to what you want to communicate, and to your audience.

## TASK 5.7

**A** In your group, agree on a central idea that you wish to convey in your drama, such as:

- It is dangerous in the city
- A character behaves heroically
- Technology can be harmful.

**B** Then experiment with the following ways of communicating the idea:

- Have a narrator or narrators explain the idea to the audience.
- Create a movement sequence that demonstrates the idea.
- Improvise a scene between two characters to explore the idea.
- Develop a comic scene in which two actors play a number of different characters to comment on the idea.

**C** Discuss if any of these methods would be helpful to the development of a style for your piece. If not, can you think of other methods to convey content and style? Also consider whether the style of your piece will be used consistently or just in a certain section.

## TASK 5.8

**Status** is one aspect of characterisation that can be usefully explored. Choose a scene from your piece and decide who has the highest status in it and who has the lowest status. Assign each an appropriate number. For example, in the *Great Expectations* example at the beginning of this chapter, Miss Havisham might have a status of 9, while the young boy, Pip, might have a status of 2 or 3. Then experiment with how you can use acting skills to convey their status to the audience. For example, Pip might lower his head or bow to Miss Havisham, while she might raise her chin and point imperiously at him.

PIP WAITS ON MISS HAVISHAM.

An illustration from an early edition of *Great Expectations*, showing the young Pip and a haughty Miss Havisham.

**KEY TERM:**

**Status:** Social, economic or political importance in relation to others; holding power.

## WHAT THE SPECIFICATION SAYS...

Learners should know and understand:

- How to make plans for the structure/ form of an artefact – set, costume, lighting, sound.

### TIP:

As with the performers, you must remember what your intentions as a designer are and how they support the piece as a whole.

### LOOK HERE

For an example of a lighting cue sheet, see page 226, and for a sound cue sheet, see page 229.

# Communicating ideas through design

For some audiences, their first hint of the meaning of a play is provided by design. A realistic set with furniture from the 1960s will lead to one set of expectations, whereas a set comprised of large black boxes and geometric drawings on the floor will lead to different assumptions. When devising your piece, you must consider how design can contribute meaning. Ask how your design will help the audience to understand:

- Where and when the drama is set
- The style and tone (Is it realistic? Is it a comedy?)
- The action of the plot (when time passes or scenes change, for example)
- The characters and their relationships.

## Design roles

The design specialisms from which you can choose the role in your group are:

- **Lighting**
- **Sound**
- **Lighting and sound** combined (but only if there is not already a separate lighting and/or sound designer in the group)
- **Set**, including props and multimedia staging
- **Costume**, including hair, make-up and masks.

If you choose to take a design role rather than a performance role, you must be prepared to fulfil the minimum requirements which are listed in full in the course specification.

### Lighting

This requires a full lighting design for the performance, with a cue sheet that details lanterns to be used and the different lighting states. The production must have a minimum of six lighting changes evident, excluding lights up and lights down. You need sufficient lighting equipment to produce the design and be able to operate the lighting desk during the performance.

### TIP:

For each design specialism, be aware of the supporting materials you must provide.

### Sound

You will need a full sound sheet with original and copied cues leading to a finalised sound CD or MP3 playlist on a memory stick for use in the final performance. A minimum of six sound cues should be evident in the performance. You must operate the sound desk during the performance.

## Lighting and sound (combined)

This can be a combination of the requirements for sound and lighting, again with a minimum of six cues each in performance.

## Set

You must produce a scale model and a detailed ground plan of the set. You will need to source set (and props) for the performance and supervise the construction of the set, where appropriate. You will dress the set ready for performance, and one set design must be realised in the final performance.

## Costume

This needs to be a final design of one of:

- One full costume – including hair and make-up detail – that is sourced and realised in performance
- One full costume – including mask(s) – that is sourced and realised in performance
- Two costumes for characters – *excluding* hair, make-up or masks – that are sourced and realised in performance. (These costumes may be for different characters or different costumes for one character.)

### TASK 5.9

A Choose one of the design specialisms discussed above and make notes, with detailed examples, about how it can support your devised piece and help to communicate its meaning to an audience.

### TASK 5.10

A Take your ideas from Task 5.9 to your group and, together, list any obstacles in achieving what you want, such as budgetary constraints, lack of technical knowledge or lack of time to complete the construction.

B Explore how these obstacles might be overcome. For example, you could use projections, as shown in the production of *Peerless* by Company One, below, rather than fully realistic painted sets.

> **TIP:**
>
> If you do not have a designer in your group, you should create a minimal amount of lighting, sound, set and or costumes as necessary for your piece to be engaging and clear, but you will be assessed as a performer.

 **LOOK HERE**

See pages 223–235, for more information about design, including practical advice.

> **TIP:**
>
> Remember that your contribution as a designer should have at least the same amount of challenge as the performers. Consider if your design involves as much work as learning lines and blocking, performing before an audience, and so on.

## WHAT THE SPECIFICATION SAYS...

Learners should know and understand:
- How to communicate meaning to an audience through engaging drama.

Learners should be able to:
- Apply performance or design skills to performance for an audience.

### KEY TERM:

**Ad lib:** An improvisation by an actor, which usually occurs when a mistake has happened on stage, such as a missed line or entrance, or when there is an interruption to the performance.

# Performing before an audience

As either a performer or a designer, you will be assessed on your contribution to the devised performance. Your fulfilment of an artistic vision, reflection of the stimulus and the effectiveness of communication will all be considered, as well as your performance or design skills. For an actor, this could mean creating a well-developed individual character or participating as a highly skilled ensemble member, whereas a designer could support a production in many ways, including through a detailed and varied lighting design or a creative and well-finished costume, make-up and hair design.

## Common performance issues and possible solutions

### Performance problems

### Potential solutions

Performance is under or over the specified time limits.
- Throughout rehearsals, time your work and make additions and edits as you go along.
- Create a piece that is definitely over the minimum amount of time, so that if lines are forgotten or rushed, you will still be within the time limits.
- For pieces that are too long, see if any dialogue or scenes could be cut without losing the intentions of the work. Are any scenes or lines of dialogue repetitious? Are there points when your audience will lose interest?

Performance does not show a high level of acting skills, such as characterisation.
- Consider what you want your audience to understand about your character and be consistent in your choices.
- See if your research or the characterisation exercises in this chapter can help.
- Ensure that you have a character who is appropriately challenging for you and allows you to demonstrate your skills.

Vocal skills are limited, such as lack of volume, poor diction or monotony.
A good vocal warm-up and asking a friend to check your work could help.

Physical skills are limited, such as repetitive gestures, wandering movement, stiffness or uncertain movements.
- Ask a friend or someone in your group to help you to spot common problems like these.
- A physical warm-up will loosen you up.
- Specific movement rehearsals should build confidence.

Lines are hesitant or forgotten.
- You must know your lines so thoroughly that even if something goes wrong you are able to carry on.
- Try speed-runs of lines, in which you run the piece double-time, to make sure you are confident.

Nervousness or stage fright.
- Practise relaxation exercises.
- Focus on your character and their world.
- Visualise success.

Something goes wrong in performance.
- Carry on! Stay in character and continue.
- You might need to **ad lib** a few lines to cover for something that has gone wrong or pick up a dropped prop, but keep in the world of the play.

# Common design issues and possible solutions

| Design problems | | Potential solutions |
|---|---|---|

**Design problems**     **Potential solutions**

**Design is too simple.**

- Ensure you have chosen a design specialism for which you have the appropriate skills and equipment. Don't choose lighting if you don't have access to a lighting rig, or sound if you are unsure how to record it.
- While devising, note how your design can be integral to the drama.
- Make sure your design demonstrates your skills and has sufficient challenge.

**Design does not contribute to performance.**

Collaborate throughout so that your design works towards the goals of the piece. For example, if the drama is to be naturalistic, your design should reflect that, or, if it is stylised, that should be evident in your design choices.

**Design is incomplete.**

- You must demonstrate at least the minimum contribution as detailed in the specification. To do this, plan your time carefully.
- Arrange fittings for costumes or test runs for placing and changing sets and props well before the final performance.
- Costume designs, model boxes, ground plans and lighting and sound cues should all be prepared well in advance.

**Something goes wrong in performance.**

- The best solution to technical difficulties is prevention: hold careful technical and dress rehearsals in which you check that everything is in good working order.
- A sound check to ensure correct volume levels should be completed.
- Carry out health and safety checks, for example making sure cables are taped down to avoid trips.
- Be prepared, for instance by having a sewing kit on hand for repairs or back-up equipment for sound effects.

# Evaluation

Evaluation should be ongoing throughout the devising process when you are making choices and changes that you will need to justify in your portfolio.

In order to test how effective their work is and to make the necessary adjustments, some groups have 'work-in-progress' performances at which their work is viewed and commented on by a small audience or other groups. Feedback from these, in the form of questionnaires, buddy assessment or question-and-answer sessions, can help a group to adjust and polish its work.

## Making improvements

Your analysis and evaluation are marked throughout your portfolio, so, make sure that you have analysed and evaluated:

- The devising progress, including decisions made during it
- Changes made during development and why they were made
- How your choices can communicate meaning to the audience
- How successful your final performance was and how it could be improved for future performances.

**WHAT THE SPECIFICATION SAYS...**

Learners should know and understand:

- How to examine in detail the process of creating drama and measure the impact on a live audience.

Learners should be able to:

- Analyse and evaluate decisions and choices made during the process of creating drama.
- Evaluate their final piece of devised drama
- Use accurate subject-specific terminology.

**TASK 5.11**

Create two targets for improving your performance or design and explain how you will achieve these improvements.

## WHAT THE SPECIFICATION SAYS...

Learners should be able to:

- Clearly document the development of the performance during the devising process through the use of a portfolio.

# Creating your portfolio

Throughout the devising process, and afterwards, you will be completing a portfolio. The portfolio has three sections:

1 Research and initial ideas

2 Creating and developing drama, including analysing and evaluating the work in progress

3 An evaluation of the final piece of devised drama.

## The format of the portfolio

Your portfolio may be one of:

- Twenty sides of A4 paper, which might include notes, sketches, diagrams, scripts, storyboards, photographs and annotations

- A 12-minute recorded presentation, which could include a video diary or blog, a recording of performance activities created through the devised performance and slides or titles with audio commentary

- Two thousand words of continuous prose.

Or, it may be a combination of the above, as fully detailed in the specification, for example: ten sides of A4 notes and drawings accompanied by 1000 words of continuous prose.

KNITTED BURGUNDY SCARF

TORTOISESHELL PATTERNED SUNGLASSES

BASIC BLACK SWEATSHIRT

BLACK OVERSIZE COAT

SHORT PLEATED SKIRT

BURGUNDY CITY BAG

HIGH-HEELED LEATHER BOOTS

GREY SOCKS

### TIP:

Refer to the OCR specification for the most detailed and up-to-date guidance on the portfolio.

## Portfolio example: *Great Expectations*

The excerpts on the following pages from candidate-style portfolios are from the same group, using the stimulus of Miss Havisham from *Great Expectations* on page 192. One is by a performer; the other by a designer.

**Candidate 1: Performer**

### Section 1: Research and initial ideas

Our initial ideas based on this stimulus led us to look at the theme of **marriage**. We wondered why **Miss Havisham** had such a severe reaction to her rejection and if that was particularly relevant to the Victorian times. Some of our early work involved researching the Victorian age. I found a popular pamphlet, written in 1854, called 'The Angel in the House' which shows an idealised version of how a woman should 'please' her husband because 'him to please is woman's pleasure'. The idea is that a **woman's place** is as a wife and mother within the home. However, for someone like Miss Havisham, whose hopes of marriage have been dashed, this would be a social was well as personal **tragedy**.

We considered setting our piece entirely in the Victorian age, and discussed basing it on Miss Havisham's relationship with her fiancé, but eventually decided to update our story to the present day, as we felt that might make it more **relatable** to our audience. We also thought, however, that we could keep the image of Miss Havisham as a **symbol**, so we could contrast her with our modern heroine. The dramatic question we decided to ask is:

How have attitudes towards marriage changed since Miss Havisham's time?

### Section 2: Creating and developing drama, including analysing and evaluating the work in progress

Given our audience and our strengths as performers, we decided to use comedy and stylised movement in our piece. One group member suggested that we could create comedy by having a young woman on a reality television programme who, rather than playing along with the idea of finding her ideal mate, instead creates chaos. We thought that this tied in well with the stimulus because Miss Havisham was, in her own way, a **disrupter**. In order to develop this idea, we spent three rehearsals improvising the 'dates' **Hetty, our main character**, goes on and how each of them goes wrong. One of our ideas was having her go to a fancy restaurant and the evening ending in a food fight. Although we liked the basic idea, it just seemed sloppy and silly when we put it on its feet. I suggested that, instead of just flinging the food around, it would be more effective and show more skills if we created a **slow-motion movement** sequence. Using a song called 'Crashed the Wedding', we employed **Frantic Assembly** techniques to create a sequence with lifts and partner work to show the violence of the date going wrong – but in a way that was also quite beautiful. However, we noticed that the piece was over-running by about five minutes, so, a week before the performance, we had to cut one of Hetty's dates and shorten the movement sequence slightly.

### Section 3: An evaluation of the final piece of devised drama

Our overall piece was successful, as we were aiming to explore attitudes towards modern weddings and contrast these with Miss Havisham and Victorian times. We also wanted to create a drama that would be interesting and engaging to our **teenage audience**. One sign that it was successful was the **laughter** from the audience. For example, the audience was amused by the whole 'reality show' which they understood to be a send-up of these shows.

One of the roles I played was the show's host and, in the beginning, I used a confident, upbeat tone and remained cheerful in the face of everything that happened. However, as the piece continued and Hetty caused more and more problems, my character became more bedraggled and my voice sounded weary and desperate. The audience was amused as I lost status. The other character I played was 'Miss Havisham' where I recreated **tableaux** of her in the play's opening and ending scenes. I felt this was a little less successful. One reason is that while the audience seemed **intrigued** by the first image, from comments afterwards, it was clear they didn't really know who this character was and what her relationship was to the rest of the piece. The final image was Miss Havisham winking at the audience and then getting up and dancing with Hetty. The dancing worked quite well, but I'm not sure that the wink registered. In a future performance, it might be worth considering how to highlight that moment more clearly and also to create a dance that was more obviously joyful – perhaps by including all the other cast members.

**Candidate 2: Costume designer**

## Section 1: Research and initial ideas

I was immediately inspired by the description of Miss Havisham's outfit – something that had once been elegant and beautiful and carefully made, was now aged and ill-fitting. In order to get a better idea of how this outfit might look, I researched book illustrations and film stills from productions of Great Expectations to see how other people had interpreted it, as well as Victorian wedding dresses and conventions. Here are some examples I found.

In my research on Victorian wedding customs, I saw the importance of veils and I thought this could be an important part of my design. Inspired by both the film stills and watching other versions of *Great Expectations*, I saw how the veil could look like a big web and Miss Havisham like a spider in it. It could also seem like a dust cloth, as if she were an ancient, immovable piece of furniture with her 'cover' gradually being covered in dust. However, the group did not want to just set the piece entirely in the Victorian age, so I decided to create two costumes – one for Jenny who was playing Miss Havisham at the piece's beginning and ending and one for Tobi who was playing our modern 'bride'. I thought the contrast between these costumes would be a challenge, but would communicate to the audience the difference between Victorian and modern weddings – and our attitudes towards them.

Miss Havisham book illustration by Charles Green, 1877.

Martita Hunt in the 1946 film of *Great Expectations*.

## Section 2: Creating and developing drama, including analysing and evaluating the work in progress

I created several sketches of the Miss Havisham dress. My first design was very close to the book illustration as you can see.

This dress has an empire line and a flowing skirt and short sleeves. However, since we have a young actor playing the role, I thought it would be better to create a dress that hid her youth and helped to give her the appearance of being older. In order to achieve this, I created a high neckline and long sleeves, both in a lacy, semi-transparent fabric, attached to a long satin dress.

The image I wanted to achieve was too complicated to make from scratch, so I visited a number of charity shops before sourcing an inexpensive, long, white polyester wedding dress. I adapted this by adding chiffon to the hem, a long, lace veil and lacy neckline and sleeves. When Jenny put this on, it gave an eerie effect, making her seem almost ghost-like. I ran into problems, however, when attempting to dye the dress a more yellowish shade. The polyester fabric did not take the dye, but the lace did. So I added lace to more of the dress, to give a general effect of being yellowed with age. In contrast, I designed and sewed a slim-fitting white jumpsuit for Tobi to wear as Hetty.

An old woman in an empire line full-length white dress, with short puff sleeves. She has messy hair and a long veil.

## Section 3: An evaluation of the final piece of devised drama.

I was very pleased with Tobi's modern outfit as Hetty. We had arranged several fittings and it showed, as it fitted perfectly, but also allowed her freedom of movement for the choreographed sequences. However, I sometimes wished that we had chosen an easier colour as some make-up marks appeared on the white jumpsuit between the dress rehearsal and final performance, so it didn't look as absolutely pristine as I would have liked.

The Miss Havisham costume was always going to be a big challenge and I believe it was only partly successful. The overlong veil worked very well and I heard the audience gasp when Jenny was first seen with the light pouring through the veil, making her look almost supernatural. However, the dress itself felt like a compromise. For a future performance, I would check that I had a dress that could be dyed successfully. The extra pieces of fabric sewn on made the dress look too patchwork and not like authentic to a rich person like Miss Havisham. However, it did contrast well with Hetty's jumpsuit and, when the two danced together at the end, it was clear that the outfits came from different eras.

### TASK 5.12

A Re-read the two candidate-style portfolio extracts and highlight every example of analysis and evaluation you find.

B Write a similar evaluation of your own final performance. Consider what went well and what could have been improved.

### TIP:

Some groups use audience feedback forms to help with their evaluation of their final performance, but do not just include these comments. Select highlights from them or quote selectively and then sum them up in your own words within your own overall appraisal.

### TIP:

Reflect on your intentions. In the end, did you accomplish what you wanted?

### CHECK YOUR LEARNING: Devising Drama

**Do you know…?**

✓ How many performers can be in a group.

✓ What designers can be in a group and what those roles involve.

✓ How you can collaborate well in a group.

✓ The specified minimum and maximum length for your devised piece.

✓ How to create, and use, a rehearsal schedule.

✓ The types of stimuli you can respond to.

✓ How to research an idea that comes from the stimulus.

✓ How to develop a drama from your stimulus and research.

✓ How to define your intention and assess whether it was met.

✓ The sections of your portfolio and what they should consist of.

✓ How to identify and overcome problems with performance and design.

✓ How to evaluate your work.

## WHAT THE SPECIFICATION SAYS...

Performers will be assessed in **two** extracts performed as part of the showcase.

Performance skills are assessed through the realisation of a live performance that must be prepared and rehearsed thoroughly so that the final outcome is polished and complete.

Designers must:

- Work with a performance group whose performance meets the minimum times.
- Realise the designs in any **two** performance extracts from **one** text in the showcase.

Design skills are assessed through the realisation of a final design in a live performance.

## ASSESSMENT OBJECTIVES

AO1 – Create and develop ideas to communicate meaning for theatrical performance

AO2 – Apply theatrical skills to realise artistic intentions in live performance.

This component is assessed by a visiting examiner.

## HOW YOU WILL BE ASSESSED

In this component, you will produce a performance of two extracts from one performance text and complete the concept pro forma describing their performance intention.

Component 03 is an exciting and challenging one in which you can demonstrate and celebrate your skills as a performer or designer. You will be involved in performing or designing for an audience two extracts from a single play. You will be assessed on your:

- Research and interpretation of the text – in your concept pro forma document
- Theatrical skills and ability to communicate meaning and intention to an audience – in your performance or design of the extracts.

# Choosing a text

There is a wide range of texts that could be chosen for this component, each with different demands. You may choose a naturalistic piece, which could require you to develop a realistic, detailed acting style. You may choose a period piece, which could involve a different set of physical and vocal skills, such as specific handling of props, moving in period costumes or speaking in verse. Or you may choose a stylised piece, which might require skills such as mime, choreography or choral speaking.

Whatever the genre of the texts, they must give you the opportunity to demonstrate your ability to handle dialogue and create a character. If a role is not a sufficient challenge, it will be difficult for you to demonstrate a full range of skills. Equally, designers must have the ability to show their skills in the chosen extracts. The needs of each student and each centre are different, so there are many choices that can be made. A small example of the range of texts is given on the following page. They are not recommendations, but have been successfully used in learning centres.

Play: **Neville's Island**

Author: Tim Firth

Genre: Naturalistic comedy (1992).

Four men are stranded on an island during a team-building exercise.

Play: **The Crucible**

Author: Arthur Miller

Genre: Naturalistic, historical drama (written in 1953, set in 1692.)

Members of a religious community are accused of witchcraft.

Play: **A Taste of Honey**

Author: Shelagh Delaney

Genre: Naturalistic drama (1958).

A neglected 17 year old becomes pregnant and moves in with her gay male friend.

Play: **A Midsummer Night's Dream**

Author: William Shakespeare

Genre: Period comedy (written in the 16th century, set in ancient Athens).

Romance and magic as lovers lose and find each other.

Play: **Private Lives**

Author: Noel Coward

Genre: Period comedy (1930s).

A divorced couple are reunited for a battle of wits.

Play: **The Gut Girls**

Author: Sarah Daniels

Genre: Period drama (written in 1988, set in the Victorian era).

A group of women endure difficulties and find solidarity working together.

Play: **Things I Know to Be True**

Author: Andrew Bovell

Genre: Naturalistic and stylised modern drama (2016).

The struggles of Fran and Bob Price and their adult children.

Play: **Shakers**

Author: John Godber

Genre: Stylised multi-role comedy (1985.)

Four waitresses present a typical night working in a bar and their hopes and dreams for their lives.

**TIP:**

You can achieve high marks from a wide variety of style and genre of texts. What is important is to choose a role and text that suits your interests and skills.

## WHAT THE SPECIFICATION SAYS...

Learners should know and understand:

- The features of the text including:
  - Genre
  - Structure
  - Character
  - Form and style
  - Dialogue
  - The role of stage directions
- How to communicate effectively using:
  - The semiotics of drama
  - The skills of a performer or designer
  - Performance conventions
- How performance texts can be presented to an audience.

# Performers

## Approaching a naturalistic text

### Example: *Leave Taking*

When preparing a naturalistic text, you must ensure that you understand the characters, their backgrounds and their motivations. Below is an example of an approach for a scene from *Leave Taking* (1987) by Winsome Pinnock. Set in London, it is the story of a Jamaican immigrant, Enid, and her two teenage daughters, Del and Viv, whose secrets are revealed in a visit to an obeah woman, a Caribbean healer. Del, who is pregnant, leaves the family home to move in with Mai, the obeah. In the extract below, Del is visited by Viv, who tries to convince her to come home.

The scene is annotated with the sorts of questions that actors might ask. (Answers can be found by reading the whole play, undertaking additional research and making discoveries during rehearsals.) It is followed by some advice for performing this style of text.

**[1]** Where is Mai's house located and what is unusual about it? What is this room like? What objects might be in it?

**[3]** Why is Viv confronting Del now? What is their relationship as sisters like? What is the age difference between them? What are they wearing and what do their outfits say about their characters?

**[6]** What does this question tell the audience about Viv?

**[7]** Del frequently responds with a joke or a deflecting remark. What does this reveal about her personality?

**[9]** What do we learn about the school? Why does Viv mention these girls? What do they mean to Del? Why is Debbie Foster mentioned in particular? What kind of character might she be?

**[12]** What does this tell us about the differences between the girls and their attitudes?

**[13]** Does Viv mean this? What is the subtext of this line?

VIV:   You can't have a baby here. **[1]**

DEL:   Why not? Anyway, I'll be out of here soon. Council puts you on the top of the list when you're pregnant. I might get a garden. **[2]**

VIV:   That why you did it? **[3]**

DEL:   No, it is not why I DID it. **[4]** God, Viv.

VIV:   I'm not gonna let you have my niece here. **[5]**

DEL:   First I heard aunt's got rights.

VIV:   You got milk yet? **[6]**

DEL:   You are such a pervert. **[7]**

VIV:   Wouldn't surprise me if you don't.

DEL:   I look after meself.

VIV:   Don't look like it. Place smells damp. Be horrible in the winter. **[8]** Baby'll get fungus on its lungs. (*Beat.*) They're dropping like flies in the sixth form: Sharon Gibbs, Glenna Murphy, Debbie Foster. **[9]** Debbie Foster was so far gone she couldn't fit the desk in the exam room. Then she had to go to the loo every five minutes.

DEL:   Probably had the answers written on her belly. **[10]**

VIV:   How you gonna manage? Baby's gonna need clothes, nappies. I'll help look after it if you come home. **[11]**

DEL:   Let me get on with my life, can't you?

VIV:   I want to be there when it comes.

DEL:   Hold my hand? Be escaping yourself in – what? – coupla months? You'll be going to wild parties, they'll be sex, drugs, booze. **[12]** (*Looks VIV up and down.*) No, you won't, will you? You're such a good girl.

VIV:   I'm not as good as you think. **[13]**

DEL:   Why, what you been up to?

VIV:   Wouldn't you like to know? So what d'you do all day? **[14]**

**[2]** How many months is Del pregnant here? How does Del feel at this point? Confident or frightened? Strong or weak?

**[4]** How does Del feel? Is she angry? Sad? Exasperated?

**[5]** How can Viv make this point strongly? Where is she positioned in the room? Does she move or make a gesture?

**[8]** Does the room smell? Is it warm or cold? Is it tidy or messy? How might Viv and Del's reactions to it differ?

**[10]** Why does Del make a joke? How does the discussion of these girls make her feel?

**[11]** How might this attempt by Viv to convince Del differ from her previous ones? Does she alter her movements or voice to signal a change?

**[14]** What should the audience understand and feel about the two characters?

Seraphina Beh and Sarah Niles as Del and Enid in *Leave Taking* at the Bush Theatre.

## Examples of naturalistic rehearsal techniques

### Sense memory

Try to recall a time when you experienced a similar sensation to one depicted in a scene you are rehearsing. It might be how something felt, tasted, sounded or smelled. Then transfer that precise memory to your rehearsal. In *Leave Taking, for* example, Viv claims that the room is smelly and damp. Close your eyes and try to remember a specific time when you smelled something unpleasant. How did you notice the odour? Did your facial expression change? How did it make you feel? Be aware of your reactions and apply them as precisely as you can to the scene.

### Observation

Seek out people who seem to look or act like the characters in the scene and observe their behaviour. This is a way of making original, honest depictions rather than reverting to stereotypes. For the scene from *Leave Taking*, for example, you might observe how pregnancy might affect a character's movements or how sisters physically relate to one another.

### Actions

Try to discover active ways for the characters to pursue their objectives by stating what their action is before a line or movement. For example, Viv's actions might be 'to confront', 'to coax', 'to discover', while Del's might be 'to boast', 'to avoid', 'to tease', 'to shut out'. After choosing actions, ensure that they are conveyed in the way you move and speak.

### TASK 6.1

Look at an extract from a play you have chosen and create a series of questions similar to those in the annotations on the previous page. You will need research and rehearsals to discover some of the answers.

### EXTENSION

'Sense memory' is a technique made popular by the theatre director Konstantin Stanislavski, who created exercises to make performances more lifelike. Other techniques involve the use of given circumstances, tasks and actions. Use the many online resources and books available to investigate Stanislavski's work and how it could be applied to a naturalistic performance.

Anne-Marie Duff and Rory Kinnear in *Macbeth* at the National Theatre.

# Approaching a period text

## Example: *Macbeth*

The challenges of a period text can prove rewarding. Many of the questions that apply to a naturalistic text also apply to a period one. It is important, however, to make sure that you have a good grasp of the meaning of the text and how to speak the language effectively, especially if you find the language confusing or unusual. Below is a short extract from Act 2, Scene 2 of Shakespeare's *Macbeth* (1606). The scene begins with Lady Macbeth waiting for her husband to return after she has convinced him to murder the king, Duncan. Around the text are some questions that student actors might need to answer.

[1] What are the main events before this scene? Why does Macbeth decide to kill the king? How has the king treated him?

[3] This scene is written in **iambic pentameter**. This is why some words are elided, such as 'done't, instead of 'done it' so that they are spoken in one beat. How can the actor playing Lady Macbeth observe the metre of the speech without making it sound odd or artificial? What words should they stress?

[5] This series of short lines are usually performed very quickly in order to maintain the metre. How might this also increase the tension?

[7] Macbeth is reacting to the blood on his hands. How might his reaction be different from Lady Macbeth's?

LADY MACBETH: [1] Alack, I am afraid they have awaked, [2] And 'tis not done. The attempt and not the deed Confounds us. Hark! I laid their daggers ready; He could not miss 'em. Had he not resembled My father as he slept, I had done't. [3]

*Enter MACBETH* [4]

My husband!

MACBETH: I have done the deed. Didst thou not hear a noise?

LADY MACBETH: I heard the owl scream and the crickets cry. Did not you speak?

MACBETH: When?

LADY MACBETH: Now.

MACBETH: As I descended?

LADY MACBETH: Ay. [5]

MACBETH: Hark! [6] Who lies I' the second chamber?

LADY MACBETH: Donalbain.

MACBETH: This is a sorry sight.

*Looking on his hands* [7]

LADY MACBETH: A foolish thought, to say a sorry sight. [8]

[2] This scene takes place late at night. Lady Macbeth is waiting to learn if her husband has killed King Duncan. How might this situation affect the mood of this scene and how Lady Macbeth uses her voice?

[4] How should Macbeth enter and how will Lady Macbeth react? What will their proxemics be at various points in the scene?

[6] Why does Macbeth say this? Has something alarmed him?

[8] What do you think the audience should feel about the Macbeths at the end of the scene?

**KEY TERM:**

**Iambic pentameter:** Verse, which may be rhyming or unrhymed, which consists of five metrical feet (ten beats), each consisting of one unstressed and one stressed syllable.

# Examples of period rehearsal techniques

Although many of the rehearsal techniques you can use in a naturalistic text also apply to a period text, you might want to pay special attention to the vocal and physical demands of a Shakespearean text.

## Breath control

This is important in being able to speak the lines fluently. Take Lady Macbeth's first speech in the extract and practise it by taking breaths in different places, for example at the end of every two lines or at each full stop or exclamation mark. Decide when you need to take a breath and when it is more effective to speak a long phrase without a breath.

## Word emphasis

Go through the script and highlight one word in each line that you think is the most important, and experiment with different ways of emphasising it. You might want to decrease the volume on a word like 'afraid', for example, and increase it on an exclamation such as 'Hark!' You could try to say a word like 'deed' quickly and sharply, while drawing out more slowly a word such as 'father' to give an indication of how Lady Macbeth feels about her father.

## Body language

The Macbeths are both powerful, important characters. How might this affect their movements and posture? Create a series of still images showing how they carried themselves before this scene and how, during the scene, their guilt and fear might alter their posture and body language.

## Status

Assign numbers at key points in the scene to show which character is more in control and when this changes. For example, you might decide Lady Macbeth's status drops to a 5 or a 6 when she is nervous, but increases to an 8 or a 9 when she scolds Macbeth for saying 'a sorry sight'.

**TIP:**

The extracts on these pages are given as examples of approaches to different genres, but you will need to perform longer sections from the plays in order to fulfil the time requirements of the exam.

**EXTENSION**

The theatre director Max Stafford Clark uses playing cards to explore status and relationships. With ace as low and king as high, try playing a scene with different levels of status, as determined by randomly pulling a card from a deck.

Michelle Terry uses small, precise gestures and an intense expression in an earlier scene as Lady Macbeth.

# Approaching a stylised text

## Example: *Metamorphosis*

You may choose a text that requires a non-naturalistic, heightened acting style. This might require you to be confident in techniques such as:

**Breaking the fourth wall (talking directly to the audience)**

**Mime**

**Synchronised group movement**

**Choral speaking**

**Multi-role**

**Narration (shared or individual)**

**TIP:**

Steven Berkoff's work is known for its physicality and inventiveness.

Below is an excerpt from *Metamorphosis* (1969) by Steven Berkoff, based on a short story by Franz Kafka about Gregor Samsa, who wakes up one day to find himself transformed into a giant beetle. This extract is from the beginning of the play, when each member of Gregor's family enters. It is annotated with some of the techniques that could be used in performance.

[1] Non-naturalistic movement. This section might begin with each performer assuming a still image.

[2] Narration.

[3] Synchronised, non-naturalistic movement.

[4] Choral speaking.

[5] Multi-role: Gregor's sister briefly becomes a clock.

[6] Shared narration.

---

*As each speaks they form a line behind each other. On the last line they take on the movement of an insect by moving their arms to a particular rhythm.* [1] *As no front lighting is used, this has the effect of an insect's leg movements.*

MR S: [*enters*] As Gregor Samsa awoke one morning from uneasy dreams… [2]

MRS S: [*enters*] He found himself transformed in his bed into a gigantic insect…

GRETA: [*enters*] His numerous legs, which were pitifully thin compared to the rest of his bulk, waved helplessly before him.

[*Movement starts.* [3] *GREGOR is in front. Suddenly the movement stops – FAMILY dissolve the beetle image by moving away – leaving GREGOR still moving as part of the insect image.*]

[*Front lights come up revealing FAMILY.*]

GREGOR: What has happened to me?

FAMILY: He thought. [4]

GREGOR: It was no dream.

GRETA: [*as clock*] He looked at the alarm clock ticking on the chest. [5]

GREGOR: Half past six and the hands were quietly moving on.

MRS S: Gregor, Gregor?

MR S: Said a voice.

GREGOR: That gentle voice…

GRETA: It was his mother's… [6]

The cast of *Metamorphosis* form a line at The Vaults theatre.

## Some rehearsal techniques for stylised pieces

### Proxemics

Experiment with performing in a very restricted space. You could mark a small area, say a metre square, for all the characters to stay within. Find inventive forms of movement, such as moving under or over characters or reaching out between each other's arms or lifting the character who is speaking.

### Gestus

This is an acting technique developed by the theatre practitioner Bertolt Brecht. It combines gestures with an essential aspect of the attitude of a character. Try it by creating one identifying movement or mannerism for each character. An obsessive or worried character, for example, might mime checking a watch or wiping their hands on an apron. Experiment with exaggerating your chosen gesture so that is unusual and very noticeable.

### EXTENSION

Bertolt Brecht was a theatre practitioner famous for his development of epic theatre, a non-naturalistic style of theatre aimed at educating the audience and inspiring them to action. Many theatre companies continue to be inspired by his work. Research examples, including work by Splendid Productions.

# Performing as a pair

If you are working in a pair, it is important to develop a strong rapport with your acting partner. The audience will want to see the relationship between the characters and how they react throughout a scene.

Some scripts might require you to use pauses effectively or to deliver lines in a quick-fire fashion. Plays like *Hansel & Gretel* by Carl Grose or *Rosencrantz and Guildenstern are Dead* by Tom Stoppard might require a double-act in which the characters depend on each other. Other duologues, such as those in *A Taste of Honey*, might emphasise the differences between the characters and their unspoken desires and hopes.

It is not difficult to find duologues with rich opportunities for both actors. The challenge is for each member of the partnership to contribute fully.

There is 'Nothing to be done' in Samuel Beckett's *Waiting for Godot*, so actors (here, Ian McKellan and Patrick Stewart) need to engage the audience and convey themes, such as hope and the absurdity of life, through very little action.

**TIP:**

Stay alert while you are on stage, even if you are not the focus of the scene. It is very noticeable if an actor 'turns off' during a performance. Always be aware of your posture and focus.

**TIP:**

In group movement or choral speaking, it can become obvious if some members of the group are less prepared than others. Make sure that you are not relying on or copying others. Demonstrate that you have a firm grasp of your role.

Amanda (Gemma Jones) dispenses a lengthy piece of advice for Laura in this monologue from *The Glass Menagerie*.

**TIP:**

It might be best not to address your monologue directly to the examiner. This can be distracting for them and could also disrupt your focus, particularly as they might be making notes or appear stern.

# Performing in a group

Group work can provide exciting opportunities for movement and dynamic, powerful scenes. Depending on the size of the group, the recommended minimum and maximum performance time is longer than for a pair, which can give you more scope to develop the characters and demonstrate your skills. The challenge is in finding extracts that will offer appropriate opportunities for everyone, but a well-chosen group will show off each group member and demonstrate their ability to realise the drama and fulfil the playwright's intentions.

# Performing a monologue

An advantage of working on a monologue is that you have entire control over your performance; you are not reliant on others. A well-chosen monologue should allow you to demonstrate a range of skills. There is no hiding in a monologue, however, so your knowledge of lines and movements, or lack of, will be fully exposed.

## Techniques for monologues

### Create the world of the character

Where was your character before the scene began and where is the character now? Improvise a short scene showing what the character was doing before they began speaking.

- Will that influence where and how will you enter?
- When and where will you move during the scene?
- Will there be any props or furniture on stage?

### Who are you speaking to?

- Is your character speaking to the audience or another character? If it is to another character, where are they located on stage?
- Do they move at any point?

It can be useful to rehearse a monologue with another actor playing the person you are speaking to so that you can accurately recreate the presence of that character.

## Avoiding potential pitfalls of timing

A common problem with monologues is rushing them. In extreme cases, students speak so quickly, or leave out lines, that they do not manage the two-minute minimum time, risking lost marks. Some solutions for this are:

- Be aware of the length of your monologue and periodically check the timing. It is a good idea to select a piece that is at least a little over the minimum time so that, if nerves affect your performance, you will still be within the limit.

- If appropriate, incorporate some changes of pace or movement into your performance. Although on paper the monologue might look like a block of words, it should be a fully realised performance. In a play like *Sucker Punch* by Roy Williams, much of the action takes place in a boxing gym, so an actor would need to explore the physicality of that world.

- Keep in mind that you are speaking to someone, not 'at' them. You need to use your voice and movement to communicate ideas and feelings to your audience. Investigate the subtext of the extracts through techniques such as thought-tracking.

Physicality is an essential part of characterisation in *Sucker Punch* at Victory Gardens Theater.

> **TIP:**
>
> You cannot perform monologues for both of your extracts. If you have a monologue for one of your extracts, the other needs to be a duologue or group piece.

# Designers

If you choose to design for this component, you may select from the following roles:

- **Lighting**
- **Sound**
- **Lighting and sound combined** (but not if there is already a separate lighting or sound designer in your group)
- **Set**, including props and multimedia staging
- **Costume**, including hair, make-up and masks.

## Selecting a suitable design role

Before choosing a design specialism, you must ensure that the chosen extracts, the facilities of the centre and your skills will allow you to meet the specification's minimum requirements. If you are confident at sourcing and/or making costumes, can imagine one or two costumes suitable for the extracts and you have the resources necessary to complete your vision, then costume design could be a good choice for you. If you are not confident, however, or the actors want to wear their own black T-shirts and jeans, or you have little interest in costume design, it would be a poor choice At the same time, you should ensure that your choice provides sufficient challenge for you to stretch yourself and develop your skills.

The minimum requirements for design are specific. So, if your chosen extracts will not allow for six lighting changes, for example, and your centre does not have an adequate lighting rig, lighting design is not a suitable choice for you. Design is, however, a rewarding choice for many candidates.

> **WHAT THE SPECIFICATION SAYS...**
>
> Designers must:
> - Work with a performance group whose performance meets the minimum times set out.
> - Realise the designs in any **two** performance extracts from **one** text in the showcase.
>
> Learners should know and understand:
> - How the different aspects of design impact on the whole creative experience for both performer and audience.

## TASK 6.2

Read the three extracts on pages 216, 218 and 220 from *Leave Taking*, *Macbeth* and *Metamorphosis* and make notes on the following:

- What design role you would like to take on for the extract, and why
- How your design could support characterisation
- How your design might contribute to the action of the extract
- How the design can suit the mood, genre or style of the text.

Just as the performers must study the text, designers must also:

- Demonstrate their understanding of the text
- Have an artistic vision for the extracts
- Know how they want the audience to respond to the performance.

In addition, a designer should consider how their design choices will support the characters, create or contribute to atmosphere and enhance the style or genre of the chosen text.

### WHAT THE SPECIFICATION SAYS...

The minimum requirements for lighting designers in total across both performance extracts are:

- A full lighting design for the performance with a cue sheet detailing lanterns used and the differing lighting states
- A minimum of **six** lighting changes evident in the performance. Lights up and down are **not** included in this number.

Students must discuss with appropriate staff the selection, rigging and plotting of lights.

During the performance learners must operate the lighting desk.

# Lighting design

If you choose to work as a lighting designer, your work will need to support two extracts from the same piece.

The best lighting designers do more than simply respond to stage directions to inform their design. Their lighting design has an artistic vision that adds to the audience's understanding of the characters and play. They can create a mood or provide a focus that makes the performance more powerful. A well-timed black-out or fade, for example, will add to the comedy or drama of a scene.

A typical approach to lighting design would be:

**1** Read the play, making notes on the chosen extracts of potential lighting demands and possible effects.

**2** Explore your lighting equipment and performance space, noting the available lights and lanterns, the size of the stage and the staging configuration.

**3** Draw a plan of the stage space and note which areas need to be lit. Consider: angles, directions and position and types of lantern.

**4** Experiment with different colour and intensity options.

**5** If appropriate, experiment with special effects, such as strobes or gobos.

**6** Under supervision, arrange hanging, setting and focusing of lights.

**7** Create an initial lighting plot and cue sheet (see page 226).

**8** Work with performers and/or other designers to ensure that lighting supports the performance.

**9** Run a technical rehearsal to ensure that all lighting timings are correct.

**10** Finalise the lighting cue sheet.

# Lighting equipment

You will need to become familiar with the lighting equipment available and how to operate it.

### Lighting rig
This structure holds the lighting for a theatre. You might have a permanent structure or an adaptable rig, such as one mounted on a three-legged telescopic lighting stand.

### Lanterns
This is a general term for the various sources of light, such as spotlights. Some typical lanterns are shown here:

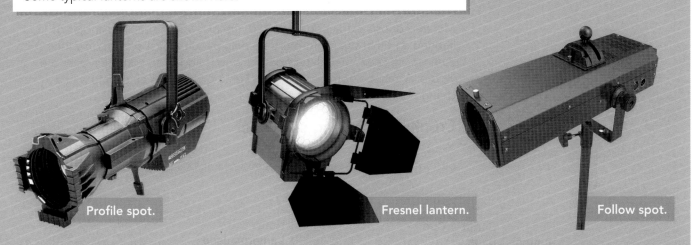

Profile spot.

Fresnel lantern.

Follow spot.

### Lighting control desk
The means of controlling your lighting, including which lights are on or off, the different levels and how transitions are achieved. These might be operated manually or through a computerised system.

### Special effects
You might have access to lighting that can create special effects. Consider if any of the equipment shown here would enhance your design.

Strobe light.

Colour filters.

Gobos: cut-out filters that fit over a lens to project patterns.

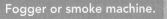

Fogger or smoke machine.

> ## TASK 6.3
> Make a detailed list of the lighting equipment available. Add comments on how you could use it in your final design.

225

**TIP:**

There are a number of video lighting tutorials and lighting education packs available online to give you advice on the technical aspects of creating your design and plot.

## Creating your design

After you have annotated your script with lighting ideas and questions and discussed these with the performers and other designers, you should draw a ground plan of the stage you will be lighting (see page 231). On it, add a series of circles, usually six or nine, to indicate the areas of the stage that need to be lit. Mark them with which lanterns will light those areas. Typically, the circles will overlap and at least two lights will be used for each stage space. Ensure that all necessary areas of the stage are covered.

For each area of the stage, choose the appropriate lantern, colour and beam size. You will also need to focus the lights to make sure, for example, that a performer's face is the focus of a beam, rather than their feet.

Consider how the angle of the beams could create specific effects. In the *Metamorphosis* extract on page 220, the playwright specifies angles of lighting and that the performers are only backlit at first so that only their outlines are seen, then, later front lighting is added so that their faces are visible. A change from back to front lighting would be an example of a change of lighting state.

## Creating a lighting cue sheet

A cue sheet contains the information needed to operate the lights during the performance. An excerpt from a simple sample is given here.

| Cue number | Script page | Cue | Notes<br>Lanterns used |
|---|---|---|---|
| 1 | 1 | Preset. | Houselights up. Single blue spotlight centre stage. |
| 2 | 1 | Opening, Act One, Midnight, in the woods. | Houselights fade out. Backlighting, upstage. C enters holding torch. |
| 3 | 2 | Line: 'What's that?' | Snap on uplighting from downstage. |
| 4 | 4 | Phil's exit. | Cross fade to morning light; fade out backlighting. |
| 5 | 5 | Thunder crash. | Sound cue: Strobe. |
| 6 | 7 | Angela stands centre stage. | Visual cue: A arrives centre stage. CS spotlight up. |
| 7 | 10 | Line: 'He's gone.' | Slow fade to black. |

Some cue sheets contain more details, such as lengths of fade times, more information about specific lanterns and levels or references to lighting computer software. Whatever style of cue sheet you choose, make sure that it is one that you understand, as you will be using it to operate the lighting desk during the performance.

# Sound design

Sound design can add to a performance in many ways. It can provide practical sound effects, such as a telephone ringing or gunshots, or it might provide atmospheric sounds that influence the audience subconsciously. It could involve music or specially created soundscapes.

Arranging how sound is amplified and projected is also part of the sound designer's job.

A typical approach to creating a sound design would be:

**1** Read the play and note sound and music ideas appropriate for the chosen extracts.

**2** Discuss your ideas and requirements with performers and/or other designers.

**3** Consider technical requirements and limitations of the performance space. What types of speaker or sound software are available?

**4** Decide which sound effects can be recorded and which rely on pre-existing sound effects recordings. Will any sounds be created live during the performance, or will all of them be recorded or sourced in advance?

**5** Record or source sound effects and music.

**6** Create cue sheets, including volumes and durations of sounds.

**7** Decide if there are any live cues and, if so, rehearse them.

**8** Hold a technical rehearsal, making sure that all cues are accurate and volume levels are correct.

## WHAT THE SPECIFICATION SAYS...

The minimum requirements for sound designers in total across both performance extracts are:

- A full sound sheet with original and copied cues leading to a finalised sound CD or MP3 playlist on a memory stick for use in the final performance
- A minimum of **six** sound cues evident in the performance.

During the performance learners must operate the sound desk.

An actor in *Hype Man*, using an onstage sound board.

## TIP:

Make sure that you consider health and safety and that all speakers are secured and wires are taped down.

## Sound equipment

Equipment you might use in your sound design could include:

**TIP:**

Note that, as the performers are being judged on their vocal production and enunciation, they can only use microphones when they are singing, not when they are speaking.

### Microphones

If appropriate to the text's content and style, actors could use visible microphones that become a feature of the singing performance (as in *Hype Man*, below).

Additionally, if you are recording original sound effects or music, you will need a recording microphone.

### Mixer

Also called a mixing console, this is a desk with a number of channels through which sound signals, such as those from microphones, recording and instruments, can be routed to speakers. It is used for combining, balancing and boosting sound.

### Speakers

Speakers transmit amplified or recorded sound. The placement of speakers will affect how the audience perceives the sound.

### Sound effects

You may record original sound effects or locate the specific ones you need from sound archives or specialist sound effects providers.

---

## TASK 6.4

Go through your chosen extracts and make notes on:

- Sound effects specifically required by the script
- Sound or music that you believe would add to the atmosphere and/or meaning being conveyed
- Opportunities for sound or music during transitions
- Ideas about how the sounds or music could be made or sourced.

## Creating a sound cue sheet

A cue sheet contains the information needed for sound during the performance. An excerpt from a simple sample is given here.

| Cue number | Script page | Cue | Notes | Duration |
|---|---|---|---|---|
| 0.5 | 1 | Pre-show music. | Pre-show music: Motown hits: low volume. | 10 minutes. |
| 1 | 1 | Pre-show music stops. | Sound of shower off stage. | Slow fade. |
| 2 | 6 | High violin noise. | Visual cue: Sam looks out of window. | 15 seconds. |
| 3 | 7 | Music: 'Can't Hurry Love'. | Visual cue: Alex enters. | 20 seconds. Snap. |
| 4 | 9 | Telephone rings. | Line cue: SAM: You have to go now. Visual cue: Sam picks up phone. | Approx. 10 seconds (three rings). |
| 5 | 10 | Door slams. | Alex's exit. | Snap. |
| 6 | 11 | Reverb voice. | Visual cue: Sam sits in chair. | 20 seconds – gradually fade up. Snap off. |

Whatever style of cue sheet you create, make sure that it helps you to deliver the sound design accurately and sensitively.

> **TIP:**
>
> There are online sources of sound effects and free industry-standard downloadable sound software that you may use to help with your design.

# Lighting and sound combined

Combining lighting and sound design can give you more opportunities to demonstrate your design and technical skills. Your lighting and sound designs will demonstrate your artistic vision for the extracts. You will need to fulfil a combination of the requirements of lighting and sound design and so create a cue sheet that encompasses both.

**WHAT THE SPECIFICATION SAYS...**

You must provide a combination of the requirements for sound and lighting which are approximately equal in weighting and which total **six** cues in performance.

> **TASK 6.5**
>
> Choose one of the three extracts from pages 216–220 and create a combined lighting and sound cue sheet for it. This should show how you could present your thoughts about the extract and your ideas on how to realise these through sound and lighting.

## WHAT THE SPECIFICATION SAYS...

The minimum requirements for set designers in total across both performance extracts are:

- A scale model and a detailed ground plan of the set
- Sourcing set (and props) for the performance and supervision of the construction of set where appropriate.

Learners must dress the set ready for performance and **one** set design must be realised in the final performance.

### TASK 6.6

After studying your chosen extracts, quickly sketch a series of design ideas for the setting. Annotate them with thoughts about potential colours, fabrics, textures and props, as appropriate.

# Set design

A typical approach to creating a set design is:

**1**
Read the script, noting particular practical set requirements and your initial artistic ideas.

**2**
Discuss with your group the likely setting requirements, as well as the atmosphere and style of the text.

**3**
Consider the practical capabilities and limitations of where the drama will be staged. What budget will you have? How big will the stage be? How sturdy will the set need to be (will items need to bear weight or are they just decorative)? Will the set be changed, perhaps for the second extract, or require a special effect to be added at any point?

**4**
Research: Use the internet, art books, photographs and so on for inspiration from other sets, images and scenes.

**5**
Put mood boards together – collections of your ideas, such as picture inspirations, colours, samples, textures and quotes.

**6**
Sketch initial ideas and plans, and revise them after discussion with your group and after assessing your stage space.

**7**
Measure the stage area and make a ground plan.

**8**
Make a model box of the set.

**9**
Explore some performance points with your group, using your ground plan. Check entrances and exits and whether there is enough room for physical performance actions.

**10**
Create and assemble the set.

**11**
Check your design and the performance space for health and safety issues.

**12**
Use a technical rehearsal to make the necessary changes.

**13**
Dress the set in readiness for the first performance.

# Making a ground plan

This is an accurate scale drawing of the stage space. It is important to know the exact size of the space so that you can ensure that your design ideas will fit. Identify where entrances and exits will be, where the audience will sit, and any special requirements your set has, such as ramps or stairs.

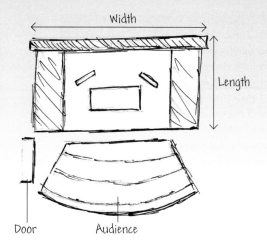

# Making a model of a set

A model of your set is an accurate small-scale representation of what the set will look like and how it will operate. Use your set design to explore colours, position objects and furnishings, and see how scene changes can be accomplished. It is also a chance to experiment with the overall style of you set and details such as texture. You might also notice and have a chance to correct any problems with lighting, such as unlit areas or unwanted shadows.

A model box by Laura Ann Price for *Talking Heads* at the West Yorkshire Playhouse.

Making details for the model of the set.

**TIP:**

You may be able to produce your models through digital means, if appropriate to your learning centre.

# Creating special effects

Some productions might require a set with special effects, such as snowfall, dropping balloons or a poster that will be ripped down. You will need to plan and test out your ideas carefully.

This digital 3-D set design by Laura Ann Price, for *Woman Caught Unaware*, was for a thrust stage at the Arcola Theatre. This scene includes the special effect of rose petals dropping.

How the rose petals appeared in the final realisation.

WHAT THE SPECIFICATION SAYS...

The minimum requirements for costume designers in total across both performance extracts are:

- **Either one** full costume including hair and make-up detail which is sourced and realised in performance
- **Or one** full costume including mask(s) which is sourced and realised in performance
- **Or two** full costumes for characters (excluding hair, make-up or masks) which are sourced and realised in performance. These costumes can be for different characters or different costumes for one character.

# Costume design

A possible approach to costume design is:

**1** Read the script, noting any practical requirements and your first creative ideas for the extracts.

**2** Discuss with the performers which character or characters you might be designing for and their perceptions of the costume needs.

**3** Research the features of the design. This could involve, for example, looking at magazines art books and photographs and visiting fabric shops.

**7** If making the costume, find or create a pattern and source materials such as the main fabric and any trim.

**6** Draw initial sketches and begin sourcing costume items.

**5** Take measurements of performers and establish sizes, such as shoe and hat sizes.

**4** Put together initial mood boards. These could include colour palettes, photographs, fabric swatches and inspirational images.

**8** Arrange costume fittings as appropriate.

**9** If you are designing hair and make-up or masks, discuss these with your performers and sketch ideas.

**10** Source any accessories required.

**11** At dress rehearsal, make any necessary adjustments to the fit and appearance of costume. Assess how easy it is to perform in (in terms of movement, for example), and to change in and out of if costume changes are needed.

**12** Check the details of costume, hair, make-up and masks (as appropriate) before the first performance; that items are secure and make-up tools and so on are to hand.

# Costume choices

It is important to design costumes that fulfil the needs of the extract and the performer who will be wearing them. Your design should combine your creative, artistic vision for the play with its practical demands. If you design a costume that unnecessarily impedes the performer's ability to move or express the character, you will not have done your job correctly, so bear in mind any requirements of movement and characterisation.

Some important decisions you need to make are:

- Type of costume: Modern, stylised/fantasy, period
- Made or sourced: Will you be sewing/constructing a costume or will you be finding it, for example from a second-hand shop, or both?
- Complete or suggested: Will it be a complete head-to-foot costume or a partial one, such as items layered over a basic outfit?

## TASK 6.7

A Examine the costumes in these photographs. Identify the type of each costume and how you believe it was created.

B Does the costume appear effective to you? If so, why? If not, how could you change or improve it? Consider, for example (as appropriate):

- Fit, colour, silhouette
- Details such as embroidery and trim
- How well the accessories suit the outfit
- How authentic to the period it appears to be
- The effect it might have on the audience.

Zastrozzi.

Shockheaded Peter.

Song for a Future Generation.

## Thinking outside the box

Sewing a complete costume would show a high level of skill, but there are other valid options to showcase your talent and effort, such as:

- Designing and screen-printing a fabric or T-shirt
- Dyeing and/or adapting existing items of clothing
- Embellishing an outfit with trim, embroidery or stencils, or adapting it with padding
- Creating accessories such as hats, aprons and handbags.

Whatever choices you make, your design is not a test of how much money you can spend, but how well you can create a costume that makes real your artistic vision.

## Make-up and hair

A make-up design can give polish to your overall costume design or create a special effect of its own. Your make-up and hair choices might include:

### Period

Research and recreate make-up and hairstyles from a specific era. For make-up, you might think about appropriate dominant colours, which features are emphasised and use of special products like powders. For hair, you could consider length, colour, styling products such as pomades or hairspray, as well as any hair ornaments, such as grips and headbands.

### Fantasy

Create a design – for example through face painting or prosthetics – to suggest a magical or mythical character, such as Puck from *A Midsummer Night's Dream* (below), or an animal from *Animal Farm*. You could use wigs, hair pieces or temporary hair colour to create suitable effects.

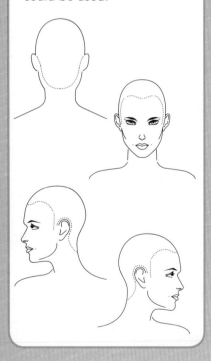

**TASK 6.8**

Draw an outline of a face and create on it a make-up design for one of the characters in the extracts you are using. Annotate it with ideas about colours, styles (including hair) and specific products that could be used.

### Character

Design make-up to suggest a character that is very different from the actor's usual appearance. This could be make-up to age or suggest that the character is ill, for example. You could also consider facial hair, such as a beard, moustache or sideburns. You might experiment with ways of greying hair or using wigs.

## Masks

The three basic types of masks you could consider are:

**Plot-motivated**
Masks that characters assume as part of the plot, such as the masquerade half-masks that Romeo and Juliet wear at the ball (right).

**Mime**
Stylised masks used for movement pieces.

**Character/fantasy**
Masks that could be used to create an animal or fantasy character.

Masks can show a high level of skill and creativity, but they must be appropriate for the play and performer. Be especially conscious that, in most cases, the expectation is that the performer will be able to move and speak in their piece, so the mask must not impede that. Additionally, be conscious of the materials used to construct the masks, as they can cause allergic reactions.

# The concept pro forma

Whether you are a performer or a designer, you will need to complete the concept pro forma. It gives you the opportunity to explain your process and goals, as well as demonstrating your understanding and interpretation of your performance text. You will be assessed on AO1 (Create and develop ideas to communicate meaning for theatrical performance) and given one overall mark for your written concept pro forma.

Typically, you will be asked four questions. Below are some examples, along with additional prompts on what you might cover in your answers, depending on your text and approach.

> **1 What are the major demands of the text?**

**You should consider the structure of the extracts in the context of the whole performance text and the original intentions of the playwright.**

- What is the genre and style of the text?
- Where in the text do your chosen extracts occur?
- When was the play written?
- What was the social, political and/or historical context of its first performance?
- What was the playwright's original intention?
- What are the difficulties or challenges of the text for a performer, designer or the audience?

**WHAT THE SPECIFICATION SAYS...**

Learners should know and understand:

- Why the extract is significant in the context of the whole text
- The structure of the whole text and the extracts' place within it
- The social, cultural or historical context of the text the features of the text including:
  - Genre
  - Structure
  - Character
  - Form and style
  - Dialogue
  - The role of stage directions
- How to communicate effectively using:
  - The semiotics of drama
  - The skills of a performer or designer
  - Performance conventions
- How performance texts can be presented to an audience.

**TIP:**

When discussing structure, don't just retell the plot of the play. Explain the extracts' importance within the play as a whole, such as 'This is when the protagonist is introduced.'

**TIP:**

Ensure that you refer to both extracts in your answers in the concept pro forma.

**2  What is your artistic vision for the two extracts?**

- What do you want to communicate about the role(s) or the play?
- What artistic choices are you making?
- What connections, developments or contrasts do you see between the two extracts?
- Where and when have you set the extracts? Why?
- What choices have you made about style and dramatic conventions?
- How does your artistic vision relate to the playwright's original intention?

**3  How did you develop your role(s) or design(s)?**

As an actor, you should consider semiotics, the use of language, gesture and expression.

As a designer, you should consider proxemics, mood, supporting characters and supporting the chosen genre and style.

- How did you rehearse your role(s) or create your designs?
- What key aspects of the character or design have you developed?
- What examples can you provide of how your preparation work has affected your performance or design?
- At what key moments do you demonstrate particular skills?

**4  How do you want the audience to respond to your presentation of the extracts as an actor or designer? Give specific examples from each extract.**

**TIP:**

To avoid repetition, make sure that you answer specifically what is being asked in each question.

- What emotions do you want the audience to feel?
- Are there any ideas or messages that you want to convey in the extracts?
- Can you provide examples of when you want the audience to:
  - Laugh?
  - Feel sad?
  - Feel sympathy?
  - Be surprised?
  - Have greater understanding of an issue?
- Are there moments in the extracts where the audience's reaction might change, such as from annoyance to sympathy or from laughter to sadness?

## TASK 6.9

**A** Below are a few candidate-style pro forma comments. Decide which of the four questions on the preceding pages each comment seems to answer. Do you think that the candidates have given enough information and detail?

**B** Highlight how the responses explain the candidates' intentions and how they achieved these.

*The play is a naturalistic drama set in the 1950s, exploring the social problems of a young single girl who becomes pregnant.*

*The ending should be moving for the audience as they become aware of the difficult decision Tom has made.*

*When rehearsing the balcony scene, it was clear that the language would be a challenge. Although written in verse, I wanted it to sound fresh and spontaneous.*

*I want to show the deterioration in the relationship between Bill and his mother between the two extracts. The body language in the second extract will be more distant and Bill's tone will be harsh and suspicious.*

*The scene takes plays in purgatory and we have interpreted this as being like an old warehouse, with big dustsheets covering the furniture. These can be removed to reveal the relevant set furnishings when appropriate.*

*The play is a comedy and our goal is for the audience to laugh. My sound design contributes to this by the humorous sound effects I have created, especially for the fight scene, in which they provide a comic-book feeling.*

*As the play is set in the 1930s, I studied films from this period to get a sense of the correct silhouette and styles before preparing my costume sketches.*

*The stylised movement sequences provided a particular challenge for us. We used techniques we learned from practitioners like Frantic Assembly and filmed two of our rehearsals in order to polish the look of our work.*

# Polishing a performance

There is much more to rehearsing and polishing a performance beyond learning your lines and movements. As you did for your devised drama, you should have a clear rehearsal schedule with specific goals (see page 199). Some students fall into a habit of simply running lines and repeating the same movements without fully exploring the characters, places and relationships. Without this deeper investigation, it is easy to repeat mistakes or to create shallow characters.

## The importance of designers

Designers should be involved throughout the process, contributing to the rehearsals. A costume designer, for example, might help to find rehearsal outfits which approximate the final costumes, such as long skirts and high heels, so the actors are comfortable moving in them. A set designer could create a rough version of the set, so that the actors are secure in where they will be able to move and the designer will know if his planned design will fit in the space and fulfil the needs of the scenes.

WHAT THE SPECIFICATION SAYS...

Learners should know and understand:
- The importance of rehearsal including time management and preparation
- How performance texts can be presented to an audience.

# Types of rehearsal

Three rehearsals that can be particularly helpful for polishing performances are:

- A work-in-progress sharing
- The technical rehearsal
- The final dress rehearsal.

Many groups find it useful to have at least one work-in-progress showing, when they can become comfortable performing in front of a small invited audience (possibly others in the class) and receive constructive feedback. Even if there is not a formal arrangement for these sharings, you might find it helpful to run lines or scenes with friends, so that you will be less nervous for the actual performance.

The technical rehearsal is when all the final technical aspects of the performance, including sound, lighting and set changes, are perfected. A technical rehearsal usually involves a lot of stopping and starting, as it is often necessary to refocus lighting, adjust sound levels or improve timing and cues.

The final dress rehearsal should have all technical and costume elements in place and, ideally, be played through as if it were the first performance to the audience. This is your last chance to make any small improvements and to ensure that everything is in place and ready for a successful performance.

## LOOK HERE

You could adapt the rehearsal schedule on page 199 as part of your preparation for your chosen text performance.

# Overcoming difficulties

| Common performance problems | How to overcome them |
|---|---|
| Stage fright/nerves. | • Be over-prepared, so that you feel you could perform the role in your sleep.<br>• Practise in front of an audience and/or friends.<br>• Before going on stage, try relaxation or breathing exercises and imagine a successful performance.<br>• Forget about yourself and enter thoroughly into the world of the character. |
| Lack of commitment, skills or characterisation. | • Explore your character thoroughly and break down the specifics of how you can use your vocal and physical skills. Don't just settle on what is easy for you.<br>• Know your own strengths and weaknesses. If you tend to speak softly, be aware that it is something you will need to improve.<br>• Remember that acting is communication. What do you want to communicate to the audience? |
| Lacks energy and precision. | • Break the extracts down into smaller units and rehearse them individually, deciding what each character wants in each section and when their objectives might change.<br>• Polish each section. Don't allow there to be one weak unit.<br>• Speed-run the lines and use it to discover if there are any unnecessary pauses or drops in energy levels. |
| Dull; lacks variety. | • Look at the stage pictures you are creating and try to find opportunities for movement and use of stage conventions.<br>• Experiment with changing levels and making full use of the stage.<br>• Explore opportunities for variety, such as changes of pace or volume. |

## Common design problems

| Common design problems | How to overcome them |
|---|---|
| Little or no evidence of design preparation. | • Be aware of the minimum requirements for your specialism and make sure you have fulfilled each element.<br>• Best practice is to keep all of your work, including early research and sketches. This will enable you to improve your design and will enrich what you write in your concept pro forma. |
| Design does not contribute to overall performance or lacks artistic vision. | • Your design should do more than simply fulfil the technical requirements in the stage directions. Make sure that you have a concept of how your design choices will help to convey genre, style, mood and/or characterisation.<br>• Your design must be sensitive to the needs of the performers. Lighting should enhance the contributions of the performers and/or other designers. Sound must not drown out the dialogue. Costumes should be functional, with performers able to move in them.<br>• Keep checking your work and adjust costumes, set, props, levels, cue sheets, and so on, as appropriate. |
| Insufficient challenge | • Make sure that the time, effort and imagination spent on the design is at least as great as that put in by the performers. |

## CHECK YOUR LEARNING: Presenting and performing texts

**Do you know…?**

✓ How you will be assessed.

✓ The types of play you might choose to perform or design.

✓ The types of research you might do in order to explore a script.

✓ The differences between monologue, duologue and group work, and their potential benefits and drawbacks.

✓ How to rehearse a performance, including what types of rehearsal to hold and when.

✓ The different design options and their minimum requirements.

✓ The different stages of preparation for your design choice.

✓ What the concept pro forma is, what it should contain and how to complete it.

✓ How to polish a performance or design ready for an audience.

✓ Common performance and design problems and how to solve them.

The cast of *On the Town* congratulate Misty Copeland after her debut performance as Ivy.

# GLOSSARY OF KEY TERMS

**Abstract:** Not realistic or lifelike, but instead using colours, shapes, textures, sounds and other means to achieve a particular 'unnatural' effect.

**Ad lib:** An improvisation by an actor, which usually occurs when a mistake has happened on stage, such as a missed line or entrance, or when there is an interruption to the performance.

**Allegory:** A story that uses its characters and events to explore reallife people and events, often making a moral point or political criticism.

**Ambivalent:** With mixed feelings; unsure or unconcerned.

**American dream:** The concept that anyone in the US, with enough hard work, can achieve success and prosperity.

**Amplification:** How sound is increased, for example through speakers.

**Apron:** The area of the stage nearest the audience, which projects in front of the curtain.

**Artistic vision:** The choice of what is going to be emphasised in a production, for example where it is set or what themes will be stressed. These decisions influence the staging, performance style and design requirements. Also called 'artistic intention' or 'concept'.

**Audience interaction:** Involving the audience in the play, for example by giving them props, using direct address or bringing them on stage.

**Bodice:** The upper part of a dress.

**Blocking:** The actors' movements. These are usually set during rehearsals and noted by the stage management in the prompt book.

**Boned:** A garment stiffened with strips of material, such as plastic or bone, in order to give it a particular shape.

**Bookended:** A structural device in which the beginning and ending of a play are similar and, like bookends, appear at either side of the main action of the play.

**Box set:** A set with three complete walls, often used in naturalistic designs to create a believable room.

**Catharsis:** When a tragedy reaches a climax and there is a moment of emotional release.

**Character:** A person or other being in a play, novel, film or other story.

**Choral speaking:** Several characters delivering lines in unison, as in a choir.

**Chronological:** Presenting events in the order in which they occur.

**Circular:** A literary structure in which the ending returns the action to the beginning, perhaps in the use of setting, wording or content. In some cases, it suggests that the same or a similar story will be repeated.

**Climax:** The most intense moment in the play, often shortly before the resolution.

**Collaborative:** Working with others; team work.

**Colour palette:** The range of colours used, for example earth tones, primary colours or pastels.

**Concept:** A unifying idea about a production, such as when it is set or how it will be interpreted and performed.

**Context:** The circumstances of the setting of a play, such as the location, period of time or conventions.

**Cross:** Movement from one part of the stage to another.

**Cross-cutting:** Changing back and forth between different scenes or episodes. This can occur in a finished piece or be used as a rehearsal technique, with someone calling 'Cut' to switch between scenes.

**Counter-cross:** Movement in opposition to another character's: so, one going stage left when the other goes stage right, for example.

**Deadpan:** Without showing expression; blank.

**Dialogue:** The words/lines spoken by the characters.

**Direct address:** Speaking directly to the audience.

**Documentary theatre:** Theatre based on real people and events and using documentary material, such as interviews, letters, reports and newspaper articles, often without changing the actual words, in order to create a play.

**Domestic drama:** A play focused on the ordinary lives of middle- or working-class characters, frequently set in a home environment.

**Downstage:** In a typical end on or thrust configuration, the area of the stage closest to the audience.

**Dramatic irony:** When the audience know something that one or more characters on stage do not.

**Ensemble:** A group of actors. The term can be used for actors who form a chorus of a play or musical, or it might refer to a group of actors who all play equal roles, with no single actor being the lead or 'star'.

**End on:** A configuration in which the whole audience directly faces the stage.

**Episodic:** A structure involving a series of scenes, or episodes, which are usually short and might take place in many different locations. They often 'stand alone' without relying upon a previous scene to explain their meaning. This is in contrast to traditional dramatic narratives, which usually have scenes or acts covering a restricted period of time, taking place in a limited number of locations and ultimately building to a climax.

**Exposition:** A literary device in which background information is explained to the audience.

**Expressionistic:** Using exaggeration or stylised elements to show emotions and ideas, rather than a realistic depiction.

**Flashback:** A scene from an earlier period of a character's life than that shown in the play's main timeline.

**Fly:** To raise or lower scenery, items or actors onto the stage from the fly space by a system of ropes and pulleys.

**Fly space:** The area above the stage where scenery can be stored and lowered to the stage.

**Foreboding:** A feeling that something bad will happen. Associated with **foreshadowing**.

**Foreshadowing:** A warning or hint of something that is going to happen.

**Fourth wall:** An imaginary wall between the audience and the stage. A performer might 'break' the wall and speak directly to, or otherwise interact with, the audience.

**Gender-blind:** Non-traditional casting where parts usually played by men might be played by a woman, or vice versa.

**Genre:** A category or type of drama, such as comedy, tragedy or musical theatre, usually with its own conventions.

**Historical drama:** A play set in an earlier period of time than when it was written and explores events of that historic period.

**Hot seat:** A technique in which a performer sits in a chair (the 'hot seat') and answers questions in character.

**Iambic pentameter:** Verse, which may be rhyming or unrhymed, which consists of five metrical feet (ten beats), each consisting of one unstressed and one stressed syllable.

**Immersive:** A type of theatre that often includes roles for audience members, takes place in a specific, unique environment and has different narrative strands.

**Incongruous:** Out of place; appearing wrong in a certain location or situation.

**Irony:** Using language to suggest one thing but meaning another.

**'Letter' sweater:** A knitted cardigan or jumper decorated with a large capital letter, awarded to high school or varsity athletes.

**Linear:** A sequence arranged in a straightforward or chronological way.

**Mannerism:** A slight movement or habit that a person does repeatedly, such as a hand gesture or a facial expression, perhaps without knowing they are doing it.

**Mime:** To act without words. This might involve using gestures or movements to express emotions or creating a scene to suggest the presence of props or other physical items when none are present, such as 'pretending' to open a door.

**Minimalistic:** Simple, using few elements, stripped back.

**Model box:** A box representing the walls of a theatre space into which a cardboard scale model of a set can be placed.

**Motif:** A repeated musical theme or tune, often associated with a character or location.

**Monologue:** An extended speech by one character.

**Motivation:** The feelings behind what a character wants or needs.

**Narration:** A commentary or background to a play or other story.

**Narrative:** A story and how it is told.

**Naturalistic:** Lifelike, realistic, believable.

**Non-linear:** A sequence that is not arranged in a straightforward or chronological way.

**Nostalgia:** Remembering an earlier time with longing or affection.

**On the dole:** Being out of work and receiving unemployment benefit from the government (from 'doling' or handing out of money).

**Performance conventions:** Theatrical techniques used in particular types of performance, such as speaking directly to the audience (direct address) or miming the use of props rather than having them on stage.

**Performance style:** The way in which something is performed, such as naturalistically or stylised.

**Peter Pan collar:** A flat collar with two rounded ends at the front.

**Physical theatre:** Theatre in which physical movement, such as mime, choreography and other stylised movement, is important and prominent.

**Props:** Small items that actors can carry onstage, such as books, walking sticks or boxes.

**Protagonist:** The main character of a narrative.

**Proxemics:** How spatial relationships between one performer and other performers and between performers and their stage environment work and create meaning.

**Psychological:** Referring to a mental or emotional state and the reasons behind it.

**Raked auditorium:** A sloped seating area, with its lowest part nearest the stage.

**Raked stage:** A sloping stage.

**Rapport:** A strong understanding or communication between people.

**Received Pronunciation (also called RP):** A way of speaking that is considered the 'standard' form of British Pronunciation. It is not specific to a certain location, but is associated with education and formality.

**Recession:** A period of economic unproductivity or decline, which is often associated with high unemployment and rising prices.

**Register:** How formal or informal language is, or language used for a particular purpose or in a certain setting, such as the language of medicine or law. Informal language tends to use less precise pronunciation and might include more slang.

**Religious mania:** An abnormal mental state with symptoms of high energy, extremes of emotion and impaired judgement, which involves an obsessive interest in religion and personal faith.

**Repressing:** Hiding, pushing down, controlling or preventing something, such as a thought or emotion.

**Resolution:** The solution or bringing together of loose elements of a plot; an ending or conclusion.

**Rostrum:** A portable platform upon which actors can perform. Some are constructed using modules, so that they can provide different levels.

**Semiotics:** How meaning is created and communicated through systems of signs and symbols. All the elements that make up a theatrical performance have meaning and an audience 'reads' or interprets them to understand the performance.

**Sightline:** The view of the stage from the audience.

**Site specific:** A performance in a location other than a theatre, such as a warehouse, office, museum or town square.

**Slip:** A thin, sleeveless, undergarment worn under skirts or dresses.

**Social drama:** A genre of plays that deal with the interactions between different social groups, an exploration of a social group, or the place of an individual within a society.

**Stage directions:** Instructions in the script indicating how the play might be performed or staged, including physical actions, location and sound and lighting effects.

**Stage picture:** A still image created on stage. It might include the positioning of the actors in relation to each other and the set. It can also be called a *tableau*.

**Status:** Social, economic or political importance in relation to others; holding power.

**Still image:** A frozen image showing the facial expressions and physical positions, including posture and gesture, of one or more characters.

**Stimuli:** Artefacts, such as photographs, letters, art, stories or poetry, used as a starting point for original creative work.

**Stole:** A strip of fabric or fur that is draped over the shoulders.

**Stylised:** Not realistic; done in a particular manner that perhaps emphasises one element of the play or production.

**Sweetheart neckline:** A heart-shaped neckline that emphasises the neckline and upper chest.

**Symbolic/ism:** Using something to represent something else, such as a rose to symbolise love or an oversized map to symbolise property or a journey. Symbolic design might be dressing characters in white to suggest purity, or using the overly loud ticking of a clock to indicate the passing of time.

**Theatrical metaphor:** Comparing something in the play to something else in order to make a point. For example, if you want to indicate a conflict, you could use the theatrical metaphor of placing the action in a boxing ring or at a football match.

**Tiers:** Rows of seating arranged so that they slope upwards, and the people behind can see over the heads of those in front.

**Tragic flaw:** A defect, failing or weakness in the tragic protagonist, such as jealousy, ambition or pride, that brings about their downfall.

**Tragic hero:** The main character in a tragedy.

**Upstage:** In a typical end on or thrust configuration, the area of the stage furthest away from the audience.

**Upward mobility:** A movement where a person's status, power and/or wealth are improved.

**Verbatim play/theatre:** A type of documentary theatre that uses the words of real people.

**Wings:** Spaces to the side of the stage, where actors can wait to enter unseen and where props and set pieces can be stored.

# INDEX

# IMAGE ACKNOWLEDGEMENTS

pp6 top and bottom, 21, 38 bottom, 40, 60, 78 bottom, 79, 100, 169 top, 170, 179, 180, 184, 206 right, 231 top and 232 top emc design ltd;

pp8, 42 and 195 top Granger Historical Picture Archive / Alamy Stock Photo;

p9 bottom Philip Vile;

p10 top Anthony Coleman-VIEW / Alamy Stock Photo, bottom Q Theatre;

p11 top Harrogate Theatre, bottom OnTheRoad / Alamy Stock Photo;

pp12, 22 top, 57, 58 bottom, 77, 78 top, 97, 98, 118, 119 bottom, 139, 159, 160, 201 and 212 bottom Neil Sutton at Cambridge Design Consultants;

p13 Emily Cooper;

p14 TAO Images Limited / Alamy Stock Photo;

p18 AF archive / Alamy Stock Photo;

pp19 and 144 Colm Hogan;

p20 *Equus* Kerry Bradley, *Odd Couple* Timothy Mackabee / Karen Almond, *55 Days* Catherine Ashmore, *Hotel Cerise* Peter Dazeley;

pp22 bottom and 231 centre and bottom-left Laura Ann Price;

pp24, 41 and 235 WENN Rights Ltd / Alamy Stock Photo;

p26 Adam Vaness;

pp27 top, 28 bottom and right, 29 top, 30 top, 67 centre and bottom Trinity Mirror / Mirrorpix / Alamy Stock Photo;

p27 bottom Mike Goldwater / Alamy Stock Photo;

pp28 centre, 46 top, 47 centre and bottom and 56 ClassicStock / Alamy Stock Photo;

p29 bottom Jeff Morgan 13 / Alamy Stock Photo;

p33 Manilla Street Productions;

p34 David Cooper;

p37 Jen Maufrais Kelly;

p38 top The National Trust Photolibrary / Alamy Stock Photo;

p39 Encore Theatre Company;

p45 Manuel Harlan;

p46 bottom Everett Collection Historical / Alamy Stock Photo;

p47 top-left Simon Webster / Alamy Stock Photo,

p50 Henry DiRocco;

p51 John Lamb;

p53 Idil Sukan / Draw HQ / WENN.com / Alamy Stock Photo;

p54 top The New York Public Library, right South Coast Repertory;

pp54 bottom and 218 Brinkhoff/Moegenburg;

pp55, 82, 148 top, 172 (1 and 3), 188, 202 and 221 Geraint Lewis / Alamy Stock Photo;

p59 Maya Michele Fein;

p66 Paul Doyle / Alamy Stock Photo;

p67 top Fantasy Films / Warner Bros;

p68 top Sally and Richard Greenhill / Alamy Stock Photo;

p75 Youth Action Theatre, Caterham School, Footscray City College;

p80 Craig Stennett / Alamy Stock Photo;

p84 GMA Network;

p85 top Tony Bartholemew, bottom-right RichardBaker / Alamy Stock Photo;

p86 top Warner Bros;

p91 bottom Artists Theatre School;

p94 TripAdvisor;

p95 ffotocymru / Alamy Stock Photo;

p99 Detroit Repertory Theatre;

p102 Charlotte Westernra;

p104 Mark Sepple;

p105 mauritius images GmbH / Alamy Stock Photo;

p107 bottom Stephenson / Stringer / Topical Press Agency / Getty Images;

p113 Daniel Beacock;

p114 Catherine Ashmore;

p115 Philip Erbacher;

p116 keith morris /Alamy Stock Photo;

p124 aberCPC / Alamy Stock Photo;

p142 DJ Corey Photography;

p148 centre Argosy Pictures / Paramount Home Entertainment;

p151 Diana Popovska;

p156 Max Dorey;

p164 Teresa Wood, Alex Brandt / Rosco, Alex T / Rosco, T Charles Erickson;

pp172 (2) and 219 Johan Persson;

p172 (4) Simon Dack Archive / Alamy Stock Photo;

p173 Kevin Berne;

pp178, 181 right, 182 top, 207 left, 227, 228 and 233 Paul Fox;

p181 left Royal Lyceum Theatre Company Ltd, centre Cylla von Tiedemann, bottom Gary Mamay / Guild Hall East Hampton;

p182 centre Avalon Promotions Ltd / Theatrereviews. design, bottom Richard Hubert Smith;

p193 World History Archive / Alamy Stock Photo;

p194 top SHAR Music;

p196 PictureLux / The Hollywood Archive / Alamy Stock Photo;

p203 Dave Clements / DWC Photography;

**p205** right Chronicle / Alamy Stock Photo;
**p212** top Victorianweb.org, centre Cineguild;
**p217** Helen Murray;
**p220** The Vaults;
**p222** Tristram Kenton;
**p223** Michael Courier;
**pp224** and **225** (profile) Musikhaus Kirstein;
**p225** (fresnel) Sashkin, (followspot) 3DMI, (strobe) Feel Good Events, (gobos) Dedolight;
**p231** bottom-right Robert Workman;
**p234** centre Debra Hely / ABC.

All other images: Shutterstock:
**p4 top** and **214** frantic00;
**p4** bottom ThomsonD;
**p6** left Meilun;
**p7** top Master1305, left, metamorworks, right NDT;
**p9** top Aerial-motion;
**p16** GaudiLab;
**p28** top terry bouch / Shutterstock.com;
**p30** left FrimuFilms, right jonesyinc;
**p47** top-right Everett Collection;
**p58** top Stokkete;
**p61** Adriana Iacob / Shutterstock.com;
**p62** AimPix;
**p68** bottom Robert J. Gatto;
**p71** Stig Alenas;
**p72** Galushko Sergey;
**p85** left Pressmaster, centre Greta Gabaglio / Shutterstock.com;
**p86** bottom Ldprod;
**p87** AlternativeVintageCo, Serg Zastavkin;
**p88** MARCELODLT, Lee Yiu Tung;
**p91** top Nadezhda V. Kulagina;
**p101** Supawadee56;
**p107** top and **109** top Roman Nerud / Shutterstock.com;
**p108** Varlamova Lydmila;
**p110** dagma / Shutterstock.com;
**p119** top Delpixel;

**p120** Marsan;
**p122** Sabphoto;
**p126** Gail Heaton;
**p127** (Barker) yakub88 / Shutterstock.com, (Hamble) Kevin Eaves, (cadets) Jonny Essex / Shutterstock.com;
**p128** Dmitry Sedakov;
**p129** Perry Mastrovito / Alamy Stock Photo;
**p134** TINNAKORN MUSIKASARN
**p140** FotoDuets;
**p145** Anna Andersson Fotografi;
**p146** Berna Namoglu;
**p147** Scott Woodham Photography / Shutterstock.com, Patryk Kosmider, Lenico;
**p148** bottom Thoranin Nokyoo;
**p149** MIGUEL G. SAAVEDRA;
**p161** Boris Rabtsevich;
**p163** UMB-O
**p168** lapandr;
**p169** Radu Bercan /Shutterstock.com
**p175** A. and I. Kruk;
**p187** filefoto;
**p190** FrameStockFootages;
**p191** Rawpixel.com;
**p194** bottom Vladimir Wrangel / Shutterstock.com;
**p195** left Paopano/NASA, right Featureflash Photo Agency / Shutterstock.com;
**p200** Pavel L Photo and Video / Shutterstock.com;
**p204** Gunnar Assmy;
**p205** left PUSCAU DANIEL;
**p206** left reddees / Shutterstock.com;
**p207** right Mirdred;
**p210** top Mayrisio, centre and right Africa Studio, left Dmytro Zinkevych;
**p225** (colour filters) Rido, (fogger) Studio KIWI;
**p234** left old-cowboy;
**p239** lev radin / Shutterstock.com.